New Jersey's Multiple Municipal Madness

New Jersey's Multiple Municipal Madness

ALAN J. KARCHER

Rutgers University Press
New Brunswick, New Jersey, and London

Library of Congress Cataloging-in-Publication Data

Karcher, Alan J.
New Jersey's multiple municipal madness / Alan J. Karcher.
p.   cm.
Includes bibliographical references and index.
ISBN 0-8135-2565-9 (alk. paper)—ISBN 0-8135-2566-7 (pbk. :
alk. paper)
1. Municipal government—New Jersey—History.   I. Title.
JS451.N55K37 1999
320.8'5'09749'dc21

98-15606
CIP

British Cataloging-in-Publication data for this book is available from the British Library

Manufactured in the United States of America

Dedicated to my sister Evelyn Graff, who has spent a lifetime watching out for me. She has been a friend, supporter, and colleague. Without her abiding interest and enduring encouragement this book would never have been done.

CONTENTS

ACKNOWLEDGMENTS

I wish to thank Pam Hersh for the countless hours she devoted to modifying my baroque style and shaping this text into readable English. Also, Paul Armstrong, Esq., is not only a marvelous lawyer but has been a good friend. Paul helped enormously in marketing the idea for a book such as this, and I'm grateful for his efforts.

My sister Evelyn Graff was a source of constant encouragement, as were other members of my family. Particular thanks must go to my son Tim, whose computer skills made the production of the final manuscript almost easy.

I never visited a library, local museum, or historical society anywhere in the state where I did not find helpful, courteous, and friendly staff. Many of these were professionals, but many more were simply volunteers performing labors of love. Our state should be proud of the people involved in our libraries and in historical and cultural preservation.

In providing graphics for the text I want to express my appreciation to the Department of Environmental Protection and to the commissioner, my friend and former Assembly colleague Robert Shinn, for permission to use the invaluable materials that John P. Snyder had prepared for the department in reference to the civil boundaries of New Jersey. While preparing his work on the civil boundaries, Mr. Snyder demonstrated a commitment to his task that reflects fascination and affection. He obviously loved maps and enjoyed the pursuit of the esoterica that constitute the history of our state's multiple divisions. I am forever grateful for his work, which made mine so much easier.

My friend Cathy Frank-White, one of the last members of the state's Study Commission on County and Municipal Government, was very helpful, and also assisted me in securing from one of the commission's final staff members, Michael Egenton, the loan of all the commission's publications. My friend and former Assembly colleague Greta Kiernan offered some wonderful insights into the complexities of Bergen County's seventy communities. Louis N. Rainone, Esq., is one of the most knowledgeable municipal practitioners, and offered many valuable contributions to this work.

I wish particularly to thank my special friend of long standing Karen E.

Kotvas, both for her helpful suggestions on the work-in-progress and for the interesting photographs she has taken to supplement the text.

The late Donald Stokes, dean of the Woodrow Wilson School at Princeton, deserves a double thanks: first, for his efforts in 1980, educating me on the principles of fair apportionment, and second, for championing the cause of consolidation in 1996 at a time when we were forced to prove that advocates may disagree without being disagreeable. He was truly a gentleman and a scholar.

Finally I must thank the hundreds, if not thousands, of real, live, flesh-and-blood, practicing politicians of both parties with whom I've had the pleasure to work over the last thirty-five years. They have provided me with an education that could never have been acquired in any academic setting. I am sure if asked about the subject matter of this book, the vast majority of them will indicate that it is just another of my pie-in-the-sky ideas, but privately will say that they think we have a few more hundred municipalities than the state needs. It is the enormous disparity between public statement and private opinion that makes New Jersey's politicians a particularly interesting and unique breed, and the state's politics endlessly fascinating.

New Jersey's Multiple Municipal Madness

Introduction

*L*ines divide. They separate and define. They exclude and include. They get drawn with the toe of a sneaker in the sand of a school yard, and they get drawn with red ink around certain neighborhoods by bankers and insurance executives. They get drawn in the form of bell curves to predict who may aspire to reside on an estate and who will be condemned to live in a slum. In New Jersey lines define crumbling cities and delineate exclusive enclaves—they are drawn around airports and golf courses, and the areas contained within those lines are called municipalities.

This is a book about how and why the boundary lines of New Jersey's 566 municipalities got drawn. It describes the economic considerations, the political pressures, and the personal agendas that guided the pens as they boldly stroked a straight line here—only to jiggle and squiggle a twisted line there. The designs are cantilevered and circumlinear, they form rhomboids and parallelograms—geometric rectangles and chaotic fractals. There are zigs and there are zags, and *every line has a story.*

The explanations for the often bizarre configurations are based on extensive research and analysis. The information provided by the canon of municipal histories cannot be verified by direct testimony. The persons who drew each and every one of the lines defining our municipal boundaries are now deceased. In large measure that fact reveals the very purpose of this book. The men who drew these lines are now departed, and with them often passed the justification, rationale, and motivation for the lines having been drawn where they were. The configurations are no longer defensible based upon the factors that originally moved the hand of the drawer, but the boundaries remain, immutable and very expensive memorials to those who drew them. Either these designs should be justified anew, in terms relevant to contemporary problems and priorities, or we should consider alternative ways to allocate, pay for, and deliver basic government services.

However, before we get into that debate, and even before we begin to explore the origins of New Jersey's many municipalities, let me explain a little about the genesis of this book. When I am asked how long I served in elected office, my normal reply is: "most people think it was too long." In all candor, that group described as "most people" sometimes even includes me. While I cannot deny the satisfaction of the experience or disclaim my intense interest in the issues of the

1970s and 1980s, the statement does reflect the frustration that resulted from my inability to persuade as many of my colleagues as I would have cared to, that perhaps it was time for us all to take a long, hard, and critical look at just what we and our predecessors had wrought.

In 1981, the New Jersey Legislature was mandated to reapportion the state's forty election districts so that each might conform to the results of the decadal census. My position as the majority leader of the General Assembly brought me the opportunity to serve as one of the five Democratic members of the commission charged with the responsibility of adjusting the districts so that each would be roughly equal in population. The unwritten agenda for the five of us was somehow to outmaneuver the five Republican members and thereby gain some partisan advantage for the elections scheduled for November of that year and subsequent biannual elections, until the next census retriggered another reapportionment process.

Our sessions often went into the early morning hours, particularly the strategy sessions involving the members of our own team, who would huddle for hours plotting our next move. We held the abiding hope of confounding the opposing team and having them acquiesce to one of our proposals. The process of designing the maps showing the possible new configurations was slow, tedious and exhausting. Computers were still a novelty so we had, at best, hand-held calculators. More often than not the use of even those calculators was eschewed for simple, old-fashioned, hand-scrawled columns of numbers on yellow legal pads. We would then be forced to reserve some time on the state computer to verify our numbers and assure ourselves that not only did our calculations add up to forty districts of equal population, but that the municipalities in each district were contiguous, that the design was relatively compact, and, most of all, that we had not left any of the state's then 567 towns missing and unaccounted for.

This last injunctive may sound humorous now, but back then we were bedeviled by the chimera of beautiful maps that properly assigned 99 percent of all governmental subdivisions to one or another district, but somehow had overlooked the existence of Elk Township in Gloucester County, or forgotten that West New York was still in New Jersey. The crestfallen sensation was akin to completing a jigsaw puzzle only to find three pieces missing, and you are sure that the dog, or one of your children, has eaten them. I was constantly reminded of my first (and last) effort to fix my own car back in 1960. The heady exhilaration of self-satisfied pride in my technical skill in reassembling the carburetor was deflated unceremoniously upon discovering, just as I was ready to close the hood, that I still had a screw and a wing nut left in my hand.

I still recall nights passing in a blur of numbers. Days spent with eyes glued to a palette of colors as districts were defined in pinks and reds, blues and greens. Weeks were consumed in negotiations that led nowhere except to partisan deadlock. Ultimately the tie-breaking eleventh member, Dean Donald Stokes of Princeton's Woodrow Wilson School, had to be appointed pursuant to the statute, by Chief Justice Robert Wilentz. Shortly thereafter, a plan, acceptable to a majority, was finally forged. That ultimate configuration was adopted by a six-to-five vote. I emerged from that exhausting ordeal with little sense of victory, but with a deep and abiding respect for the stamina, integrity, and intelligence of all my fellow commissioners, with some new friends, and with a wholesome respect for the process.

There was a time somewhere about halfway through that long process when the ever-shifting kaleidoscope of numbers, colors, and lines resulted in my asking myself certain questions. The first question was: who am I, that, by taking a magic marker and coloring in a specific configuration of a district, I may dramatically affect the career of someone else? If my design were to be adopted, the configuration of that district could mean either defeat or victory for someone with whom I was presently serving in the Assembly. Who was I to have that type of power over someone else's destiny?

The second, and more enduring question was: how did these municipal boundaries get drawn in the first place? I vividly remember articulating this question to my colleagues, who in turn looked at me, startled that such a question would be posed. The general response was—this is the way the state is subdivided, and "that is that." We had our hands full as it was without exploring the history or sociopolitical dynamics that had rendered our state into its unique condition.

I did not really expect an answer during that tense and hectic time, but the question of the number of towns and the origins of their configurations lingered on long after the new election districts had become operative. Over the following decade I took every chance I had to inquire of people, some whose opinions I respected, and others whose historical knowledge I highly regarded, what they could tell me about how we had arrived at this sorry state of affairs. Many could tell me how their home town came into being, but had little else to offer on the subject. Some possessed vague, often anecdotal, stories concerning certain towns.

As time passed, the original question developed nuances, subsections and variants. How could the State delegate the same municipal powers to the City of Newark, with a population once approaching 500,000, as it did to Teterboro and Pine Valley, with populations of under 20? Why are there five different types of towns? Why are some towns called towns while others are cities, boroughs, townships, and villages? What had happened in the past? Who had permitted this to happen? Who had made this happen?

I even started to ask extremely stupid questions, such as why places such as Glassboro and Plainsboro were so designated? Did the borough officials not know how to spell? The most interesting, albeit incorrect, answer I received to the spelling issue laid responsibility for these spellings on President Theodore Roosevelt. He knew how to spell, but despite knowing that borough was a term in English usage for over 900 years, he was set on simplifying the language. Allegedly his contribution to the crusade for Esperanto led him to direct the Post Master General to refuse recognition to any community that attempted to use the suffix, "borough," and had thereby forced them to adopt the shortened form, "boro."

This explanation proved to be apocryphal, as did dozens of others I heard about the origin of one town or another, as I delved deeper into New Jersey's rich and colorful history. One thing I did discover was that much of the oral and written history of towns and their origins is laden with folklore. It also became obvious that many communities had attempted, over the course of time, to cloak their true origin in the mists of memory and to create ennobling legends about the courage and vision of their founders. The principal cause for these municipal fantasies turned out to be that the town was created as the result of some very petty or highly personal reason; often a reason that today would be deemed to be "politically incorrect."

The genesis of the present political map of the state is a story that, while usually interesting is not always charming, while often fascinating is also far from edifying. Little in the history can be called quaint. Rather it is a story of separation and exclusion, of division and greed, of preservation of prerogatives and prejudices. It is a story that supports the conclusion that these lines are rarely the product of chance—rather, they were drawn by politicians with very human foibles and frailties, and with very narrow agendas.

The tradition of adjusting lines to suit political and economic agendas is long and time-honored in this state. Even the very first line—the one dividing East and West Jersey—was subject to revision and recalculation.

The other grand tradition of New Jersey is the legacy we inherited from the tax-evaders, or, more euphemistically, the tax-avoiders who were our founding fathers—the ones who helped finance the Revolution with the profits they had built up by circumventing the Molasses Act of 1763 and other import duties imposed by the British Crown. Our national heroes were, by the definition of King George III, scoundrels and thieves. That legacy of minimizing the payment of taxes is not unique to New Jersey, but here it was brought to a high art. The skills of the smuggler were passed down from generation to generation, ultimately to be manifested in the creation of tax-free zones such as Teterboro and Rockleigh Township in Bergen County. The same acumen that managed in 1770 to disguise sugar from Barbados as mere ship ballast was developed to the point where golf courses could masquerade as boroughs.

The lines on the geopolitical map of New Jersey were drawn by men with political and/or economic agendas. Even where borders are constituted by a natural dividing line such as a river or a stream, the line was endorsed by some one or some group to further a personal agenda. While those personal agendas may have been inconsequential and innocuous at the time, today the costs of maintaining New Jersey's multiple and redundant jurisdictions mounts into the billions of dollars.

It would be impossible to do justice to every one of the 566 municipalities. It is important to recognize from the outset that 177, or almost one third of these municipalities, are less than two square miles in area, and over 100 of them have populations under 2,000. Most disturbing of all is that approximately 200 of them have tax bases so small, narrow, and unexpandable that their very existence is solely and exclusively a matter of state aid.

The common themes running through each town's genesis generally sustain a simple proposition: every significant decision made on the state level regarding taxes, schools, housing, transportation, preservation of natural resources, and doz-ens of other issues starts with the given that it must accommodate 566 local gov-ernments. New Jersey solutions, when and if they are found, must come in the single variety of "one size fits all." The configurations of these local units are the products of economic and social dynamics operating primarily in the nineteenth century. Those reasons are not extant today, yet they still dictate public policy. The municipal boundary lines weave a web that fetters, tangles, and ultimately ensnares the governor and legislature in their attempts to address critical contemporary problems.

It is my intention to conduct a full-scale examination and analysis of how these lines got drawn—the public policies that allowed and even encouraged the drawing of these lines and the political dynamics that formed those public poli-cies. Also, this book will address the hows and whys of the public policies that have thwarted every effort of a major New Jersey metropolis to emerge into the front ranks of American cities.

This work is divided into four sections. The first four chapters are devoted to: identifying the major motivations behind the unparalleled experience of New Jersey's municipal multiplication; an initial discussion of the consequences of the unique New Jersey experience, with some suggestion of the incredible costs asso-ciated with our political inertia; and presenting two detailed case studies of how sprawling colonial townships, consisting of hundreds of square miles, were divided and redivided and redivided again to become the municipal entities we see today.

The second section delves more deeply into the primary causes of new lines being drawn. When a particular factor or area of controversy, such as road appro-priations, the location of a railroad station, the control of a local school district, the regulation of alcohol sales, and the preservation of exclusivity prior to the ac-ceptance of zoning, resulted in the creation of twenty-five or more communities, it has warranted its own chapter. The other chapter includes stories of town cre-ations that were miscalculations, "acres of diamonds," war orphans, and other mis-cellany demonstrating just how diverse the motives were.

Section three is devoted to an analysis of the political processes and the public-policy positions of the state that have operated since the seventeenth cen-tury to frustrate the possible emergence of any city as a contender for national prominence. The external forces, as well as the more critical internal myopia of the state's policies, are investigated in detail. These chapters explore: how the Quaker settlement of Burlington City and the Scottish stronghold of Perth Amboy, despite their respective designations as the capitals of West and East Jersey, were considered suspect and restrained from growth by the Anglican Royal Governors; how the unequal apportionment of political power operated to drain the cities of wealth and opportunity for 200 years; and how and why the efforts of Camden, Newark, and Jersey City to broaden their bases and increase their powers were unsuccessful.

Finally we shall assess the present situation and what has occurred in the past sixty years since the municipal multiplication madness has ceased. Some sug-gestions are offered about taking another look at the matter. However, the ultimate judgment as to whether there might be a more sensible modern approach to the delivery of local services and the future course of action, if any, is left to you the reader.

Allow me to conclude, however, with one observation concerning our attitude toward municipalities in New Jersey. The present configuration of municipal boundary lines, settled now for a period of almost sixty years, has assumed a political status approaching the sacrosanct. How did we allow this to happen? Thomas Jefferson volunteered a great deal of advice. Much of it was followed, a great deal of it is revered, but some advice has been ignored, such as his recommendation that a government's constitution be reviewed and rewritten every twenty years. New Jersey has managed to survive with only three major overhauls of its organic document. However, since the last constitution was adopted in 1947, there have been almost fifty amendments to our most important and fundamental instrument of government, an average of one change per year. During the same time virtually no changes have occurred to our municipal boundaries. We change our constitution as we change our clothes, but are satisfied that our municipal boundary lines are immutably carved in stone. An electorate as ready to vote on changes in the constitution should at least be open to the possibilities that maybe some improvement and economy might be realized by taking a stitch here and a tuck there on the threadbare sections of the municipal quilt we've patched together.

PART I

Background and Case Studies

CHAPTER 1

Motivations for Municipal Multiplication in New Jersey; or, What Moved the Hands that Drew the Lines

Never be surprised by how quickly self-interest can inspire a politician to rise above principle.
Common wisdom

For about the price of a dinner at a decent restaurant, you can purchase a software program for your computer called SIM-City that, without undue risk to either your digestion or cholesterol level, provides you with hours of entertainment. And since its introduction a few years ago, this software has spawned a number of even more sophisticated versions. Whatever program you choose, it is crafted and designed to provide you with almost limitless opportunities to exercise your creativity and imagination in building model communities. The options are manifold: laying out street and traffic patterns; constructing centers for mass-transit alternatives; assigning low-rise housing to the inner ring while placing single-family, larger-lot housing judiciously on the perimeters; centering high-rise office and commercial uses advantageously near the well-conceived vehicular arteries; segregating industrial and manufacturing uses from populated areas buffered by parks and open space—everything one could want in a well-planned community. Conversely, since the conditions and parameters of your project may be programmed from the beginning, it is possible to fail, or to be overtaken by disaster. All of these alternatives provide promise that the time spent engaged in this program will be both challenging and stimulating.

No longer does one have to spend a fortune on a degree in architecture or urban planning and then endure years of apprenticeship as an educated automaton with some huge firm where early assignments are limited to the refinement of details. Instead, for an extremely modest sum, one may enjoy the fantasy and power of creating novel and unique cities. All that is required is the proper software, a computer, and unlimited imagination.

The designs of New Jersey's 566 municipalities were not the products of so-phisticated software programs currently available on the eve of the twenty-first century. The present political map of New Jersey, in large measure, is the product of the nineteenth century. The map is so much a part of the past century that it can be defined as being pre-Euclidean—not in the geometric sense, but in the legal context that it largely predates the advent of zoning. The U.S. Supreme Court placed its constitutional imprimatur on zoning only in 1926 in the case of *Euclid v Ambler Realty Co.*, 272 U.S. 365, and the New Jersey Constitution was amended in 1927 to validate municipal zoning ordinances. By this time New Jersey already had over 540 municipalities, and the majority had constructive zoning schemes. The distribution of land use had often been the simple corollary of municipal in-corporation.

The advent of zoning was the defining event in the history of municipal in-corporations. After zoning, many of the factors that had driven the dividing and redividing of territory were able to find expression in the municipal zoning code. The fever that had raged throughout the state during the period of 1850 to 1927 abated. Those in political power could now exercise their new, constitutionally rec-ognized powers to "zone-in" what they found attractive, and conversely, exclude through zoning what they considered to be "undesirable." In large measure zon-ing rendered moot the option of creating a new municipality and negated the ne-cessity of exercising that option to preserve the status quo.

As a mechanism for preserving the status quo of the de facto, segregated housing patterns of the vast majority of the state, zoning proved to be extraordi-narily effective for the fifty years between its authorization by constitutional amend-ment in 1927 until the *Mount Laurel* decisions in the New Jersey Supreme Court. In those three landmark *Mount Laurel* cases, the Court became progressively more aggressive and ultimately prohibited the type of exclusionary zoning that had re-placed municipal proliferation as the accepted vehicle for protecting the existing social, economic, and cultural landscape.

The psychological mind-sets and political interests operating in the twenti-eth century that resulted in some municipalities zoning all available land within their borders for either industry or agriculture, or, as in the case of some commu-nities, zoning for housing almost exclusively on five-acre lots, first exercised it-self in the nineteenth century in the proliferation of municipalities.

The driving forces that had drawn those town boundaries, however, were much more ancient than the contemporaneous pressures of nineteenth-century American life. The forces at work in establishing New Jersey's municipalities were the raw and primitive forces of ambition, avarice, and acrimony. Added to this list were efforts to enforce abstinence, and, in some rare instances, plain and simple accident. The final dynamic, so unpleasant yet so obvious, was the quest for ex-clusivity. In other words the attempt to build walls between *us* and *them*.

The literature on the subject of town origins is extensive. Texts have been written in the fields of law, sociology, architecture, geography, political science, and even anthropology dealing with the formation of communities. However, the works dealing specifically with the historical development of New Jersey's municipalities are distinctly less profound. Most authors are long on providing a plethora of names, dates, and assorted data, but somewhat short on analysis or suggestion as to motivations. Most writers recount the basics of who was involved, and how and when the incorporation took place, but rarely does one find a commentary that candidly addresses the question of *why* a particular community sought recognition as an independent entity. The comments of some authors approach what might be considered as real candor and attempt to provide credible explanations as to how New Jersey experienced municipal multiplication to a greater extent than any other state. More often than not, commentary on the origin of a particular community can only be labeled as civic boosterism or politically correct revisionism. Some municipal histories place a spin on the story to make the motivations appear less petty or more politically correct. There are also various studies that have made a broader attempt to justify the veritable explosion of political subdivisions in this state, but, here again, while it would be needlessly pejorative to characterize these efforts as myth, they are misconceived.

The previous work done in the field of New Jersey municipal history may be divided into four general categories:

• The first category consists of works that might appropriately be grouped under the generic heading of *commemorative publications*. These publications range in length from those that are book-sized efforts by serious students of a particular area to slim pamphlets put together by a centenary committee without any pretense to serious scholarship. These books are normally site-specific and usually contain detailed recitations of the genealogy of the area's first settlers. Almost universally they are divided into sections describing the religious organizations, the school system, the industry and commerce, the volunteer and civic associations, and the parks and recreational opportunities provided by the community. These commemorative publications invariably ascribe to the town's founders the highest and noblest motivations: the American aspiration for self-governance and desire to be independent are often invoked, as is the dream of being destiny's master.

Well intentioned and often well written, these accounts are interesting and often candid enough to acknowledge, albeit casually, that the new town had emerged as the result of an ongoing altercation over some road appropriations, or involved a political faction breaking free from the perceived oppression of another faction. For others, it was just the existence of an irresistible economic opportunity. While for many it was the desire to create a community of like-minded people, interested in preserving their "way of life."

• The second category consists of historical studies of the entire state—political texts that require that some comment as to how the state arrived at its present condition. The historical analysis provided for the extraordinary situation of the present existence of 566 municipalities is often cursory at best, the broad-but-thin-brush approach. This usually appears in works that attempt to compress into a few hundred pages the entire history of the state's complex and colorful political development. Given projects this ambitious in scope, one hates to criticize them for providing shallow and general explanations for the proliferation of the state's municipalities.

It is difficult, however, to understand how a recent volume could attribute the multiplication of municipalities to the "up-ticks" in the economic cycle. The claim asserted that the number of municipalities increased in direct ratio to the general level of national prosperity; depressions and recessions therefore flattened the numbers, according to this argument. It would appear that the opposite was true. Following the bank panics of 1837 and 1873 New Jersey experienced two of its most active periods of municipal expansion. A study of the statistics would lead one to conclude that, in periods of tight money, property-tax payers became more anxious to exercise closer scrutiny over how their taxes were being spent, and resorted to the creation of new towns to insure a more direct influence over the use of their property-tax payments. For example, President Grover Cleveland personally interceded to prevent a collapse of the market in government bonds during the Financial Panic of 1893. Still reeling from that crisis, the country witnessed the labor turmoil of major strikes in the mining, garment, and railroad industries, as well as the march of Coxey's Army on the nation's capital in 1894. Despite these convulsions in the economy, 24 new boroughs were in the process of being formed in Bergen County, in that year alone. The origin of these new towns was directly related to changes in the state's school laws and had no relation whatsoever to the condition of the national economy.

Similarly mistaken is the theory that the potential for political patronage served as an inducement to create more communities. The logic of this argument proceeds along a simple straight line: the more towns, the more jobs to fill. However, in the era prior to civil service, political power was vested in the county bosses, who would have been loathe to encourage additional fiefdoms that might exhibit any degree of political independence. The additional patronage argument, while being superficially attractive, does not hold up well under scrutiny. It is just too easy to explain any phenomenon in New Jersey by saying political patronage was at its core. Given New Jersey's reputation, this facile, but specious, claim is too readily accepted, without additional examination.

• The third category consists of government publications—primarily those produced by the County and Municipal Government Study Commission, whose work, as far as it went, was significant. It is regrettable that the Commission's agenda was confined to technical matters and that they were restrained from addressing larger issues that cried out for attention. Sadder still is the fact that a false sense of economy terminated the Commission in the early 1990s. The majority of their publications addressed the morass of problems confronting a system that was already out of control. Their recommendations were often cogent and practical, and were, in many instances, followed by the Legislature.

That having been said, however, one should note that the Commission tended to confuse the symptoms with the disease itself. They observed the constant conjunction of events and mistakenly assumed that they were identifying cause and effect. For instance, one of their earliest pamphlets entitled *Consolidation: Prospects and Problems*, published in 1972, contains the conclusion that the increase in the number of boroughs from 5 to 193 between 1850 and 1917, had "resulted from the existence of very permissive legislation." No comment is offered or suggested as to why the permissive legislation existed. Lenient standards and minimal requirements for incorporation did not cause the creation of 188 new boroughs. Permissive legislation may have facilitated the proliferation of municipalities, but the law did not cause them. The political establishment in Trenton was merely responding to the pressures of local leaders who liked the system and who wanted maximum flexibility to exercise their ambition, avarice, religious tenets, tax policies, or other particular agenda. In many cases the legislators were the same people who were benefiting from the political subdivision proliferations, which, at the very least, were deflecting attention from state-wide problems. Therefore, when one reads that liberal incorporation statutes caused the creation of an overabundance of towns or that the passage of the school law of 1894 encouraged the creation of many Bergen County boroughs, one must consider the legislators who passed the laws and how they had arrived in their seat in the Senate or Assembly chamber. Their most powerful and influential constituents were the "power elites," who were asking, importuning, and lobbying for the creation of additional jurisdictional ponds, where these "power elites" would be large fish. The permissive incorporation legislation was merely a symptom—the underlying illness was just the operation of human nature.

• The fourth category of works on New Jersey history is by far the most entertaining, consisting of rich, amusing, and authentic folklore. The authors of these volumes were engaged in a labor of love, which is evident in every tale and story they record. The people about whom they write are genuine, and their motivations understandable. The characters we meet in these tales are most often common folk, real flesh-and-blood people, concentrating on feeding and sheltering themselves and their families—not the larger-than-life hero types that populate the anniversary editions. Here can be found the anecdotes of schemers and the dreamers, so far removed from the political happenings in the capitol to ever worry about whether the laws governing municipalities were too rigid or overly permissive—too involved in their fantasies to pay much heed to the business cycles or worry about partisan patronage.

The folklorists present stories of people who are capable of ambition and avarice; who are willing to respect the rights of others as long as their rights are respected as well; who believe that good fences make good neighbors; who will pay their own way, but resent being made to pay for others; who love their independence and their way of life to the extent that they want to preserve it free from interference or intrusion. Thus, these are people who exhibit all of the foibles, follies, and frailties that make us human. In these stories we glimpse all of the forces that forged this state, while at the same time allowing it to shatter into 566 individual local jurisdictions.

I would theorize that it is possible to examine the origin of each of New Jersey's 566 municipalities and categorize the genesis of every one as the product of one or more of the following factors:

1. Ambition manifested as avarice or self-aggrandizement—often both.
2. Particular economic conditions, unique to the time, place and circumstance.

3. The actions of a single individual, or, in some cases, a tightly knit group of like-minded men engaged in a common venture, involving the implementation of a very narrow, personal and/or provincial agenda.
4. The attempts to impose a policy as to the sale or consumption of alcoholic beverages.
5. The preservation of existing tax benefits and/or the anticipation of a new tax system that held a special advantage.
6. The unique priorities of areas adjacent to railroad passenger stations, motivating commuters to want greater control over the expenditures of their property-tax dollars on those specific priorities.
7. The exercise of the political maxim: divide and conquer.
8. The use of municipal incorporation as a means to attain exclusivity and enforce de facto segregation along ethnic, racial, and economic lines.

The overarching issue that becomes so clear after examining the gestation and birth of each individual town is relevance. Indeed, there are identifiable, demonstrable, and timely reasons not only for the existence, but also for the configuration, of each separate community. However, those reasons were the reasons of people long dead—motivations and justifications for actions of men long departed, and remembered now only on dusty plaques, and with passing references in seldom read histories.

The town founders were men of action, energy, and enterprise to match their ambition, avarice and ego. Persons who if they were with us today and confronted by a challenge to justify what they had done, would answer with simplicity and candor, "it seemed like a good idea at the time."

Our generation and those that follow must inquire if that reason is sufficient, or if the problems of our current time dictate different reasoning and require a new answer.

CHAPTER 2

Historical Context of Municipal Creation

$\mathcal{A}$t one time, every line on the map may have seemed like a good idea. The draftsmen probably took little thought of the potential consequences of their actions; if some risks were seen, they were ignored, because the immediate benefits outweighed future problems. Ask people why they are willing to take a chance, and the odds are they will reply that it seems like a good idea at the time. Native New Jerseyans' ability to understand and calculate the odds is legendary. The talent has existed for generations and occurs in direct ratio to the proximity of one's birth to Jersey City (the capital of East Coast gambling from approximately 1910 to 1978)—a fact once acknowledged by former Governor Brendan T. Byrne—or Atlantic City (the legitimate capital of East Coast gambling from 1978 to present).

In 1973 when I ran for the Assembly on a ticket headed by Brendan T. Byrne, the Middlesex County Democratic candidates met with candidate Byrne at the old Brass Bucket Restaurant in Woodbridge. During the course of the evening one of the veteran legislators asked him his position on the hotly debated issue that had been raised during a number of the previous sessions: a constitutional referendum to authorize casino gambling. (The question of state-wide casino gaming was defeated in 1974, but when the issue was limited to Atlantic City in 1976, it gained voter approval.) In the summer of 1973, Byrne noted his support of extending gambling to casino-type games, but added that in the case of Jersey City a constitutional amendment wasn't necessary—a mere validating act would suffice.

As was seen in the previous chapter, the canon of literature covering Jerseyana and serious New Jersey history is relatively extensive, but other sections of the library offer some pertinent information. In addition to the obvious areas of political science, sociology, and urban planning, the literature on mathematics yields fascinating information, particularly the use of statistics and probability in attempts to predict the future or explain the past. One of our species' most consistent, enduring, and defining attributes is the insatiable desire to know the future. In a state endowed with an inherent attraction to odds, probability is relevant to the state's history. Probability theory is used, with equal persuasiveness and credibility, to explain the past as well as to foretell the future. For instance, many believe that organic life sprang from inorganic elements, because of a particular moment in time when the elements within the primordial chemical soup were at exactly the right temperature and conditions. Although it may seem improbable that life could emerge from inorganic matter, it became possible because of the law of large numbers—in this particular case, five billion years. Similarly we are told by the law of large numbers that provided enough time and opportunity, anything might happen. For example, if a zillion chimpanzees were placed at a zillion word processors, then sometime over the next zillion years—one of them would bang out an exact replication of Shakespeare's collected works—or so the theory goes.

I have digressed upon this discussion of probability to underscore that in New Jersey it helps to know the odds. This applies not only at the tables in Atlantic City, but equally as well if one chooses to participate in the state's public life. Using the theoretical laboratory of the hardworking chimps, I would be willing to wager my entire earthly possessions that even if they were forced to work double shifts armed with the most sophisticated computer-assisted design software, in ten zillion years no chimp would accidentally redesign the municipal boundaries of New Jersey's 566 towns or the lines of its 611 school districts.

You may caution me that the bet is unwise, since over an extended period of time it is highly probable that chimpanzees will evolve intelligence equal to, and ultimately far greater than, the present human intelligence. This proposition of evolving intelligence is, I believe, a safe bet. However, the smarter they get, the less likely it becomes that any species, chimps or humans, would replicate the map in its present configuration.

The message is simple: Given the opportunity to redraw the political boundaries of the region, no one would ever break the state into the same irrational, wasteful, and counterproductive patterns that presently exist. Why then have we as a society been so willing to remain voluntary prisoners in these expensive historical anomalies? To explore this question we can visit other shelves in the library, such as law or fiction, particularly Gothic horror novels. Under both headings we will find reference to something known as *mortmain*, literally the dead hand. Just as it is necessary to have a full understanding of how irrational and artificial the present boundaries are, it is equally important to comprehend how extensively and expensively our political culture is being controlled by dead hands.

British monarch Edward the First signed a statute in the year of 1279 prohibiting the practice of mortmain. What exactly is mortmain, why is its prohibition so historically important, and why is this issue relevant to our inquiry?

The problem Edward addressed had been brewing for more than two hundred years in England. The religious establishment persuaded members of the aristocracy to either will or gift to the churches large and productive properties with the understanding that such properties were to be held by the Church in perpetuity, i.e., never resold or placed upon the open market, and of course to be held by the Church tax-free. Edward was troubled, not by the practice of his aristocracy attempting to buy their way into heaven, but by the constant erosion of his tax base. Let the aristocracy pay for their indulgences in cash, believed the king. Of equal importance was the establishment of the political primacy of the living king, who must prevent the subversion of his sovereignty by decisions made from the grave. Literally, Edward was confronted by the problem of public policy being written by dead hands.

The public policy involved in thirteenth-century England implicated such familiar-sounding items as: taxation, finance, land use, housing, transportation, employment, civil rights, public safety, and law enforcement. I might suggest that for the twenty-first as well as the thirteenth century, the formulation of public policy in these important areas is best left responsive to contemporary needs—not frozen or paralyzed in place for perpetuity.

The problem of mortmain is no archaic concept, of interest only to medieval scholars tracing the rise of capitalism. The same rationale that produced the initial Statute of Mortmain in 1279 helped define the organic nature of the Common Law: evolutionary and responsive. It is the same rationale that provides for amendment to all man-made laws, even constitutions, and that today places a premium on a government's ability to adapt and respond to change, challenge, and crisis.

Times change. Circumstances change. Attitudes change. Problems change. Solutions change. Institutions should have the ability to change as well, for without it a dangerous and expensive situation arises. A syndrome of inflexibility, rigidity, and public paralysis leads to the ultimate public surrender to foolishness and excess. I think we have already witnessed this phenomenon in New Jersey.

While I feel confident that I can explain the system and recount how and why the lines are drawn as they are, I can make no good-faith effort to defend the present structure. It is doubtful that anyone could support the present boundaries with a straight face. After all, where can a credible apologist be found for a system that is bizarre in its design and ridiculous in its redundant expenses? It is impossible to defend the present system that legitimizes municipalities the size of Bill Gates's living room with populations insufficient to fill the offices of a skeleton local government. When are we as a citizenry going to look at each other and ourselves and speak the heretofore unspeakable? When are we going to acknowledge as mature, reasonable adults that we have too long tolerated a municipal framework that represents the opposite of everything this century has learned about effective management, efficient control, economy of scale. The system is simply ridiculous, in large measure because its operation is dictated to us from beyond the grave. Billions of dollars in public expenses and consequent taxes being virtually controlled by dead hands writing the bills for these costs—all this makes for a ridiculous and trashy Gothic horror story.

However, the taxpayer who wishes to find the most frightening and terrifying book in any of our state's 300 plus library systems, shouldn't bother looking in the fiction section, but should go instead to the reference section on government.

Ask if the library has a copy of comparative local budgets, a volume that compares salaries for comparable positions and contains information from approximately sixty percent of the state's communities. To protect the reader from the goriest tales, it does not include salaries of the superintendents of the 611 school districts. Nor does it carry information about such things as retirement benefits, buy-outs of contracts, or compensation for unused sick-time—items that in the course of the last year for some individuals in some communities have amounted to $250,000.00.

A remedy, however, is far from plain and simple. The problem has so far proven to be intractable, and moreover no single model presents itself as a clearly superior alternative. Part of the reluctance to change can be attributed to the promises of a paradigm that have failed miserably. Our proximity to New York City, which in 1998 observed the centennial of its formation from 400 separate units, has provided us with a close look at the problems experienced by a city that perhaps over-consolidated.

Is there an ideal-sized municipality or an administrative unit that might be replicated in cookie-cutter fashion? I doubt that such an ideal organization exists even in theory. *The goal should be to create a political framework that is responsive to change and challenge.* My intention is not to suggest some panacea, but rather to provide a more complete examination of the historic dynamics that designed the present map and then froze its configurations. It is offered in the context that a problem well stated and thoroughly understood is closer to a solution than is a situation that is merely ignored with a shrug of the shoulders of the body politic.

We have grown so accustomed to the multiple jurisdictional lines that one forgets how prior to those lines appearing on any maps a satisfactory system of governance existed for centuries. Our present system replaced a Native American system of governance that had been operational for millennia. The governance of the Lenni Lenape (the original people) tribe had been eminently successful in resolving territorial questions, in providing adequate housing, food, health care, and recreation, in governing markets, in administering a system of justice. The governance accomplished this in a manner that made this tribe legendary for peace and prosperity. The Lenni Lenape maintained regular settlements, but built no cities. They traveled, unaccosted and unthreatened, throughout their land, summering along the shore, and moving inland for the winter, where the fuel supply was as abundant as the game. In these annual migrations, they used settled and well-trod routes without extracting taxes for maintenance and improvements and without divisive quarrels as to jurisdiction. One of those Pre-Columbian routes was the Minnisink Trail, which stretched from the Navisink River northward across the Raritan River and upward toward the Kittatinny Mountains.

The Minnisink Trail bisects the town in which I was raised and is located just a mile or so from where I lived the majority of my life. It is to this same area that I now invite you for our first case study. It is there that we can investigate how the once sprawling South Ward of Perth Amboy came to be nine separate municipalities.

CHAPTER 3

Case Study of
Perth Amboy's South Ward

These are good people here. Be good to them and they'll be good to you.
Quaid family wisdom

I was raised walking distance from the confluence of the South River and the Raritan, where my father's family had lived for generations. I listened attentively to story after story concerning the history of how the area on the south bank of the Raritan River had developed. Later in life, and for a period of sixteen years, I had the honor of representing a good portion of this same area as a member of the General Assembly.

As a result of my familiarity with this particular region of the state, I want to use it as a case study of the nineteenth-century dynamics that ultimately resulted in nine separate municipalities being formed entirely or in part from what had originally been just a single large township. The location and configuration of each of these nine towns is obviously unique, but the political and psychological factors that drew the boundary lines creating each of these nine communities are representative and reflective of how similar lines were drawn throughout the balance of the state.

The south bank of the Raritan Bay is less than twenty-five miles from Manhattan. I learned in college that the Watchung foothills, being about the same distance to the west as New York City is to the north, were the principal cause of the topography and geology of the lower bank of the Raritan. The land at the estuary of the Raritan had been built up from the aggregation and accretion of alluvial deposits laid down over the course of tens of thousands of years. My professor at Rutgers explained that the Watchung foothills were once much grander, rising higher than their present elevations by hundreds of feet, but the melting of the glaciers after the Ice Ages had caused the peaks of this range to be drastically eroded and trillions of minute particles of kaolin had washed toward the Atlantic Ocean. The erosion process continued, more slowly to be sure, once the glaciers of the last Ice Age had fully retreated into Arctic Canada. However, the enormous deposits of silt laden with kaolin from the eroded mountains had settled along the south bank of what was now the Raritan River and compressed to form deep, thick layers of clay—clay as fine in quality as any similar deposits to be found on the East Coast of North America. In more recent times, the clay deposits were thinly covered with sand; only within the last few thousand years a coating with the poorest veneer of soil developed to support meager vegetation. Salt marshes spread in from the river itself for hundreds of yards before giving way to stunted scrub oaks and pines. However, the farther in from the river you traveled, the quality of the soil and the flora it sustained dramatically improved.

From the perspective of geography, as opposed to geology, the lower bank of the bay had some distinct value. It is located on the strategic route from Philadelphia to New York. Anyone in the seventeenth, eighteenth, and even the early nineteenth century wishing to make the shortest possible trip between these two urban centers would ferry from Manhattan to South Amboy and then on to Philadelphia via ferry connections at Bordentown, or vice versa. There were alternative routes, but South Amboy had convenience and speed. Lawrie's Road, named for the provincial governor, opened in 1684 and connected the *South Ward of Perth Amboy* to Bordentown. The road passed through a place on the old maps designated as *Spotteswood*. Most of the road traversed a huge township called Piscataway, which constituted over seventy-five percent of what is today Middlesex County, as well as a good portion of Mercer. But not until the eighteenth century would these areas be set off as South Brunswick and the Windsors.

This particular case study focuses primarily on what occurred in the Township of South Amboy from the time it demonstrated an independent existence in the late seventeenth century to the turn of the nineteenth century. The history of the region could have been traced even further. Indeed, if we had started with Piscataway Township in 1664 and traced all municipal subdivisions originating from that point, the study would be unwieldy, as Piscataway was the root source of virtually dozens of present-day municipalities on both the north and south of the Raritan River.

The early maps indicate that a substantial new area had received a designation, named the South Ward of Perth Amboy or South Amboy Township. This new place on the map contains well over 100 square miles and will maintain its configuration for the next one hundred and fifty years.

By the time of the Revolutionary War, South Amboy was a tiny, but bustling, community edging out from around the dock where the ferry boats came and went in relative synchronization with the comings and goings of the stage line that had been in continuous scheduled operation since 1703, albeit that was only once a month for the first fifty years.

The Township of South Amboy's ferry dock and stage depot constituted less than a small fraction of one percent of the land usage. Surrounding the actual settlement along the waterfront spreading to the south were miles of desolate woodlands. To the west along the river bank were thousands of acres of salt marshes. Interspersed throughout were a few large farms that in spite of their size were barely able to sustain their owners.

In the vast expanse of what now are the Townships of East Brunswick, Monroe, and Cranbury, the forests were being cleared for farming, and the wood harvested for fuel or lumber. The village of Spotteswood stood along Lawrie's Road, and here and there around a grist, cider, or saw mill, a hamlet had emerged. If a church, a blacksmith's forge, and a tavern were present it became a place of significance, such as the historic village of Cranbury.

In the late eighteenth century, some of the more enterprising farmers, closer to the river banks in present-day Sayreville, were supplementing their incomes by extracting clay and making whisky jugs and other items of pottery on a modest scale.

The stagecoach line that moved travelers to and from the ferry dock in South Amboy throughout the eighteenth century was rendered obsolete by the railroad line, built in 1832. That first railroad line connected South Amboy and Bordentown and from there Camden. This line was the *Camden-Amboy Railroad Company*, destined to be the most profitable and infamous railroad in America. Eventually the railroad company became so powerful and dominant that the usage of its name became synonymous with the state itself. The company's virtual control of the political life of the state for nearly thirty years justified the nationwide usage of the term.

By 1838 the railroad was no longer a novelty and it had become the preferred mode of travel across the state. South Amboy envisioned a future for itself as a railroad hub, and with little regret it first jettisoned almost half its territory for the creation of the new township which was to bear the honored name of the late president, Monroe. On February 23, 1838, the Legislature acted on the petition of certain residents of the area to create the new township; with only one stipulation—that the existing poorhouse was to be owned jointly by the two townships.

The *Centennial (1938) Review of Monroe*, prepared as part of the Federal Writers' Project of the depression era, speculates that the "split, no doubt, was due to basic economic differences between the needs of an agricultural, versus industrial community." The truth of the matter was that even at this very early date the impact of the railroad, was already at work. The tension centered on the expenditure of tax dollars for roads. The farmers of Monroe felt that they were getting short-changed and wanted more money allocated for the purpose of maintaining the rural network of roads that were the lifeline of the agricultural economy. South Amboy, on the other hand, had been taken under the thrall of the industrial age, and wanted to spend the money on upgrading the roadways in closest proximity to the depot and the ancillary warehouses, taverns, and stables that had sprung up around the depot. The attitude in the farming district is accurately reflected by the conclusion expressed in the anniversary volume: "The inhabitants of land-locked farms in Monroe-to-be probably felt that they had too little to say as to how their taxes were to be used."

It is also reasonable to assume that those land-locked farmers by the 1830s fully adjusted to the fact that New Brunswick had supplanted Perth Amboy (and its South Ward) as the market and administrative center of the region. Internal roads were important, but, it was equally important that the local network tie into roads leading toward New Brunswick. That city, loyal to the Revolution, had displaced Perth Amboy, stronghold of the Tories, as the county seat in 1778.

The dispute over the distribution of taxes collected for maintaining roads continued within the new Township of Monroe. While the original network of roads for the township was laid out in 1838, the year of their incorporation, the plan was not fully completed until 1900. In the interim, squabbling over the road appropriations led to the creation of additional subdivisions and then additional towns. Political infighting was vigorous and sometimes vicious, particularly with regard to *Road Districts Number 2* and *Number 11*. Charges and countercharges of misfeasance flew back and forth with regularity. By the mid-1850s there were competing factions fighting over who was legitimate holder of the title of "road overseer" for District 2.

The township committee intervened and succeeded only in exacerbating the fight. Eventually cooler heads prevailed, and the problem was resolved by splitting the road district into two jurisdictions, thereby allowing each claimant to have his own bailiwick. However the problems involving road maintenance were widespread. The Solomonesque resolution of the quarrel in *District Number 2* served as an impetus for some of the leading citizens, including Andrew Snowhill, who had been instrumental in Monroe's achieving independence from South Amboy, to determine that the creation of another municipality might be the ultimate solution. They started plotting this possible move.

The dispute over *Road District 2* had been resolved amicably, if only temporarily, unlike the altercation swirling in District 11. James Buckelew, who was a prominent citizen and the official collector of taxes, took it upon himself to arbitrarily close down the turnpike in *District Number 11*. The township committee responded to the outcry of the citizenry by referring the matter to the road overseer for the district. No accommodation could be reached between the overseer and Mr. Buckelew, and the public outrage mounted. The committee escalated the conflict by authorizing the overseer to bring suit against Buckelew, but failed to appropriate funds for an attorney. The public now mobilized and collected fifty dollars to pay the lawyer. The great *District Number 11* "road war" culminated in 1860 with creation of the Township of East Brunswick from a portion of Monroe and from some area that had previously been a part of North Brunswick. James Buckelew was not happy or satisfied, but consoled himself by addressing his energies to the development of that area of Monroe Township that would become the Borough of Jamesburg.

Before going on with the story of the Buckelew family, it must be pointed out in an attempt to retain chronological order that in March of 1872, Cranbury became an independent township. The area of Cranbury Township embraced not only the historic village, which was situated in South Brunswick Township, but also surrounding farms and the freight depot along the Camden-Amboy rail line known as Cranbury Station, located in Monroe. Three factors may have been at work here:

1. Cranbury wished more control over the maintenance of roads serving the village;
2. The potential of some special tax benefit from the presence of a rail depot;
3. Within the village was an inn that dispensed alcohol, a practice not generally approved of by the farmers of Monroe and South Brunswick.

Whatever the reason(s), the officials of Monroe interposed no objection to the aspirations of those who wanted Cranbury to stand on its own.

Jamesburg seems to have been an entirely different story—a story filled with acrimony and recrimination. The Buckelew family is credited with transforming the area from a sleepy little mill site into a thriving industrial town and something of a railroad hub. In the year of 1887 a special election was held in which 151 of the 167 voters casting ballots endorsed the creation of a borough commission. This allowed the commission to address certain concerns of the people living clustered near the rail depot—concerns such as sidewalks and street lights within the geographic limits of the borough. However, Jamesburg was not an officially independent community. Property taxes were still assessed and collected by Monroe Township with a portion of same being allocated to the area designated as an unincorporated borough. The authors of the Federal Writer's Project provide an almost blow-by-blow account of the tensions, as they escalated, between the Township Committee of Monroe and the Borough Commission of Jamesburg. The borough commissioners had an ally in the form of the local newspaper, the *Jamesburg Record,* whose editorials reflect the mounting division between the interests of the agricultural township and the rapidly urbanizing borough. The township's response to the historic blizzard of 1888 generated this comment from the newspaper: "The snow bill is the most iniquitous thing, however, $500 being paid out—most of it, we wager, being paid for labor used in digging out pigs, cows, etc." The bias is evident, and perhaps with just financial cause. The township committee not only was too prone to allocate money to advance the farmers' interests, but also got much of that money into its coffers as the result of unfairly high assessments on borough property, while the farms of Monroe were given too much of a break.

The disparity in tax assessments between the township and the borough generated this no-holds-barred editorial in the *Jamesburg Record:*

> There are men tampering in our township affairs who have been false to every trust. Are such worthies, safe men to put in office to continue their vicious practices? What have our committee and assessor to say regarding farms worth $20,000 and $30,000, now assessed at $3,000 and $5,000? Underestimating with the few, increases the burden of the many. Such rascally work should cease. Turn the rascals out!

The festering conflict was only resolved in 1896 when Jamesburg took the final step. In early 1897, by virtue of a confirmatory referendum, it became a completely separate entity, with much greater powers, such as the ability to borrow money by bonding and to enforce, locally, laws against disorderly conduct. This completed the divorce from the township and its assessing and bookkeeping practices. It also confirmed that Jamesburg, as a borough, would have local jurisdiction of the school district that was coextensive with its municipal boundaries.

Many other municipalities were being formed during this specific time period. Some of these will be identified as "railroad towns," while others will be identified as "school-district boroughs." Jamesburg shares characteristics of both types, as do many other communities throughout the state.

Even the divorce did not end the fighting. The quarreling over financial matters apparently continued for another two years until the Spanish-American War diverted everyone's attention from a bitter dispute. But of such disputes is the geopolitical map of the state drawn.

Spotswood dropped a *t* and an *e* from its original spelling and became a separate community in 1908, with all the attendant powers of regulating liquor sales and providing a potable water system.

Helmetta was created from a snuff mill in 1888. Cigar and snuff making were major industries in the area as early as the seventeenth century. The various interests of John D. Outcalt, David Snowhill, and William Dill were consolidated into the Helme enterprise whose chief executive at the turn of the twentieth century was John Herbert, an intimate of presidents. Herbert was so powerful that it was an easy matter for him to have a separate municipality created for his company. Indeed, he is given the credit for maneuvering Passaic County Senator Garrett Hobart on to the national Republican ticket in the position of vice-president and making Governor John Griggs the Attorney General of the United States. At the end of this chapter I'll unveil the mystery of how this town got its unique name.

While the Township of South Amboy had kept its configuration intact from 1685 to 1838, it took only 22 years before the creation of East Brunswick Township altered the configuration of Monroe. East Brunswick Township, in turn, found that the residents of the Borough of South River had developed a commercial orientation distinct from the fundamental rural character of its host township. South River, first known as Washington Town when it became a town within the township in 1870, would totally separate from East Brunswick in 1898 and concentrate its focus on the industries and trade that resulted from its access to shipping opportunities. In 1902 East Brunswick would surrender another piece of the township to help create the Borough of Milltown.

Actually, the Boroughs of Milltown and South River must be marked with an asterisk, since the creation of East Brunswick, although constituted primarily by land from Monroe, also contained a contribution from North Brunswick Township. Milltown and South River are included here because their lineage from North Brunswick was merged into the creation of East Brunswick.

Meanwhile, although the citizens of South Amboy had great expectations for the rail line that carried its very name, the owners of the railroad did not have reciprocal affection for South Amboy. As soon as the railroad could ferry passengers across the Hudson to embark on through-trains from Jersey City to Trenton, South Amboy was abandoned as a major passenger station and relegated to handling mostly freight. Thrown over for a faster and safer route, South Amboy was left to console itself that the famous line still bore its name. It also consoled itself that it had retained a good share of the freight handling and all that went with it; former outposts of the township that had served as stagecoach post stations such as Spotteswood, still a portion of Monroe, had been completely by-passed by progress.

South Amboy's absence from the march of progress was relatively short-lived. Like a medieval courtier with underestimated attributes—spurned, scorned, and exiled, only to be called back by a remorseful monarch to be elevated to a new height—South Amboy sat in the middle of the planned extension of tracks to the profitable vacation market at the Jersey shore, as the railroad kings realized.

When the Pennsylvania line decided to push its coast line to the newly popular holiday center of Long Branch, South Amboy became a major railroad center with railroad yards spreading across hundreds of acres adjacent to the water front. Almost as if to compensate for past neglect the railroad decided to use South Amboy for a switching facility and major maintenance area.

After the Civil War, the hottest political battle waged state wide was the effort to rein in the influence of the railroads, influence that every historian reports to be pervasive, enormous, powerful, and corrupt. The state constitution adopted in 1844 was extensively amended in 1875. Among the most important and controversial of the amendments was one that is contained in the latest state constitution adopted in 1947. The genesis of what is now designated as Article Eight, Section Two, Paragraph Two of our constitution was to prohibit the wholesale donation of state, county, and municipal property to the rail lines as an inducement for the companies to build or extend their tracks, a practice that had been rampant in the mid-nineteenth century. As the result of its location, the Township of South Amboy needed no such seductive tactics to attract railroad development. Far from begging the railroads to come to South Amboy, it was the other way around.

South Amboy Township that had existed since 1685 was actually a large township even by colonial standards. The township's northerly boundary was the Raritan River, and on the east it was the Raritan Bay or the Atlantic Ocean, depending on how one wished to define that body of water at the mouth of the river. It originally stretched south all the way to the dividing line between Middlesex and Monmouth Counties.

The next meaningful division of South Amboy after the formation of Monroe Township was in 1869 with the breaking off of Madison Township, containing almost 40 square miles of land inhabited by fewer than 250 families. The dynamics of the creation of Madison Township, now Old Bridge Township, are relatively clear:

- It was so sparsely populated as to be insignificant to South Amboy.
- Its pockets of population were so distant from South Amboy's center that travel by horseback was challenging and by horse and wagon, difficult at best.
- It had virtually no taxable enterprises.

- The widespread expectation of the possible passage of the state's first Railroad Tax Act after the Civil War gave the residents of South Amboy's central district the hope that they could set themselves on a tax base that need not be shared with the outlying areas of the Township of South Amboy. Up to this time the railroads had been completely exempt from local taxation, but significant agitation had begun to require that the extensive lands owned by the railroads, but not actually used as the main lines be subject to local assessment.

The focus of discussion of future taxes on the railroads was that the main lines, or rail stems as they were called at that time, were destined to be the exclusive tax domain of the state. Discussion had already begun, however, about the prospect of allowing municipal taxation on the ancillary properties owned by the railroads.

Very little economic activity occurred in this area, to be known as Madison Township, the vast and marshy expanse to the south—so little activity that the railroad to the shore did not even contemplate a station of any size within the geographical boundary of the new township. After the station at South Amboy the next stop would be in Matawan, Monmouth County. Madison Township was an engineering challenge to the railroad, and a political problem for South Amboy.

For their own part, the residents of the area were satisfied to go it on their own as the political powers in South Amboy continued to allocate the majority of the tax revenues to the improvement of the area near the station.

- The most important of all factors was accessibility to the new center of political and economic gravity that had formed in New Brunswick, which continued to eclipse Perth Amboy in economic importance. New Brunswick, the county seat, was also the center of political and legal administration. Moreover its economic strength was growing. Previously it was important to keep roads open and passable to South Amboy and from there rely on the ferry to Perth Amboy to conduct any legal, commercial, or banking business. Now it was essential to maintain in good condition the line of communication and transportation to the village of Old Bridge, the nearest market center, and through that village directly on to the county seat in New Brunswick. Except for the shore route along the bay, there was no reason to spend much money maintaining other roads that ran toward the Amboys. The legendary report of Barbour and Howe, originally published in 1854, reported that the village of Old Bridge already contained more buildings than did the center of South Amboy by a margin of 35 to 25.

The rumors about the railroad tax proved correct, and the next two efforts at amending the Railroad Tax Act in 1873 and again in 1884 proved the point. The main traffic line, identified as the stem, together with fifty feet on either side of the center of the stem, would be exempted from ad valorem (percentage of value) property tax—the main track would not be subject to local assessment, nor subject to local tax levy—taxes on the value of the main line would continue to go to the State.

South Amboy, having jettisoned Madison Township, still consisted of 17 square miles. Within its boundaries it had developed a large amount of taxable railroad property, consisting of sidings, coal yards, docks, and wharves, plus all of the enterprises that were associated with the operation of a rail center, i.e., warehouses and supply houses, including stables and blacksmiths, hotels and taverns, lots of taverns. Added to this were a number of small enterprises, business offices, a bank, and even a small power-generating station for the production of steam. This was necessary because a major repair and maintenance facility for the railroads was situated here, and it required power to work the machinery that forged and welded parts of the trains needing repair.

The new amendments to the Railroad Tax Act were rumored and widely discussed in the early 1870s. Each year new proposals were introduced, and it was now just a matter of time before significant change would occur. Change was in the air. The impetus for change came from many sources.

- The former special charters under which the railroads had been incorporated were about to expire, and with them the contract agreements that provided for the chartered railroads to pay taxes solely to the State.
- The system by which the old special charters for the railroads and canal companies were handed out by special legislation had proven to be so blatantly corrupt that although the arrangement had been profitable for the State, the system was so unpalatable that one of the new constitutional reforms of 1875 forbade the Legislature to grant incorporations by legislative charter.
- The county and municipal governments, growing in population, political power, and assuming ever-increasing responsibilities, wanted a piece of the railroad tax action.
- A good deal of the blame for the nationwide financial panic of 1873 was leveled squarely at the excesses of the railroads, thus making them easy targets for increased taxation.

The possibility of monopolizing the lion's share of local railroad taxes was an inordinate temptation for the politicians in South Amboy proper. Political power lay with the population that was concentrated around the hub of the railway stations. Moreover the population centered in the downtown area was separated by ethnic and religious differences from the scattered population out in the farms and brick factories of what was to become Sayreville. The river was still the major transportation modality for the brick yards and pottery manufacturers. At least four active docks were in operation along the south bank of the Raritan west of South Amboy proper. On the other hand South Amboy's life centered around the railroads. The dock and wharf of South Amboy were only relevant as they integrated with the rails, whereas the docks along the Raritan were the primary transportation option for brick companies. Finally, a significant factor in the dynamics of the separation was the intensifying ethnic and religious divisions.

It is almost idiomatic to the history of both New Jersey and the country that the Irish dug the canals and built the railroads. By the 1870s it was the rails that kept the Irish busy. The ethnic flavor of downtown South Amboy had become distinctly Irish by then, and the Roman Catholic Church enjoyed their allegiance. Meanwhile the farmers and clay manufacturers of the balance of the township remained predominantly English and German, worshipping in congregations that were Methodist, Lutheran, and Presbyterian. There were some Irish in the area but they were a distinct minority. Our family Bible records that the first celebration of a Roman Catholic mass took place in Sayreville on Christmas day 1876, in the home of Timothy Quaid, my great-grandfather. Timothy Quaid, who was known to all as "Captain," had worked since boyhood developing routes on the Raritan by which he hauled bricks by schooner from the brick yards to New York.

It was a very logical decision in all regards for South Amboy, in the parlance of modern corporate organizations, to "spin off" the township of Sayreville. A factor in the dynamic for the separation or spin-off was the ego of James R. Sayre, the leading industrialist of the area, but a resident of Newark. First, he was flattered by the idea of a community that would bear his name. This was heady stuff for a building contractor and factory owner who was neither war hero nor patriot. Secondly, he was encouraged to expect that he would have a great deal to say in the local affairs of the community. Just how strong an influence was anticipated can be clearly seen from the composition of the first township committee that consisted of five members. Committee members John H. Conger and Peter Rush both worked for James Sayre's company, the Sayre and Fisher Brick Company. The chairman of the committee, George Such, and another member, Thomas Armstrong, were employed by Such Clay, the major outside supplier to Sayre and Fisher. As to the Fisher family, Sayre's junior corporate partner, the first township clerk, was Peter Fisher, Jr., and the first tax collector was William Fisher. George H. Ludlow, later both senator from Middlesex County, and eventually governor from 1881 to 1884, was the township's first counsel. An able attorney and politician, he numbered among his private clients none other than the Sayre and Fisher Brick Company. The third factor was the encouragement given by the powers in South Amboy, who saw all of this as a once-in-a-lifetime opportunity to create a tax haven for themselves courtesy of the newly formed Pennsylvania Railroad, who had consolidated the major holdings of the previous rail companies.

The aim of the Sayre family was to create Sayreville as a company town in the same sense as others throughout the state. The brickworks was growing and prospering in the mid-1870s, and additional growth lay ahead, as construction in Manhattan and Brooklyn created an almost insatiable demand for the quality products of the famous Sayreville kilns. The goal of a company town was almost achieved, as evidenced by the operation of the company store, which accepted the company script that was issued by the brickworks in lieu of cash. In 1898, Sayreville sent to the legislature a young man who fought for a significant reform. He was particularly interested in improving conditions for those workers who were virtually imprisoned within company towns. His efforts became the stuff of family legend, for Sayreville's first assemblyman was my great-uncle and son of the

"Captain." Assemblyman John J. Quaid later became the first mayor of the newly constituted borough of Sayreville in 1919. At its high point the Sayre and Fisher Brick Company owned or leased over 1500 acres of property in the township— these holdings constituted approximately twenty percent of the entire community's high ground and stretched along almost two full miles of the riverfront. By 1900, the Sayre and Fisher Brick Company was one of the ten largest employers in the state, with thousands of men manufacturing tens of millions of bricks a year.

The bricks that built New York moved well enough by barge, but times were changing. The railroads were rapidly displacing water traffic everywhere. The Morris and Essex Canal, which had been designed to move Pennsylvania coal to the industrial centers of Paterson, Newark, Jersey City, and New York had come upon hard times. The company was as great an economic failure as it had been an engineering marvel. Just as the turnpike companies had folded under the competition of the rail lines so were the state's canal companies failing to hold their own against the power of the trains. The railroads now looked to other markets that they could take away from the remaining shipping interests. In 1888 the Raritan River Railroad began construction of a line that would service the brick yards and sand-mining operations of Sayreville. At the same time it would haul coal to fire the kilns and feed the power plant operated as a subsidiary by the brick company. By this time the city fathers of South Amboy were having second thoughts about their decision to let Sayreville go. After all, the great tax wars of the previous decade had been settled amicably.

The general law creating Sayreville had been adopted in the New Jersey Legislature and signed by the governor on April 14, 1876. It had spelled out the geographic boundaries and had directed appropriate representatives from South Amboy and Sayreville to meet at Mrs. Clark's Inn, located in South Amboy on May 10, 1876, to decide what tax ratables would fall to which community and to settle up any delinquencies. The joint determination was that residents of the new Township of Sayreville still owed taxes to South Amboy. The amount owed, to be exact, was $1,386.82. The folks out in the lands west of South Amboy proper had not been very punctual in paying their levies. This reluctance to pay taxes was another factor in the thinking of the town fathers in central South Amboy, who were willing, if not secretly anxious, to rid themselves of the few hundred families inhabiting this area, who had proven to be more trouble than they were worth. In 1877 a special election was held in Sayreville to provide for special assessments to be imposed on the residents of the new township to raise the money to pay South Amboy. Allegedly the vote was unanimous to pay the money, and to raise it by this special one-time-only tax. This seems very strange to me, since nothing in Sayreville was ever done unanimously. Moreover the imposition of the special assessment was vigorously protested by many taxpayers and by the Pennsylvania Railroad who filed an appeal claiming that Sayreville had no right to tax them for anything since their holdings were in South Amboy, not in Sayreville. Moreover, what they might own within Sayreville, was exempt. The appeals must have worked, or the people of Sayreville were demonstrating the same bad habits, and confirming the worst allegations of the South Amboyans. Whatever the case, it actually took five years before Sayreville ever paid what it owed to South Amboy. In fact, ten years after the separation, South Amboy's school district was still writing to the clerk of Sayreville inquiring why school moneys from 1881 had never been paid over.

In 1892 rumors began to spread that a bridge might be built over the Raritan. A railroad bridge had existed since 1872, but no other means except ferry brought people and goods from the one side of the river to the other. By early 1894 the rumors had become reality and much to the shock of the residents of South Amboy the bridge would be in Sayreville. South Amboy immediately responded by initiating an effort to allow South Amboy to reacquire the section of Sayreville that would be the southern terminus of the proposed bridge. At the same time they wanted to pick up some of the taxable property of the new Raritan River Railroad.

South Amboy, a full-fledged borough, made a game attempt, using its superior political clout to get a bill through the New Jersey Senate that would have reannexed parts of Sayreville. No action on that legislation was taken in the state assembly, and so the effort to annex part of Sayreville was thwarted for the time being. This defeat did not dissuade South Amboy from making three more attempts to retrieve what they came to realize they had improvidently allowed to slip away in 1876. In 1910, South Amboy, now a full-fledged city, had an annexation bill introduced in the New Jersey Senate, but this time it was referred to committee, which was, and still often is, the legislative equivalent of the Bermuda Triangle. Another effort was made during the First World War, and the final and most ambitious effort came in 1919. This proposal was to allow South Amboy to almost double in size from its self-imposed one and half square miles. Again South Amboy was rejected by the township it had spun off.

Just as railroads had been the driving economic force of the period from 1876 to 1910, munitions had become the driving economic force in the years leading up to the First World War; America happily and profitably supplied the potential European combatants and the allies after America became a participant in 1917. Even earlier, the International Smokeless Powder Company had built its first munitions works in Sayreville between 1898 and 1901 in response to the anticipated demand of the Spanish-American War. The Union Powder Company followed suit not many years later. The Union plant, later acquired by the Hercules Powder Company, was a major supplier for the U.S. Navy. During the actual conflict in Europe two additional armaments plants were constructed. By 1918 the tax base of Sayreville had grown to over $6.2 million, far more than enough to make many other communities smoke with envy.

More could be written about the specific dynamics affecting each of these individual towns. The personalities are fascinating, and the events they set in motion always interesting but often, in retrospect, merely comical. In the latter category falls the tale of how Sayreville's classification was changed from a township to a borough. It is not the material over which the eminent British legal scholar Frederic William Maitland pondered as he wrote his seminal treatise on *The Borough and the Townships* in 1895. Indeed, had he been aware of the circumstances of Sayreville's evolution to borough status he may well have abandoned his project. However, I would argue that the story actually reflects the deep historical precedents and is exemplary of the tradition of boroughs having certain immunities and privileges as asserted in the theories of Maitland and other historians who have studied the genesis and development of municipal government through the Middle Ages.

It was not the railroads that caused Sayreville to amend its charter; rather, it was events that occurred on European battlefields and within the bureaucracy of Washington, D.C. On May 20, 1918, the War Department issued an order prohibiting the sale of alcohol in any township within a certain radius of any military facility. As the crow flies the Township of Sayreville fell within the proscribed distance from the military arsenal located in Raritan, now Edison, New Jersey. As a result of this fiat from the War Department, the seven taverns within Sayreville were immediately closed. The Borough of South River on the west and the City of South Amboy on the east were exempted from the order because of their corporate status.

The proprietors of these establishments realized that it would be unpatriotic as well as futile to complain to the War Department that their order had made no sense. Finesse was required in these delicate circumstances. The legislature was petitioned and responded with alacrity, allowing Sayreville to become a borough. Notwithstanding the speed with which the tavern owners had mobilized their unique war effort, the issue was rendered moot by the time Sayreville gained its elevated municipal status on January 1, 1920. The tavern owners were successful in getting the town fathers to rebate a portion of the fees that had been paid in 1918 and 1919 for their annual liquor licenses.

Thus, contained within the history of the Balkanization of South Amboy Township are many of the factors that were described in the first chapter. Moreover, almost every one of the major causes for municipal proliferation that have been discussed will be examined more closely in the following chapters.

The creation of Monroe Township reflected the divergent agendas: the industrial interests associated with the commercial activity along the bay in South Amboy, as well as the agricultural interests of the farming communities removed from the navigable waters. For Monroe, New Brunswick became the center of gravity, replacing Perth and South Amboys.

Madison Township was jettisoned by South Amboy as it too was fundamentally removed from the commercial and industrial development that was creating a strong localized tax base incidental to the railroads' plans for the expansion of their service. Also Madison felt the attraction of devoting its resources to repairing its roads to the market village of Old Bridge and to the administrative center of New Brunswick rather than to the Old Coast Road to Perth Amboy.

Sayreville Township's creation was a combination of the ambition of the Sayre family and the desire on South Amboy's part to protect the enviable tax base it was developing as a result of its railroad freight facilities that were now expanded significantly by the opening of through service to the Jersey coast communities.

East Brunswick and Jamesburg are products of the classic street fights that occurred throughout the state over appropriations and priorities. These altercations, coupled with the private financial agendas of some local citizenry, brought about independent municipalities that would hopefully better monitor the expenditure of tax funds. The adoption of the new school law in 1894 was the final operative factor in Jamesburg's full boroughood, but it had created a commission earlier, following the pattern of other railroad towns throughout the state.

Helmetta was simply the product of the power and ambition of a single dominant political leader, who also happened to be the chief executive of the company for which the borough is named. Spotswood and Cranbury had operating taverns or inns, which made it easier for the dominant *dry* interests who controlled the balance of Monroe, with its active Anti-Saloon League, to see them go their own way, while incorporation allowed both towns to have a greater say in how their road tax dollars were spent and how the sale of liquor was regulated.

Street-fight townships, railroad towns, school district boroughs, wet versus dry towns—the only major cause that we didn't cover in this case study was exclusive enclaves. What was left of South Amboy—all one and half square miles of it—falls into that category in an unorthodox way. South Amboy contracted to such a small size to maximize its ratable base. As we shall see, other municipal boundaries were drawn on somewhat the same basis—to protect and preserve what was already there—and to keep out what was perceived to be undesirable. In the era prior to the acceptance of zoning principles, the most effective way of accomplishing this goal was to define the boundaries and then incorporate as a municipality.

Now, as promised, I will reveal the origin of the name Helmetta. As we learned earlier, John Herbert was the confidant of presidents and the intimate of the most powerful industrialists in the nation. He was also an extraordinary diplomat. The dominant tobacco company was owned by Colonel Helme. It might have been enough to suggest the new town be called Helmeston or Helmeville. The unique suffix *etta* was in honor of the colonel's beloved daughter Antoinette, whose intimate family nickname was Etta. She also happened to be Herbert's wife. It is no wonder he got so far, possessing as he did such skills.

CHAPTER 4

Shrewsbury

THE INCREDIBLE SHRINKING TOWNSHIP

I have a small-town soul.
It makes me want to know
Wee, unimportant things
About the folks that go
Past on swift journeyings.
Violet Alleyn Storey

Shrewsbury Township, one of the first half dozen recognized townships in East Jersey, has a history of municipal disintegration perhaps more unusual than that of any other community in the state. South Amboy Township had consisted of approximately 100 square miles and subsequently provided the territory for ten of our present-day municipalities. Shrewsbury Township was ten times larger than the original limits of South Amboy, and within the original borders of Shrewsbury one finds 75 separate towns spreading over two counties. An overview of the township's history demonstrates how a thriving township contracted to an infinitesimal fraction of its original size.

Shrewsbury was settled, not by an initial immigration from Europe, but, as with Newark and Middletown, by transplants from New England. In the case of Shrewsbury the migration and resettlement had been a two-step process: from New England to Long Island and then finally to the lower bank of the Navesink River. In December of 1663 a contingent of about twenty men sailed from Long Island to drop anchor in the Navesink River. They came for the specific purpose of buying land from the Native Americans. They were interested in three specific parcels or tracts of land and had to deal with three separate tribes. The Navesinks exercised control of the area north of the Navesink River; the Navarumsunks controlled the prime lands between the Navesink and the Shrewsbury Rivers; while all of the lands south of the Shrewsbury were the lands of the Portapecks.

The first five settlers were already occupying their purchased properties by the time the Duke of York assumed title to New Jersey in 1664. The duke empowered his faithful and successful colonel, Richard Nicolls, as governor of all the areas from which the Dutch had been ousted, thanks to Nicolls's seizure of New

Amsterdam. The new governor quickly promulgated rules for the acquisition of lands from the Native Americans. The settlers in Shrewsbury petitioned Nicolls in 1665 to recognize and confirm the purchases that they already consummated, and in April of that year Nicolls issued a grant thereafter referred to as the Monmouth Patent. This tract, therefore, has always stood separate and apart from all other lands in New Jersey, and the questions of political rights of the settlers of those holding title to their lands under the Monmouth Patent became a thorny issue during the period from 1665 to 1702.

The name was taken from the ancient and beautiful English town of Shrewsbury. The mother country was also remembered by Colonel Lewis Morris, when he purchased the ironworks of James Grover, an original patentee, and re-named it Tintern after his estate in Monmouthshire, England. Not quite as enduring as the Abbey immortalized by Wordsworth, the forge soon came to be known as Tintern Falls, which in turn was corrupted to Tinton Falls. Although the name was generically applied to the entire area embraced by the Monmouth Patent, most people understood the name Shrewsbury to refer to the quaint village that grew at the crossroads of the Kings Highway and the Burlington Trail. This village is now the heart of the Borough of Shrewsbury, and the southwest corner is the site of the municipal building and the Shrewsbury Historical Society, a home, as they accurately describe it, of history and remembrance.

Officially formed in 1693, Shrewsbury Township extended for almost 1000 square miles. It reached in the south to include all of what is now Ocean County. On the north it was bounded by the Navesink River, and in the west it ran all the way to the westerly edge of what is now the county line of Monmouth, separating it from Middlesex and Mercer Counties.

The total land area encompassed by Shrewsbury represented over thirteen percent of the total land mass of the entire state. To put this in some context, Burlington County, as it stretches from the Atlantic Ocean to the banks of the Delaware, constitutes the largest county in the state today, yet at slightly over 800 square miles it is substantially smaller than the original Shrewsbury Township. The figure of 1000 square miles converts to 640,000 acres. Today, amazingly, the township consists of barely 56 acres or .09 square miles.

Shrewsbury remained unchanged for almost sixty years until its lowest extremity was set off by Royal Charter to form Stafford Township, which in its turn formed the majority of the land mass of what today is Ocean County.

In 1768, on the eve of the Revolution, parts of Shrewsbury Township were separated to form Dover Township. Additional sections were ceded to Freehold and Upper Freehold Townships. Following statehood, Shrewsbury Township was included in the list of 104 townships incorporated and ratified by the famous Township Act of 1798, but it was only three years later in 1801 that Howell Township broke away and was recognized as another large and diverse free-standing municipality.

After forty-five years passed, another erosion occurred, thanks to the U.S. government. Sandy Hook was a strategic area for the protection of the entire New York Harbor, and the government in Washington, D.C., was anxious to have control over this sensitive and vital strip of land. A legal issue arises from this transfer as the original acquisition of this area included a license and easement agreement with the original Americans that provided them with the unrestricted right to enter Sandy Hook annually to hunt, fish, and harvest "beach plums." A subsequent agreement, supported by consideration of under one pound sterling, allegedly extinguished those rights. (I would enjoy the prospect of watching the fairness of that arrangement defended today in a courtroom.)

In the year of 1847, the Township of Atlantic was incorporated, and two years later the Township of Ocean was formed. These two townships took diverse courses, with Ocean being divided and redivided, fragmenting into a dozen communities, while Atlantic actually reduced its size by returning a part of its territory to Shrewsbury in 1891, but otherwise retaining its configuration until the present. It changed its name to Colts Neck in 1962.

Red Bank Town was formed within the township boundaries of Shrewsbury in 1870. Eatontown Township was created in 1873. The following year another parcel was given to the new Township of Eatontown. On Valentine's Day in 1879 Red Bank Town became Shrewsbury City. The romance with city status proved very short-lived, and the name and status were returned to Red Bank Town on May 5 of the same year. The Township of Lincoln was created in 1867, but changed its mind and asked to be reabsorbed into Shrewsbury the following year.

Between 1900 and the Second World War the break-aways continued:

- In 1907, the Borough of Rumson was formed after a referendum was held in that portion of the township.
- Red Bank, having been both a town and a city, decided it would be a borough and became such after acquiring another addition from Shrewsbury in 1908.
- Rumson received additional land in 1911, and in 1912 the Borough of Fair Haven was created.
- In 1923 the Borough of Little Silver came into existence.
- After all this time, Shrewsbury Borough became an entity in 1926 when a referendum was held to create the Borough.
- In 1928, a third parcel of land was added on from Shrewsbury Township to Rumson.

After the Second World War, yet another tract was lost by Shrewsbury Township to the Borough of New Shrewsbury, which kept that name for twenty-five years before changing it to become the Borough of Tinton Falls in 1975.

Shrewsbury Township has existed since 1950 with its present configuration, consisting of nine one-hundredths of a square mile, or roughly 56 acres.

Many of the large divisions just outlined were subjected to multiple subsequent divisions as time progressed. It is not necessary to trace every branch to the tips of its smallest twig, but it will be useful to study the major subdivisions to see why some, such as Colts Neck, remained fundamentally intact while others, such as Ocean Township, fragmented into a dozen or more pieces.

Focusing first on the territories still within the County of Monmouth, both

Freehold and Upper Freehold existed as place names long before their formal incorporations in the early twentieth century. Freehold, first mentioned in 1691, sent burgesses to the General Assembly of East Jersey at that time. Upper Freehold was noted as being "formed" from Freehold in 1731. Both townships are the beneficiaries of substantial additions from Shrewsbury in the year of 1768, and both enter the famous list of townships in the Act of 1798.

In 1844, Freehold yielded a portion of its lands simultaneously with Upper Freehold and Monroe Township to create the new municipality of Millstone Township. Later that same year, another section of Freehold was absorbed by Jackson Township, now Ocean County.

In 1847, another portion of Shrewsbury was contributed, along with lands from Middletown Township and Shrewsbury for the formation of Atlantic Township, which, as we have already seen, remained fundamentally intact until the present time, only changing its name to Colts Neck. The origin of the name Colts Neck is uncertain, but we do know the name was in use during the War for Independence. Over a square mile of the township was dedicated in 1844 for the experimental commune, The North American Phalanx Society. This venture was extremely successful at its outset, but had dissolved by 1855, much to the dismay of others who were adherents and advocates of the social philosophy of the French utopian socialist François Fourier.

The geographic stability enjoyed by Colts Neck was also enjoyed by the next two subdivisions of Freehold Township—Marlboro Township and Manalapan Township. The boundaries of Marlboro have remained exactly as they were when the new municipality was created in 1848. Manalapan's boundaries were altered only once since it was set off as an independent entity in 1848. The historic village of Englishtown, located within Manalapan, became a borough, containing .57 of a square mile, in 1888. Located within Manalapan is the famous *Olde Tennent Church* significant for its role in the Revolutionary War. Englishtown, by the way, does not derive its name from any connection with the British. In fact it was a center of anti-Tory sentiment and provided a safe haven for General George Washington. Known as Englishtown for a long period prior to the Revolution, the village was named for James English, who owned all of the village.

Marlboro, once known by its proper spelling of Marlborough, was originally settled by Quakers in 1685. As anxious as many of the present-day residents are to establish some provenance between the name and the ancient and honored family in Great Britain, none exists. The original village was called Topanemus, a name which is either Greek for "place of the worms" (*topo*-place and *nema*-thread or worm) or is a Native American place name. Rich in worms, the land consists of soils commonly called marl, which are particularly abundant in potash and phosphorous, and were used as fertilizer on poor thin soils before the widespread use of chemical fertilizers. The enormous commerce in this rich worm-filled soil led to the use of the present designation as Marlboro.

In 1869, Freehold Town was formally recognized, but existed within Freehold Township. It incorporated as a borough in 1919 and expanded by adding a piece of the township to form its present configuration, composed of exactly two square miles, in 1926.

Upper Freehold Township contributed land for the creation of Millstone in 1844 and of Jackson Township in the same year. In 1849, a piece of Upper Freehold Township went to Plumstead Township in preparation for the establishment of Ocean County, which took place in 1850. In 1851, Jackson Township returned a section to Upper Freehold to straighten the county line, and in 1869 Plumstead, now in Ocean County, also returned a section to Upper Freehold. Allentown, a historic village similar to Englishtown, but containing a few more acres, became an independent borough in 1889. As with Englishtown, Allentown Borough carries the name of its original founder, Nathan Allen, who built a grist mill there as early as 1706. Other villages within Upper Freehold carried interesting names such as Imlaystown, Cream Ridge, Prospertown, and Cabbagetown, but none of these carried enough influence to become independent municipalities.

In 1845, Millstone Township restored the portion it had received from Monroe Township, which two years later gave Millstone another piece to finalize the county line between Middlesex and Monmouth. After Millstone added a piece from Jackson Township in 1846, Millstone maintained its boundaries for ninety years until the creation of Jersey Homestead Borough in 1937. This borough, consisting of 1.96 square miles, changed its name to Roosevelt in 1945, whose story will be recounted in a later chapter. As for the balance of the Millstone Township, we know only that the Perrine family had moved to this area from New England and that by 1825 the name of Perrineville had appeared on the map.

Turning now to the north coast of Monmouth County, let us look at a major subdivision of Shrewsbury: Ocean Township. The area along the Atlantic Coast had been a haven for vacationers, starting with seasonal sojourns of the Native Americans who came to the beaches to harvest the abundant shellfish and then feast until the discarded shells formed virtual mountains on the beach. The area from Long Branch to Belmar constituted some of the finest beaches anywhere along the Eastern coastline, but it was principally the attraction to and development of the village of Long Branch that caused the creation of Ocean Township in 1849. Elliston Perot of Philadelphia had built a sizable boarding-house in 1788, and a hotel appeared by 1834. By the time of the Civil War there were a handful of hotels and perhaps as many as 75 private houses.

Ocean Township's orientation was to the sea. Its resources were focused on the improvements necessary to foster a rapidly expanding holiday trade: with a climate moderate in comparison to the oppressive heat of the plantations, it was popular with wealthy families from the South prior to the outbreak of the Civil War. Nearby were the commercial centers of New York and Philadelphia, so that long-standing trading relationships could be attended to by the heads of the household, while the rest of the family enjoyed the ocean view from the verandas or watched as horses ran at the nearby tracks. The war changed these rituals and changed the clientele. But the appeal of Long Branch as a resort continued to grow.

Long Branch in 1867 was granted a charter from the New Jersey Legislature to have its own commission within Ocean Township. The commission had much wider and greater powers than any ever extended to a township: it could control traffic, pave and light streets, license various activities, and suppress vice. The legislature had no difficulty constructing this very special charter for the community. After all, Long Branch was the Monte Carlo of America. Just as the European playground held an independent status, so too, the charter for the Long Branch Commission provided for a community *in but not of* the balance of Ocean Township.

The commission functioned in governing Long Branch for nearly forty years, but then the community, with its glory days nothing more than fading memories, reincorporated as a city in 1903. When one visits Long Branch today, it is difficult to believe that it was once a resort of worldwide fame and reputation. That ethereal status came to Long Branch along with the annual visits of President Ulysses S. Grant, who adopted the town as his home. Along with President Grant arrived the glamour and wealth that are always associated with high-profile residents. A great deal has been written about antebellum Long Branch, and the tales of conspicuous wealth and egregious excess have endured where the attraction of the city has faded.

Lending credence to Hegel's theory of an historical dialectic, there arose at the opposite end of Ocean Township a community diametrically opposite to Long Branch. Ocean Grove was as deeply committed to temperance and probity as Long Branch was to indulgence and dissipation. The Camp-Meeting at Ocean Grove was opened in July of 1869 and provided a seaside resort for those of a more sober bent than those attracted to the saloons and gambling parlors of Long Branch.

Nowhere is the tension between wet and drys more visible than in the fate of Ocean Township. The sale and consumption of alcohol was an issue that resulted in a new Mason-Dixon Line being drawn through Ocean Township, with the North being wet and the South being dry. The unity of Ocean Township could not survive, and no efforts to enforce a union of an area so deeply divided could have any hope of success.

In 1873 to 1874 Ocean Township yielded territory for the creation of Eatontown, which was named to honor the memory of Thomas Eaton, who had settled the area in 1670. Eatontown was more importantly the host to the Monmouth Park Jockey Club, whose facility rivaled any of its kind known in the world, and where the refreshments served were stronger than lemonade. At the same time, the new Borough of Asbury Park was being formed, one of the new Ocean Township communities that developed out of the temperance issue. In addition to Asbury Park, Bradley Beach, Ocean Grove (now reabsorbed into Neptune Township), Avon-by-the-Sea, and Belmar owe their existence to the temperance movement, and in large measure they were developed to stand as the antithesis of the wicked ways of Long Branch. This phenomenon was replicated further down the New Jersey coast, where the debauchery of Atlantic City inspired the creation of alcohol-free resort communities in Cape May County.

Once begun, the separatist process continued within Ocean Township with the formation of Neptune Township in 1879, Sea Bright Borough in 1889,

Allenhurst Borough in 1897, Borough of Deal in 1898, Monmouth Beach Borough in 1906, Interlaken Borough in 1922, and Loch Arbour Village in 1957. Except for Neptune Township, the other six municipalities were created for the purpose of preserving exclusivity, each being little more than a tightly controlled real estate development in its inception. That is not in any way to diminish their significance. For instance, the Borough of Deal represented an effort to restore the glory and magnificence of what Long Branch had once been, but without the tawdry elements that had been allowed to pervade that city.

Neptune Township was susceptible to the pressures and tensions of the time. It now became a question of which religious sect could prove itself the absolute driest. Neptune was divided between the township and the new City of Neptune. Two additional municipalities had managed to wedge their way onto the beach front between the Methodist-dominated communities of Ocean Grove (which would ultimately be reabsorbed by Neptune Township in 1921) and Belmar, which earlier came from Howell Township through Wall Township.

James A. Bradley was a busy man, who in 1873 had single-handedly launched the founding of Asbury Park. Twenty years later his efforts were devoted to founding the new project of Bradley Beach. At the same time he was actively campaigning to become the state senator from Monmouth County. His successful campaign became legendary, and Bradley was seated only after the Supreme Court blunted an attempt by the Democrats to bar him from the Senate as being unfit. One of the charges against him was that he had given gratuities for votes. It seems that he had handed out scrub brushes to prospective voters—a gesture rich in symbolism. Once seated, Bradley helped administer the coup de grace to his old nemesis, Long Branch, by outlawing race tracks, such as the popular Monmouth Park. But the Methodists were thwarted from unifying the beach front from Asbury to Belmar by the creation of Key East, which had been founded by a group of Baptist ministers. In 1900, the borough of Avon-by-the-Sea would replace Key East.

The development of Howell Township was in stark contrast to the pitched temperance battles that had identified the course of Ocean Township. Howell had enjoyed township status since 1801; and other than surrendering a good portion of its jurisdiction to Brick Township in Ocean County in 1850, Howell experienced only two further divisions. The major change came in 1851 with the creation of Wall Township, and then no further changes occurred until the Village of Farmingdale incorporated as a borough in 1903. Its major offspring was named in honor of General Garret D. Wall. One of the state's most interesting political figures, Wall had been among those bright young men who hooked their wagon to the national political movement led by General (and later President) Andrew Jackson. Originally from Burlington County, Wall had been selected by the legislature to be governor in 1829. He declined to serve in that position, opening the way for his fellow Jacksonian Peter D. Vroom of Somerset to become governor. In 1851, Howell Township had sparse settlement other than in the coast village of Manasquan.

It is difficult to find the same intensity of religious conviction that dominated the Long Branch/Asbury Park area along the southernmost coast of

Monmouth County. There is no question that the temperance movement did play an important and often unintended role. The separation of Manasquan from Wall in 1887 is clearly related to the newfound importance of the railroad as the center of the community's economic life. Spring Lake is in the mold of Deal, being a town that began as a private real estate development, where the interests of the developers were best accommodated by the creation of a municipality.

Sea Girt had much the same origin, but its incorporation as a borough was related to the events of the First World War, rather than a compulsion to protect its exclusivity. It appears that both Sea Girt and Brielle existed as separate boroughs, the former incorporated in 1917 and the latter in 1919, for the same reason that Sayreville became a borough—to protect the right to sell alcohol despite being within the proscribed radius of a military installation.

Belmar, of all of Wall's progeny, has the most diverse history, but also one most directly related to the temperance movement. Anyone who has ever been in Ocean Grove would readily acknowledge that it is extremely crowded, with each building virtually built on top of the other. Many residents in 1873 decided to spread out to the area to the south. They chose a beach front about three miles below Ocean Grove and started the Ocean Beach Camp Meeting Association. In 1885 it began its existence as a separate municipality called Ocean Beach Borough. The railroad was having some influence on Ocean Beach—and it soon became the City of Elcho Borough. This odd name reflects the municipality's attempt to be both a city and a borough. This was not the only time in the state's history where a municipality adopted two types of municipal status in its corporate title. Within a month the residents had changed their minds about Elcho, and had changed the name again to the City of Belmar Borough. The following year the decision-makers decided to drop the pretense of being a city and became simply the Borough of Belmar. Belmar shares in a number of municipal creation traditions. It could be argued that its genesis was controlled by the desire to create another beachhead in the battle for prohibition, but it could equally well be argued that it was the railroad and its influence that precipitated the decision to create a new municipal government.

In summary, the fragmentation of Shrewsbury represents most of the major dynamics of town creation.

- All of the divisions prior to 1850 had their genesis in quarrels concerning roads and the priorities involved. New centers of commercial and administrative gravity emerged. The county seat in Freehold drew increased attention, and it was the market center for the agricultural interests in the surrounding townships. The opening of the Jamesburg-Freehold Agricultural Railroad in 1853 made Freehold a magnet drawing roads and the expenditure for their construction and maintenance toward this administrative and commercial hub. The farmers in the townships of Freehold, Upper Freehold, Howell, Marlboro, Manalapan, and Atlantic (Colts Neck) had no interest in having decisions on roads being made by the committee in Shrewsbury. They knew where their interests lay and wanted control over what market roads would get the most attention.

- The focus of Ocean Township was indeed upon the object that its name honored. It is difficult to believe that at its creation in 1849 anyone thought this township would become a cultural and religious battleground. Yet almost all of its offspring were hatched out of the conflict between wets and drys.
- Red Bank was a port that evolved into a railroad-borough. Eatontown's existence was also railroad inspired.
- Rumson and Fair Haven, were products of the pre-zoning use of municipal incorporation as a method of preserving residential enclaves, and a particular style and way of life.
- Another dynamic that drove the balkanization of so much of the state was protection of local schools. As with road construction, liquor sales, railroad depots, and the desire for exclusivity, school districts functioned as a major influence in the fragmentation of New Jersey.

It is important to point out that school issues also played a role in the fate of Shrewsbury. In 1923 the Board of Education for the Shrewsbury Township suggested that $100,000 be spent for the construction of a new elementary school to consolidate the existing local schools and thereby require that children living in the village of Little Silver travel many miles to the new school.

The village had existed for many years, and its residents were more affluent than those living in the balance of what remained of Shrewsbury Township. How the village came by its name was always of great interest. Some thought it was from the fact that only a little silver had been necessary to gain title to the region from the Native Americans. Another theory was that the water in the area was streaked with hues of silver. In fact, the name derived from the ancestry of the first settlers who had come from the area around the Devonshire Village of Silverton, and who invoked memories of their homeland by calling their new settlement by the diminutive, Little Silver.

The residents of the village were already upset by the fact that they contributed about a third of the total taxes in the township, and received in return only about half that amount in services. The New Jersey State Legislature passed a bill allowing Little Silver to conduct a referendum on becoming a borough with a coextensive school district. The territory that had once been Monmouth County School District Number 74 became, upon successful passage of the referendum, the two-and-a-half-square-mile Borough of Little Silver.

The creation of this school-district borough lagged almost thirty years behind the tidal wave of such boroughs that had come into existence primarily in Bergen County. The effort required a special act of the legislature in 1923, whereas the 30 or more school-district boroughs created in 1894 to 1895 had no need to clear that particular hurdle. Little Silver was one of the last dozen or so boroughs in the state to come into existence as a result of a desire to control the local school, but not the last such borough in old Shrewsbury.

With this perspective the final story on Shrewsbury now should be told. In 1926, fear arose among many residents that the very heart of the historic Shrewsbury Township would be taken over by the burgeoning community of Red Bank. And of course the question of protecting the autonomy of the local school district was a factor. The residents of this area were as loathe to send their children to the new central school as had been the residents of Little Silver. Pressure mounted and the residents petitioned the legislature to pass the law providing for a local referendum. The first vote on May 11, 1926, was not quite unanimous—at least 8 of the 124 eligible voters thought it more economical to consolidate their school system with Red Bank's. Then on June 8, 1926, unanimity was achieved with the election of a mayor and council who ran unopposed.

The first problem that faced the new governing body was: where to meet? The original town hall of Shrewsbury had gone the way of other facilities. It was now serving as the seat of government for Red Bank. The most serious problem for the township was that most of their officials lived in the new Borough of Red Bank. The first meetings of the borough were conducted at the Parish Hall of historic Christ Church. Legend has it that on August 2, 1926, the heat in the hall was so overwhelming that the governing body recessed and reconvened in the adjoining cemetery. No one seemed to mind the portents implied by this move.

The loss of 2.21 square miles must have been of little consequence to a township that had already been so severely shrunken. Moreover the Shrewsbury Township still contained almost 16 square miles of territory. But then came the Second World War, which led to major land losses for Shrewsbury. As the storm clouds gathered over Europe, the military began to expand its operations at Fort Monmouth. The home of the Army Signal Corps, the fort desperately needed housing, which the federal government built in Shrewsbury for noncommissioned officers and other essential personnel The housing, just fancy barracks for those with families, was named the Alfred Vail Homes in honor of the man who had been the chief assistant to Samuel Morse and played a critical role in the development of the Signal Corps.

The contribution of Vail and of those who occupied these tax-exempt homes was quickly forgotten after the end of the war. Enormous resentment replaced gratitude as soon as the federal government ceased subsidizing the schools and other services in Shrewsbury. The patriots did their best to force the Vail residents to form their own municipality, i.e., they wanted them thrown out of Shrewsbury Township and their municipal services cut off. Thwarted in these attempts, the patriots then turned to their legislators in Trenton to protect them from these nontaxpaying parasites. Governor Alfred Driscoll agreed that something should be done. With the powerful Monmouth County Senator J. Stanley Herbert leading the way, Chapter 133 of the Laws of 1950 was enacted. It drew a line around the Vail Homes and said everyone living in the Shrewsbury Township outside the Vail

Homes would be entitled to vote in a special election to decide if they wished to be a new borough—the Borough of New Shrewsbury. The issue passed and the governor was now obligated to appoint officials to a committee in the township, which was now just the Vail Homes.

Why weren't the folks in the Vail Homes allowed to vote on the issue of whether or not they wanted to be abandoned? The slogan of the day summed up the pettiness and resentment: Vail Home residents allegedly had *representation without taxation*—damn near Communism according to those who led the drive for the divorce.

The once gigantic Shrewsbury Township was reduced to one of the half dozen war-orphan towns in New Jersey. Especially raw in the divorce of New Shrewsbury (Tinton Falls) from the historic township is the fact that the residents of the Vail Homes were literally disenfranchised from the decision. The Constitutional Amendment of 1875 prohibited the legislature from adopting legislation interfering with the internal governance of a community. However, the Constitution of 1947 had provided in Article Four, Section Seven, Paragraph ten a way to interfere:

> Upon petition by the governing body of any municipal corporation formed
> for local government, or of any county, and by vote of two-thirds of all
> of the members of each house, the Legislature may pass private, special
> or local laws regarding the internal affairs of the municipality or county.

The creation of the war-orphan municipalities was accomplished by invoking this particular constitutional provision.

The 1950 separation of the Vail Homes to create New Shrewsbury (Tinton Falls) decimated the once-mighty Shrewsbury Township and is the most dramatic example of the selfish and petty motivations—the basis for the majority of municipal entities in the state. Even assuming that the reasons existing in 1950 were somehow defensible within the context of that time, the Supreme Court's subsequent rulings (*Robinson v. Cahill,* and *Abbott v. Burke,* concerning the state's obligations for public education) have made those 1950 reasons irrelevant. The same could be said about the reasons that might be advanced for the separate existence of so many of the other separate communities that were once a part of Shrewsbury Township. The once-powerful dynamic of the temperance movement has been relegated to the same footnote status as the Volstead Act and national Prohibition. We really must ask ourselves: if the reason for separation no longer exists why, then, should the consequences of the reason still exist?

Finally, it should be noted that the entirety of present-day Ocean County was originally nothing more than the southern section of old Shrewsbury Township. All of Ocean County's 33 municipal entities now spread out over 636 square miles and house a population that has grown during the course of the twentieth century from under 20,000 to an estimated 500,000 at the next census (2000).

Ocean County's population in the 1950s was so sparse that it became the site for the state's first nuclear-power facility, located in remote Lacey Township. The population has risen substantially since the construction of the generating station, growing from under 1000 when construction began to over 23,000 on the eve of the millennium. Yet Lacey enjoys a population density less than half of the average density in the balance of Ocean County.

The dynamics of the growth of Ocean County are complex and to a large degree depressing. Low property taxes and inexpensive housing transformed the northern perimeter of the Pine Barrens into an artificial suburb of stultifying sameness. The Garden State Parkway became an escape route for tens of thousands of aging, urban whites seeking the security of sameness. Lacking mass transit, the internal network of roads became parking lots thanks to the increased traffic attempting ingress and egress to the strip malls serving as the new downtowns of Brick and Dover Townships.

However, many fine examples of the same dynamics that fragmented other areas of the state are well represented in Ocean County. Seaside Park reflects the strong temperance movement in this area of the State. On the other side of the equation is Lakewood, which once rivaled Long Branch as the destination of choice for the sybaritic. Lakehurst, as well, exists as municipal proof that a loyal soldier should be able to get a drink at the end of a tough day on the drill-field. The influence of the railroads can be seen not only in Point Pleasant and Bay Head, but also in the Township of Manchester, which was planned to take a role similar to that of its namesake in England and become the central manufacturing site for locomotives. Tuckerton's independence from its parent was also influenced by the railroads, as were a number of towns on Long Beach Island.

Exclusivity was present in the county's development and perhaps more than any other single dynamic created a number of towns along the coast of Ocean County.

Also noteworthy is the demographics of Ocean County. Shrewsbury was settled by men and women who were relocating not from England but from homes they had already established in the New World. Nowhere in New Jersey is this tradition of relocation more actively honored than in Ocean County, home to hundreds of thousands who have relocated from elsewhere in the region.

The more things change, the more they remain the same. That is not always the case. But, while we are on the subject of change it is appropriate to say a few final words about the name Shrewsbury. The suffix *bury* is a corruption of the ancient term *burgh*. Other mutations of the term, which denoted a place smaller than a city but larger than a village and usually having a wall or secure enclosure, are *burg, borough,* and *boro.* In England, after the Norman Conquest, the more Latinesque *y* sound replaced the Germanic guttural *g* sound. By the twelfth century Canterburgh and Salisburgh had become Canterbury and Salisbury.

PART II

Specific Issues that Cause Division

CHAPTER 5

Municipalities Created by Street Fights

The very word "roads" was practically synonymous with scandal.
Governor Walter E. Edge

No other state either enjoys, or suffers, the same reputation as does New Jersey for its long-standing and serious devotion to partisan politics. New Jersey's public life has been organized and led by some of the most colorful political leaders that the country has ever seen, and their questionable practices and quirky electoral rituals have been the source of legends. The history of the state is cloaked in an aura of a tough, bare-knuckled, no-holds-barred, win-at-any-cost, partisan political tradition. Every statewide campaign has had the flavor of a rough-and-tumble street fight. The reputation has been well earned and is more than justified. And, indeed, street fights, in both the literal and figurative sense, were the basis for the creation of a substantial number of the state's 566 towns.

In Chapter 3 we observed the creation of East Brunswick Township from *Road District Number 11* of Monroe. We also saw how Monroe Township and Madison (now Old Bridge) Township broke away from South Amboy Township as new road priorities evolved, and roads to New Brunswick became more vital than the roads to Perth Amboy. Those stories are just examples of what had been occurring since colonial times. The legacy of jurisdictional division as the result of road-expenditure disputes goes back so far as to warrant the designation "trail fights" rather than street fights.

It is easy to identify and delineate the conflicts that arose in the second half of the nineteenth century between commuters, who wanted lighted paved streets, and farmers, who wanted the township to concentrate expenditures on maintaining the rural roadways. However, it is somewhat more difficult to imagine that the issue of road, actually trail, upkeep could set farmer against farmer in the eighteenth century. The division of Windsor Township, which was still a part of Middlesex County in 1796, is an excellent example. The division of old Windsor Township was caused by a controversy involving whether the trail to Trenton or the road to New Brunswick would get more attention when it came to appropriation of available road-repair dollars. From this quarrel sprang the Township of East Windsor, whose focus was on keeping the way to New Brunswick passable, and the Township of West Windsor, whose residents felt it more important to be able to reach Trenton on a reliable route.

The records of the proceedings dividing the township are still intact, and the governing bodies of both East and West Windsor, as a part of their bicentennial observances, reenacted the fateful meeting that divided Windsor into east and west.

It is impossible to miss the point of these early deliberations. The spirit of independence was manifested in a simple proposition: "I'm happy to pay for what benefits me directly, but don't ask me to pay for someone else's benefit"—a view that has been as persistent in New Jersey, as it has been dominant.

In this chapter we will explore the history of road construction in various areas of the state, and focus particular attention on the dynamics of dividing jurisdictions. Ultimately, the issue of control of tax revenues and the allocation of those moneys resulted in the division and redivision of municipalities. However, it is important to understand how the evolving statutory systems governing local road construction and maintenance, designed and redesigned by the legislature over the centuries, encouraged jurisdictional fragmentation, and how those statutory schemes dovetailed with phases in the state's economic development. The emergence of economic and administrative centers resulted in the formation of "centers of gravity" that gained priority status in local budget decisions. Finally, we will take a brief look at how both the railroads and the coming of the auto age compounded the problem of resolving local budget priorities, causing additional jurisdictional splits.

The debate causing the division of the Windsors was fairly representative of the dynamics that were operating on the society at the turn of the eighteenth century. New Jersey's settlers had inherited a tradition of road maintenance that had existed in England from time immemorial. Professor Maitland discusses, in his text on the early British common law, the obligation of each freeholder in the eleventh century to contribute to the construction of new roads and to the upkeep of the roads that had been built by the Romans in the first and second centuries.

The colonists, as we shall see, enacted laws reflecting the English system or their interpretation of that system. The first legislative enactment concerning roads was adopted in 1682. The concept of separate branches of government apparently had not yet taken hold, as it was the courts who were designated to appoint citizens to serve as Overseers of the highways. Responsibility was reposed in the counties, but it was merely a matter of time before that obligation was being delegated to township committees as well.

Unquestionably, roads were the subject of early disputes. One of the earliest known roads in the state was the *Road up the Raritan,* which started in Piscataway and ran to what is now Bound Brook, where it merged with the King's Highway. Parts of this road were fenced in, or rather travelers were fenced out, thus setting the stage for litigation. The first, but obviously not the last, litigation occurred in 1718, beginning a long tradition of court disputes involving highways. The reported opinions of the courts often provide us with interesting historical summaries of the development of the law affecting roads.

Middlesex County records from the early eighteenth century indicate that it already had thirty-five public roads, which were tended by what these early records refer to as *viewers*. Apparently, road maintenance continued to be a county matter for a considerable period of time, but in 1774 the legislature enacted statutes delegating powers to the townships. The title of those in charge of maintaining the roads was now *Township Overseer*.

By an act of the legislature in 1818, townships were required to appoint Overseers of roads, and were directed to divide their territory into road districts. No township appointed a single Overseer, but rather the township's governing body would divide up the municipality into road districts of approximately equal size and then divide the moneys raised among the various road districts. The equal division of the money raised was not rigidly observed, and the disparity in treatment resulted in disputes. In other instances, the money was scrupulously divided to see that each district received the same amount, and that, too, caused problems.

The 1819 Supreme Court case of *Ward v. Folly*, 5 N.J.L. 566, is classic among the type of disputes that arose under this system. It was a nasty fight that involved a farmer named Peter Ward, who tried to block off a roadway running through his property. The Overseer, Abraham Folly, tore down the fence and repaired the road using some of the materials that Ward had piled up there. Folly had been the Overseer for this road in the prior year, but had not been officially appointed for the year in which he made this repair. Ward sued for $25—the damage to his fence and the value of the transposed materials. Chief Justice Kirkpatrick wrote that in considering the dispute on appeal, he had read all of the old acts of the Assembly, or at least as many as he could collect. While never specifically stating that the dispute is being decided under the new statute, indeed never mentioning the year in which the dispute arose, his decision must be taken as a pronouncement on the new law passed in the previous year, 1818.

His research started with the first Road Act of 1682, which was enacted not long after the first settlement of the province. The 1682 act had directed that all necessary highways be set and laid out by certain persons who were to be appointed by their specific counties. They were further directed to give an account of their work to the governor and the council so that the highways could be registered in the public records of the province. The Chief Justice said he was in possession of another act passed in 1716, but strongly implied that there may well have been additional acts that had been lost or destroyed. He then emphasized that the Act of 1716 does not require the recordation of the highways in any place either in the county seat or the state capital.

Kirkpatrick went on to say that only in an act passed in 1760 does he first find the requirement that surveyors report all roads they have laid out to the county clerk, who was given the responsibility of maintaining a special book, to be called *the road-book*. Kirkpatrick attributed to this act the origin of the term *road-book*, and determined that until that time no record of roads was actually required to be kept as a permanent record. Finally, he decided that since the road in question had been in use as far back as memory can reach, it is an "ancient road," and therefore a public thoroughfare—notwithstanding the fact that its existence did not appear in the county's official *road-book*.

The second part of his opinion deals with the section of the new act that read as follows: "The township committee are hereby authorized and directed to assign and appoint, in writing, to the Overseers respectively, their several limits and divisions of the highway within such township, for working, amendment and repair."

His judicial construction of this provision provided insight into how the system actually worked. He wrote:

> The great object of this clause is to inform the Overseer, with precision, what part of the road belongs to him, and to make him responsible for the repairing of it. . . . After a good deal of inquiry, I have found that the course pursued by these committees in very many townships, has been to lay off the township in districts, which are entered in their books and which remain unaltered, sometimes for many years together; and then at the town meeting, annually, to choose an Overseer for each district, and to make no further assignment about it.

A jury had awarded the sum of $15 to Ward, but the Supreme Court, speaking through Chief Justice Kirkpatrick, was persuaded to reverse the decision and find in favor of Overseer Folly, who was represented by the attorney general. Ward, however, was not to be denied. He brought another complaint for trespass against Folly for what he said was a subsequent event, and this time he once again prevailed with a jury. Folly appealed to the Supreme Court, and had the benefit of again being represented by the attorney general, but this time to no avail. The finding of the jury that Folly had thrown down Ward's fence, carried off his rails and stones, and dug up his property outside the limits of the road was affirmed with Justice Southard, this time writing the opinion of the court.

The opinion of Kirkpatrick in the first case provides a contemporary account of just how the system worked. It also demonstrates that by this early period the forces of reductionism and division had already been at work: the legislature originally delegated only to the counties the responsibility for roads, then to the townships; and in practice the townships by 1818 had already adopted a further division of jurisdictions by establishing "road districts." The accepted practice is acknowledged by both the wording of the statute and the opinion of the Supreme Court.

This system was operated in a period that did not require the town fathers to observe the present-day niceties of competitive bidding. The many records indicate that the names of those appointed to the position of Overseer of Roads bore a strong family resemblance to the names of the members of the township committee. The work was to be done, not only in the absence of bids, but also in the absence of any formal plans or specifications other than the mandate to keep the roads passable.

Another reported opinion of the Supreme Court 82 years later provides the same type of historical review of road legislation and brings us, not only up to date, but also to the end of the roles of Overseer and elected Commissioner of Roads. The opinion in the matter of *Allen v. Hiles*, 67 N.J.L. 135, was given by Justice Garretson,

> The duty of making and repairing the public highways was, from the earliest times, imposed upon the townships (Leam. and Spi. 459), and this obligation has remained upon the townships to the present day, unless other provisions have been made by Special Laws. The townships have always been required to provide the money and labor necessary for these purposes. In support of this assertion the court cites the various relevant statutes, starting in 1798 and running through all amendments and revisions until 1901. ("An Act Incorporating Townships," passed February 21st, 1798 (Elm. Dig. 571), and "An Act Concerning Roads," passed February 9th, 1818 (*id.* 472); "An Act Incorporating Townships" (revision), approved April 14th, 1846 (Gen. Stat. P. 3583 sec 11); "An Act Concerning Roads" (revision), approved April; 16th, 1846; "An Act Concerning Roads" (revision), approved March 27th, 1874 (Gen. Stat., page 2814 sec. 39); "An Act Concerning Townships" (revision 1899), (Pamph. L. 1901, p. 382).

In 1859 the legislature made a crucial change in the road act by establishing the position of a Commissioner of Roads (Gen. Stat., p.3583, sec. 12), to be elected in each road district as delineated by the township committee. This arrangement was continued, according to Justice Garretson, in revisions to the act in 1885 (Gen. Stat., p. 2932, sec. 528). Justice Garretson reported that he was unable to find a repeal of these statutes, but concluded that they were repealed by implication in the Act of 1891.

Between 1859 and 1891 many an elected district road commissioner, having won the support of his constituency within that district of the township, began to fantasize that if that district were an independent municipality, he would be the mayor rather than just the road commissioner. It is easy to understand how the pursuit of these day-dreams became irresistible to some.

By the time the legislature got around to changing the statute again in 1891 (Gen. Stat., p. 2853), a substantial number of new municipalities had been created thanks to disagreements on road priorities within various townships and the egos and ambitions of elected road commissioners.

The subject of the litigation in the *Allen* case was the interpretation of the new statute of 1891, which recited that henceforth, "the township committee of each township shall have the full supervision, management and control of the making and repairing of all roads in said township, and may make and repair same by hire or by contract, and for that purpose may annually appoint a competent person or persons to superintend the making and repairing of all roads . . . and he shall serve at the pleasure of the township committee."

This change in the statute was extremely significant in many ways. First, it put a stop to elected road commissioners establishing their own little fiefdoms. Second, it represented a portion of the broader context of municipal statutory reform, which during the 1890s consolidated the hundreds of various and often conflicting laws that had found their way into the statutes. Third, the trend of consolidating power and accountability in the hands of the municipality's governing body was reflected in this act, as it clearly placed responsibility on the entire committee rather than decentralizing authority throughout the various road districts. This trend that centralized appointment powers was widely criticized at the time as giving too much patronage power to the elected local officials. Finally, it should be noted, as an interesting aside, that this act, repealing by implication the power of road district "taxpayers" to elect their local road commissioner, represented a step backward in voting rights for women. The Act of 1859 had specifically provided for the right of "taxpayers" to vote for this office, and women were often the "taxpayers." The exercise of this limited franchise had led to some controversy. By this time women had won the right to vote for members of the school boards, but women's participating in road commissioner elections was considered too radical after their participation had been the swing vote in some elections.

We can see now in retrospect that the separation of East Brunswick from Monroe, in the year following enactment of the provision for elected Road District Commissioners, was probably a decision that was driven by the new act. The elected position of road district commissioner spawned other municipalities, as evidenced in the history of two Bergen County towns in which two future mayors cut their political teeth on a hotly contested election for the position of road district commissioner.

The Tercentenary Committee of Englewood Cliffs published a history written by James J. Greco. According to this publication, it seems that the referendum held in 1895 by a handful of residents from the one and one-eighth square mile along the Palisades had nothing to do with school district–borough fever that had spread like influenza through the rest of the county. Instead the explanation provided by Mr. Greco involved a controversy dating back to 1859 (cited as 1863 by Greco), when the Road District Act was amended to provide for the election of road commissioners from each district. Many years later a hotly contested election for the position of commissioner of Road District Number 1 was held between William O. Allison and Clinton H. Blake. The victory at the polls went to Blake, but Allison successfully challenged the outcome in court. Apparently Allison raised the issue of whether women could legitimately exercise the franchise under the category of "taxpayers." The court ruled that even though women had previously voted in road-district elections, they had no right to participate; and since the "women's clique" allegedly carried the day for Blake, the election had to be overturned and Allison installed. But old Englewood refused to acknowledge Allison's right to the office. This grievance to Allison and his partisans supposedly inspired those living primarily within Road District Number 1 to break away from Englewood and form their own independent borough. Allison was elected the first mayor of Englewood Cliffs. Mr. Blake later went on to become the mayor of Englewood, and in 1916 was advocating the annexation of Englewood Cliffs. However, his efforts came to naught, for, as Mr. Greco says, "We have set ourselves free and hope to remain free and separate."

Whether the Act of 1859 was the real catalyst for the creation of East Brunswick, or whether the dubious election in Road District Number 1 of Englewood resulted in the creation of Englewood Cliffs, there can be little doubt that the impact of the law was felt in many areas throughout the state. For example, the boundary lines of various road districts proved to be the lines of cleavage in the creation of new municipalities. Also, the fact that a number of road commissioners later occupied mayoral chairs of newly formed towns speaks even more eloquently of how the dynamic operated. The statutory framework governing these instances was not merely permissive. The Act of 1818 directed the division of the townships into districts, and the Act of 1859 mandated that the office of road district commissioner be an elected rather than an appointed position. The effect of these laws was "pro-active" in the creation of new municipalities. In addition to this general statutory environment, another factor in the formation of municipalities is development—how major roads, built in response to emerging industries and markets, shaped the state.

Over three hundred years ago in 1693 all of the land area of New Jersey was spoken for—in the sense that New Jersey was the first of the original colonies not to have any no-man's land. The 24 recognized townships contained all of the land mass of both provinces—East and West Jersey—with each having the equal number of 12 townships. Between that time and the onset of the War of Independence there were basically only three ways that a new municipal entity could come into existence:

- By the issuance of a royal charter or letters patent from Queen Anne, George I, George II or George III. The British monarchs had better things to do than draw lines on the map of one of their smallest colonies, so it is safe to assume that the documents granting royal charters were actually drafted by the Provincial Governor and slipped under a royal nose for execution. The Crown also had provided for the recognition of certain entities having corporate status, separate from but still within the townships. They were the cities of Perth Amboy and New Brunswick in Middlesex County and Burlington City on the Delaware river. Elizabeth and Trenton were chartered briefly as boroughs before being granted city status. The London Board of Trade functioned as the screening mechanism for royal charters, and it was this body that originally received for review applications forwarded by the Royal Governor.
- By order of the courts a total of 12 new townships were created in the counties of Sussex, Morris and Cape May. (In the case of Cape May, three townships with the very unimaginative names of Upper, Middle and Lower were created in 1734.)
- By the passage of special acts of the general assembly which created six townships in Cumberland and one in Monmouth county.

Emerging from the victory in the Revolutionary War, the new state ratified the existence of all previously chartered municipalities, and quickly added new ones. The legislature, meeting in 1798, felt it necessary to pass an act that not only would incorporate the 104 townships specifically listed, but also would designate the exact powers of the townships and regulate how they were to conduct their municipal meetings.

By the War of 1812, the economic center of Essex County (then containing Newark, Elizabeth, all of present-day Union County and a portion of present-day Passaic County) had subdivided into 11 additional and separate units. The total number of formal townships had grown to 125 by 1834, with the majority of activity centering in Essex, Morris, and Sussex Counties, and the new (1824) county of Warren.

The reason why the activity seemed to be located in these counties as opposed to other areas of the state is simple: roads. The issue of road costs dominated the majority of the decisions. The questions of constructing and paying equitably for roads were the dominant considerations in that period of economic growth.

Attempts to resolve the transportation issue controlled the public agenda in this pre-railroad era—a fact demonstrated by the extraordinary number of charters granted by the legislature to turnpike companies. A total of 51 private grants to build toll roads were voted between 1801 and 1829. Only half these roads ever moved off the drawing board, but the ones that did still serve today as the foundations of some of our best-known and most well-traveled highways in North and Central Jersey.

In 1806, charters were granted for the construction of turnpikes from Newark to Elizabeth, Belleville, New Brunswick, Springfield, and Bloomfield. Also in 1806, Newark Township was split into three wards: Newark, Orange, and Bloomfield. It was only a matter of time before the two latter entities would gain independence. The Turnpike to Springfield Township passed through Union Township, which was set off as an independent township in 1808. The issues here were straightforward. The toll road was to be a project of significant dimension, but the secondary or "feeder roads" were a matter of local jurisdiction. The residents in Bloomfield, the Oranges, and Union Township were not anxious to be underwriting the construction and maintenance of the network of streets feeding into these major arteries planned in Newark and Elizabethtown. They were adamant about paying only for the secondary roads serving the interests of their immediate area.

The toll-road alternative was viewed as a viable solution to the provincial attitudes of the farmers, who were primarily concerned about the road that led from their farm to the nearest market town. Roads that would link county seats or would serve to bring the products of the mines, proposed for Sussex and Morris Counties, to the ports of Newark and Elizabeth were supported by those who owned the mines, but enjoyed no political support among the farmers who still dominated both geographically and politically.

Everyone familiar with New Jersey knows that, while toll roads literally went out of existence in the face of the fierce competition from the railroads, they have enjoyed a renaissance in the state during the second half of the twentieth century.

New Jersey has the most extensive network of toll roads of any state based on the miles of toll road per square mile.

Economic development was not limited to the north. There was commerce in the central region as well, albeit on a much more moderate scale. A free road known as the King's Highway, or the Old York Road, had been used for a considerable time. It started in Elizabethtown and proceeded on a course westward to what is now Plainfield, and then into present-day Somerville. All of the municipalities through which it passed are now served by Route 28, but the reason they became independent municipalities was not the road, but the railroad. Starting in 1834 the railroad laid its tracks on a course parallel with the Old York Road through Union and Somerset Counties. However, after Somerville the railroad took a different course, moving northwest, whereas the Old York Road dipped southwest toward the ferry at Lambertville. Towns formed in Hunterdon County in response to the modest activity that was occurring along the rail transportation corridor in the first half of the nineteenth century.

The road, having left what is now Raritan Borough, moved into Branchburg Township, which had attempted to break away from Bridgewater as early as 1799, and only succeeded in doing so in 1845. The balance of the Old York Road after its departure from Raritan Borough was lined with classic road-fight townships. An excellent example is Branchburg, where the farmers of the more rural areas to the west of the north and south branches of the Raritan River felt overtaxed and neglected. As the railroad further encouraged population increases and growth, more attention was given to the commercial concerns of Bridgewater's developing villages of Somerville and Bound Brook. The first action taken by the new committee in Branchburg was to appropriate $400 for their apparently neglected roadways. Moreover the new township was to receive a rebate of $250 from Bridgewater as what should be interpreted as evidence that even the committee in Bridgewater recognized that they had not been giving the farmers of Branchburg their fair share of road services.

Having arrived in Hunterdon County, the Old York Road continued its course southwest for the ferry known as Coryell's—where travelers could safely cross the Delaware River into Pennsylvania and be on their way to Philadelphia. The eighteenth-century carriage riders found themselves passing through the farmlands of Readington and Amwell Townships, along a route where, in the next century, the railroad would not parallel. These areas remained rural almost to the present time, and it is significant that following some divisions in the first half of the nineteenth century the configurations of the municipal boundaries remain basically as they were, save for some minor adjustments.

The huge area of Amwell Township had divided into road districts pursuant to the law of 1818, and these survived intact for another 20 years. In 1838 Delaware Township, virtually the entire northwest section, and Raritan Township, the entire northeast section of the original township of Amwell, were created. Eight years later Amwell split again, this time into East and West by means of a referendum. The town of Lambertville came into existence in 1849, and on the hundredth anniversary of its incorporation it became Hunterdon County's only city.

The Borough of Flemington had served as the county seat of Hunterdon since 1785, when it was a village within the original township of Amwell. Raritan Township served as its satisfactory host until 1910. It is reasonable to attribute the division of Amwell to a desire to keep roads open to the most important market village. In the case of Raritan and East Amwell the roads to Flemington were of primary concern: Delaware Township viewed its destiny as linked to Stockton; and West Amwell was most interested in the quality of the roads to Lambertville.

What happened to the original Amwell Township is almost a repetition of the experience of South Amboy Township. Agricultural communities—such as Monroe and Madison in Middlesex County, and Delaware, Raritan, East and West Amwell Townships—felt the pull of new centers of administrative and economic gravity. The priority of the rural communities was to insure a reliable and passable roadway from them to that center of gravity.

Two other factors should be mentioned as to these township subdivisions. The first was the construction of the upper spillway or feeder of the Delaware and Raritan Canal. This assured that a controlled and dependable flow from the upper reaches of the Delaware would be brought to Trenton and into the canal itself so that the depth of the canal between Trenton and New Brunswick would remain stable. The construction effort brought hundreds of immigrant workers to the area of Lambertville between 1832 and 1834, and created an urban environment from which the farmers of Delaware Township wished to separate themselves. The influx of workers associated with the construction of the canal compounded what had already been a spurt of earlier commercialization. The original increase in activity came in 1814 with the spanning of the river by its first covered bridge joining the east bank with the village of New Hope, Pennsylvania.

The residents of East Amwell then felt it was time to protect themselves from the priorities being set by the commercial interests that had intensified along the river. Finally, it was the West Amwellians who thought it best to let Lambertville, with its hotels, inns, and busy streets (as well as the increased presence of immigrants), go it alone as an independent town.

The decline and ultimate termination of ferry service resulted in the town being named for captain John Lambert, builder of the famous hotel and tavern, rather than for the Coryells, who were the real founders. Emanuel Coryell had started the ferry in the early 1700s, and his son George, who lived from 1760 to 1851, continued it until the bridge made it obsolete. George Coryell was a prominent patriot and an intimate of General George Washington. So close a friend was Coryell that he had served as a pall bearer for the nation's founder. One must imagine that had the bridge not been built, the town would have carried Coryell's name.

Each of the numerous divisions of the original Amwell Township can be traced to disputes over the maintenance of roads and division of money among the road districts. It is interesting to note that none of the area bears the name of its original owner, John Holcombe, who owned most of what was Amwell, including Lambertville. Holcombe had engaged in what might be considered the prototype of all of New Jersey's road wars. His adversary in his road struggle was John Reading, a New Jersey landowner of equal wealth and stature, who at least had a township named for him. Perhaps the naming of Readington Township should be viewed as a consolation prize. Reading was, after all, outmaneuvered in the titanic battle for the final alignment of the King's Road. Reading owned a tract almost equal in size to Holcombe's holdings. The Reading tract included the present site of the Borough of Stockton, and he provided a ferry service of his own across the Delaware at approximately the location of the present bridge. Both men fought and lobbied to have their respective ferry landings serve as the terminus of the King's Highway. Holcombe won out, not only because the route was more direct, but also because he was apparently more skillful in using his political connections with the Franklins, father and son.

The true street fights manifested themselves as conflicts of orientation—commerce versus agriculture, as well as local market town versus administrative center. These street fights, witnessed as early as the turn of the nineteenth century, came to a boil as the interests of the commuters and the developers assumed political power within the townships. The farmers became frightened that more taxes would be spent on paving subdivision streets than on keeping the rural roads passable. The next chapter will look more closely at this phenomenon.

Oradell, Biography of a Borough, written by J. Irving Crump, extensively cites Oradell's original clerk, Arthur Van Buskirk. To him is attributed the simple explanation that "the inequitable and unfair distribution of our tax money was the cause of intense dissatisfaction, and resulted in the formation of our borough." Delford was formed from two hamlets within Midland Township. It also took a small piece of Palisades Township and Harrington Park. The name came from combining the last syllable of the two hamlets; the "del" of the hamlet of Oradell and the "ford" from the village New Milford. Fifty years after the break, Van Buskirk told an audience in the Oradell school that Midland Township was considering a bond issue of $50,000 for macadamizing streets in the township, and someone had estimated that while the residents of Delford-Oradell would be expected to pay $2,400 in road taxes, they would only get $600 worth of road work. Obviously no one in this section of the township was ever intending or expecting to use the roads in any other section of Midland. We are told that proponents of the borough idea discussed this blatant potential oppression *along with other instances of similar unfair taxation.*

Although the subject is not mentioned directly, the issue of the costs involved in school consolidation was probably discussed among the other instances of unfair taxation. The rhetoric on the taxation issue might just be a way to obfuscate the identification of schools as the real cause of the split. In Chapter 7 we will look in some depth at how the dynamics of local school politics generated the creation of new boroughs during this period. When one sees the formation of a new borough in Bergen County there is an almost automatic assumption that it was created to control the local school district. Many argued that the action of forming new municipalities was taken solely and exclusively to preserve local control of the school district. Many critics, including influential and respected leaders in the field of education, such as Addison B. Poland, the state superintendent of schools at the time, regarded the creation of new boroughs as being selfish, elitist, and a ruse to extract more money than they deserved from the state. A certain stigma was attached to the communities that were considered to have abused the system.

But one should note that:

- The village of Oradell had boasted of its own school since a time prior to the Revolution.
- One of the signers of the petition is listed as a D. Zabrieski. The family name was both common and widely respected in the history of the state, particularly in Bergen County. Oddly enough, a David. D. Zabrieski was serving in the assembly in 1894.
- A niece of Arthur Van Buskirk authored a remembrance for the fiftieth anniversary. It may now appear that the essay of Miss Helen Waite is a bit overdrawn, but she did have the advantage of an education in a school district not forced to consolidate with undesirable elements. She wrote: "One wonders if the founders of the borough ever saw the parallel between the birth of our nation and the development of the borough! New Milford and Oradell broke away from the townships of which they had been a part for the very same reason the thirteen colonies broke from England. The reason was— high taxes, and what was felt to be the unjust use of the proceeds."

One may never really know whether it was schools or roads that was the proximate cause of the this particular needless division, but it is interesting to note that in 1944 fights over road appropriations and expenditures were viewed as being more legitimate and tactful than the blatant elitism of wishing to preserve the ethnic and/or social purity of local schools.

Just as independence from England did not necessarily result in fewer fights about taxes among Americans, the coming of the automobile did not put an end to the street fights. The state realized its duty to improve major roadways, to finance highway maintenance and construction, and to pass registration fees and ultimately motor-fuel taxes. However, the responsibility for maintaining local roads was still an issue that could generate controversy.

The age of the auto only served to exacerbate suburban tensions, particularly in what had been the last vestige of the bucolic existence of western Essex County. Caldwell Township which occupied all of the northwest quadrant of the county, carried the name of the clergyman who made the ultimate sacrifice for his unstinting support of the Revolutionary cause. The township sprawled over dozens of square miles. The coming of the railroads had not substantially altered this rich agricultural area, but the advent of the automobile suddenly turned village against village as each in its turn expressed its dissatisfaction with its allocation of street moneys by petitioning the legislature to be set off as a separate borough.

Between 1898 and 1908 disputes centered around the disposition of road taxes led to the creation of six municipalities. Once there had only been the Township of Caldwell; now there were Caldwell Borough, North Caldwell, West Caldwell, Verona, Cedar Grove, and Essex Fells.

Essex was not alone in its reaction to the auto age. As late as 1924 major townships were being fractured by intense and acrimonious conflicts over the allocation of local tax dollars for projects in various sections of the community.

In 1921, and again in 1922, the *Camden Daily Courier* was carrying stories that reported literal fist fights at township committee meetings in Clementon Township, sparked by debates concerning road repair and construction priorities. By the end of the decade, the single township of Clementon became seven separate boroughs.

New Jersey waited until 1906 to impose a licensing fee on motor vehicles. The money collected was to be apportioned to the counties according to the mileage of improved roads in each county. By 1910 the state was collecting about $325,000. Of this sum the state retained almost $50,000 for the operation of the newly created Motor Vehicle Department, but apportioned the lion's share of $275,000 to the counties. Things had changed dramatically by 1928. In that year the state collected almost $13.3 million in licensing fees, but instead of distributing 85% to the counties, the state retained almost $8 million or about 60% of the total fund.

In 1927 the first gas tax was instituted at the rate of $.02 per gallon. In 1930 this was increased to $.03 per gallon, but with the promise that at least $5 million of the gas tax receipts would be distributed to the counties for traffic control and road maintenance.

Of course all of these funds including the state highway fund that had been created to fund state bonding of major state highways were all heavily tapped during the depression simply to pay for the emergency Workers' Relief Fund, which was consuming the state budget. However the saddest fact about road expenditures in New Jersey is cited in Chapter 223 of the Public Laws of 1912, which provided that convict labor might be used in the repair and construction of roads.

In summary, we can safely argue that road construction and repair served as a major catalyst for municipal multiplication in New Jersey, particularly in the nineteenth century for the following reasons:

- From the earliest times residents in geographically large townships disagreed on what roads should receive priority status.
- The construction of major turnpikes left the areas through which they passed with decisions on how construction and repairs of the feeder road system would be financed.
- Economic activities such as mining and forging created new economic centers, as did the construction of the turnpikes and the canals. As new centers of commerce and administration grew, certain areas within townships developed altered orientations and wanted more moneys spent on the maintenance of the roads leading to the emerging centers.
- The legislation of 1818 requiring that townships be divided into road districts expedited the many ultimate separations which broke along lines established as road districts.
- The legislation of 1859, providing that position of road district commissioners

be an elected public office, further encouraged the formation of new town-ships and boroughs; the elected road commissioner often became a moving force in the formation of the new municipality.
* The coming of the railroad and the birth of the auto age only served to in-tensify disputes over the allocation of road appropriations.

I want to leave this chapter with a short note about how roads are actually built. The word *"pave"* comes to our language via the Norman Conquest. The French word *paver* came from the late Latin *pavare* or *paviare,* which had evolved from the classic Latin *pavire* meaning "to beat down." In the Middle Ages cities and boroughs in England might work off part of the taxes levied against them by the Crown by claiming that they had engaged in pavage, and should therefore receive a credit for the improvements made to the King's roads. On the other hand local officials could make assessments against individual landowners having frontage on the roadway that had been enlarged or improved. Much of what began as feu-dal custom continues today. Many landowners of today feel beaten down when they receive an assessment. Likewise I'm given to understand that over the years many a paving contractor has been shaken down.

CHAPTER 6

Railroad Towns

JERKWATER DEPOTS AND REAL SUBURBS

In lieu of any kind of overall planning, the railroad itself defined the character
and projected the limits of the town.
Lewis Mumford

$\mathcal{T}$he history of civilization is the history of the development of transportation. Millions of words have described the migrations of populations that followed the domestication of pack animals. Libraries are filled with shelves of books detailing the conquests premised upon the use of the horse. Millions of words have been exhausted detailing how commercial cultures emerged as the consequence of harnessing the wind to power sailing craft, and how the embryos of great cities gestated and matured where two ox carts had routinely met to exchange commodities. The expansion of the Roman Empire was predicated on its growing system of roads—where the road went, so went Roman civilization.

So, too, is the history of New Jersey's municipal development. The railroads had a unique and enduring impact upon New Jersey. Every change in transportation modalities has such an impact. Such changes create and affect the environment in direct proportion, or ratio, to their usage, and in New Jersey the use of railroads was staggering.

From our vantage point in this age when airports expand to the size of small cities, with their clusters of terminals sitting invariably adjacent to superhighways, railroad trains appear somewhat slow and outdated. It is difficult to imagine the mind-set that observed the construction of the first rail lines in the nineteenth century. The changes the railroads wrought were swift, dramatic, pervasive, and permanent. Within thirty years of the opening of the first line, a cultural quantum leap had occurred that was every bit as momentous for the citizens of the nineteenth century as the coming of the auto age and epoch of flight has been for the twentieth. The railroad had the deepest and most enduring effect upon the political life of the country, and nowhere was its impact more pronounced than in New Jersey.

From the national perspective, it may be advanced that the railroad unified the country, allowing relatively open and unimpeded social and commercial intercourse, thereby narrowing the historical division between urban and rural life. On the other hand, the construction of the tracks created, at the local level, an indelible division of those on the right side of the tracks and those on the wrong side.

New Jersey is often referred to as the state of bedroom communities. Each day, millions of people awake to begin journeys by bus, train, and/or automobile that would have been unthinkably time-consuming, if not virtually impossible, a century ago. Today they are routine and in the course of the day will be retraced, so that travelers will return home for the purpose of utilizing the bedroom to recharge for the commute the following morning.

A great deal has been written in the last decade about suburbanization as a fait accompli. One cannot find many articles dealing with the subject as a prospective phenomena that should be subject to some policy analysis or debate.

The working definition of a suburb was an area that had a net deficit between jobs and population—a municipality that provided fewer employment opportunities than there were people—an area where people lived, as opposed to worked. This has changed to the degree that New Jersey's development pattern now shows evidence that the major commuting trend is suburb to suburb rather than the traditional pattern of suburb to city. The creation of exurbia is one of the compelling reasons that the entire municipal framework in New Jersey warrants a fresh look.

Despite New Jersey's penchant for classifying municipalities as cities, towns, boroughs, villages, and townships, there is no official list of suburbs *per se*. The historic Mount Laurel litigation and its progeny made much of the term *developing community*, and this terminology was apparently well understood and widely used for planning purposes. The relevance of classification terminology is suspect, since, as we have seen, a *city* can be used for Newark and Corbin with the same degree of correctness.

Anyone familiar with the state can read down the list of towns and identify with some ease those defined as suburbs, at least in a common-sense way. However, a problem arises when one must decide if East Brunswick is a suburb of New Brunswick, or really a suburb of New York City. Is Teaneck a suburb of Hackensack, or is it a suburb of Paramus, but then is Paramus only a suburb of New York City? The lines blur rapidly, and we are left with the unsettling feeling that the term *suburb* may have lost its relevancy. With the ever-increasing use of the Internet and the growing trend of people regarding either their home or their computer as their workplace, the entire concept of urban/suburban may be rendered moot, and the term *exurbia* may be one of the shortest-lived words on record.

There was a time, however, when the term *suburb* had real meaning and was subject to more-precise definition. The growth of the classic or traditional New Jersey suburb was a function of the railroads. The iron rods that spread their tentacles from the main lines changed our language as surely as they altered our landscapes.

The eminent arbiter of the American spoken and written word, H. L. Mencken, tells us that the words *commuter, commuting,* and the phrase *to com-*

mute entered the American vocabulary in the Civil War era. To this day the term *commuter* is not used in England, where someone in this category is still referred to as a "season ticket holder."

The first railroad suburb that has been identified as such is Napierville, Illinois, but that distinction is questionable, and may well be misapplied. The distinction of being the first railroad suburb might equally be claimed by any number of New Jersey towns, with the Essex County community of Orange being the first that comes to mind.

The principal fact for which Napierville gets credit is that it was purposely developed from a railroad's determination to create a suburb out of what had been nothing but farmland. In the case of Orange, a community had previously existed, and its growth was accelerated by the construction of a specific train station. Napierville was the nineteenth-century equivalent of the Levittowns of the twentieth century. It was so successful that the Illinois Central Railroad proceeded to erect a total of 38 clones. Each development was laid out in the exact same grid, and the streets even carried the same names. One legend has it that this practice was only modified when the railroad received too many complaints from commuters who had slept through their station, and subsequently found themselves in the awkward situation of attempting to gain entry to houses that belonged to someone else.

The railroads caused at least three separate types of communities to develop in New Jersey:

The first were the large commercial and transit hubs of which Jersey City is the prime example—a city abused like none other in the history of the state. Not only did the railroads steal its most valuable asset—its waterfront—they did so without contributing a penny to the city's ratable base. The railroads bought up almost a third of the entire city, rendering all these lands tax-exempt. The history of the rape of Jersey City by the railroads and the State's government is long and complex. The dynamics of the rise and fall and current attempts to resurrect Jersey City are the subject of a separate chapter in this book.

The second type of community that the railroads directly created were those that served freight lines. They functioned so that raw materials, such as lumber and farm products, could be loaded while the engine's boiler was being replenished with water. Such communities actually developed a descriptive moniker based upon the activity by the locomotive's engineer and tender while it was at the depot. These became the towns so colorfully, disparagingly, and accurately known as *jerkwater towns*. The vast majority of these places remain as only names on the map, and many have not even sustained enough permanency to support even that. They did not endure and did not develop, as the direct result of the railroads not having enough economic incentive to mold them into thriving boroughs or even villages. They served only the convenience of the railroads for the operation of the line from a mechanical perspective.

The third type of community created directly by the influence of the railroads—the type that lives on today—is the classic railroad suburb, subject matter of our present inquiry.

However, before we closely examine how these classic prototypical suburbs were created, it is important that we review the role the railroads played in New Jersey politics of the mid-nineteenth century.

Every history of the state ever written concludes that the railroad corporations virtually owned the state government, and that the legislatures of the railroad era were merely subsidiaries of the lines. The railroads' domination of the electoral process and the state governmental apparatus is taken as historical gospel. The statement of this conclusion by historians usually ends there. However, it is necessary to explore the aftermath of allowing the railroads to control the agenda, and to examine the long-term public-policy implications of their political role and the demographic consequences.

The seeds of not only present day suburban sprawl, but also the decline of the cities, were sown in the attitudes toward the railroads in the mid-nineteenth century. For a period of thirty years, starting in 1835 and ending in 1865, the railroads were sacrosanct. The Camden-Amboy Railroad and its immediate successors were immune from criticism by the governors and legislatures, despite charging higher rates than any other railroad in America. Moreover, that exorbitant rate was extracted for what was generally conceded to be second-rate service and reliability.

The railroads, however, understood the inferiority complex that was ingrained in the political culture of New Jersey. The syndrome had manifested itself in the debates of the Constitutional Convention of 1787, with the advocacy of the *New Jersey Plan,* which would require each state to have the same number of representatives in the Congress notwithstanding its size or population.

A condition akin to xenophobia and paranoia prevailed in New Jersey. Perhaps it was justified on the historical basis of New York's continuing attempts to dominate and control the political and economic life of the state. The initial resentment can be traced back to the high-handed attempts of the earliest of colonial governors, Colonel Richard Nicholls and Major Edmund Andros, who in the late seventeenth century treated New Jersey as a suburb of New York, totally within its sphere of political and economic control. The bad taste that these colonial governors had left in the mouth of New Jersey was exacerbated by the assertion that certain monopolies existed over the ferry traffic in New York Harbor. The fights required the intervention of the U.S. Supreme Court; but by the time the high court had broken the monopoly of Robert Fulton–Robert Livingston and their associates from New York, the bitterness and resentment had become institutionalized.

The railroad barons of New Jersey contained among their number some of the very people who had been cheated and humiliated by the economic monopolists of New York. They now found themselves with the stronger suit and used their control over the fastest route between New York and Philadelphia to extract tariffs that were twice as high on a per-mile-traveled basis than any other rates in the country. Merchants and travelers from up and down the East Coast screamed, moaned, and whined, but to no avail. Action was even initiated on the federal level to force the Camden-Amboy to reduce their rates, but that legislation never saw the light of day because of the enormous political clout of the railroads.

The virtual immunity the railroads enjoyed was premised upon three factors:

- The state was a substantial partner in the venture, holding thousands of shares of the stock of the company, upon which they enjoyed enormous amounts of dividend revenue and a bonus revenue of ten cents per passenger and fifteen cents per ton of freight.
- The passengers were travelers, moving between New York and Pennsylvania—a fact the railroad barons continually emphasized. The state revenue was based on a win-win-win structure. The State of New Jersey is a partner, reaping in dividends; the state gets revenue from strangers; and the revenue is so great that no other state taxes on state citizens are needed.
- The psychological factors mentioned above were very strong. The railroad interests exploited these factors, by pointing out that the criticism came from foreigners and outside agitators—the same people who had done the state wrong for many years previously, and were still trying to abuse the state economically.

The consequences of having the public policy of the state dictated by the railroads were enormous and can be seen to the present time. Among the most critical of those consequences are the following:

- The image of the state as a corridor state was ratified, reinforced, and institutionalized. New Jersey was not to be a destination, but a corridor.
- The state became spoiled from the excess of revenue it received without direct taxation. The proposition that the state could get by, without imposing taxes, became so ingrained that New Jersey was resisting broad-based taxes into modern times, with its politicians always looking for some miraculous return to the halcyon days when the railroads had picked up all the bills.
- The railroads were encouraged to buy up incredible amounts of real estate, not only at the site of their terminals in the cities, but also along the course of their rights of way. The arrangement with the state gave the railroads such large profits that their surplus revenues could be used to buy land, needed and unneeded. The state exempted the railroads up until 1884 from any meaningful property taxes payable to the municipalities.

All was idyllic for the railroads until they were hoisted on their own petard. When the passengers metamorphosed from "travelers" to "commuters," the trouble started. People demanded lower fares for in-state travel and property-tax payments from the railroad companies. The railroads responded by making up in volume what they were forced to sacrifice in reduced commuter fares, and selling the lands they had accumulated tax-free to encourage the development of commuter suburbs.

The impact of the railroads on the formation of specific and distinct municipal entities can be described as a process involving one or more of the following factors:

- Railroads recognized that they could expand their traditional consumer base from travelers journeying through the state and open an entirely new market for those who wished to have access to their employment in the city while enjoying the amenities of life outside the congestion, disease, crime, and pollution of the central urban area.

- The railroad executives profited directly or indirectly from land speculation in and around the areas that were designated as stations with regularly scheduled service.

- The interest on the part of the railroads and their executives in developing housing was accelerated by the Railroad Tax Act of 1884, which imposed municipal taxes on the surplus land owned by the railroads. The railroad companies no longer had any reason to hold the land and to pay taxes on it, when it could be subdivided and sold for a handsome profit to buyers who then became a captive market.

- The priorities created by the new commuting population were concurrent with the interests of the railroads and at variance with the agricultural interests of the existing townships in which stations were placed.

- Even prior to the adoption of the tax amendment of 1875, the method of local-purpose tax assessments fit into an established pattern. Mr. Justice Elmer described the method accurately by explaining that "for many years during our colonial government, and under our original and existing State Constitutions (1844), taxes were assessed upon land according to some ratio of value, discriminating between farm land and town property, in favor of the former" *(Rudderow v. The West Jersey Ferry Co.*, 2 Vroom 512).

This last comment perhaps identifies the most compelling reason for the initiatives that were launched by so many railroad suburbs to divorce themselves from their host townships. In Chapter 3 of this book, an editorial from the Jamesburg newspaper criticized the discriminatory assessment practices of Monroe Township. That complaint was echoed in almost every developed area, where the new homes that clustered near the station carried full assessments, while their fellow taxpayers in the rural areas of township enjoyed a de facto farmland exemption.

Some typical railroad suburbs of the nineteenth century—a variety of towns dispersed throughout different counties and serviced by different railroad companies—demonstrate the validity of this theory.

The first community is Dunellen in the northwest section of Middlesex County, a borough of about 6,500 people. By Mount Laurel terms it is an already developed community. Once a section of the large and sprawling Township of Piscataway, it had been settled for over a hundred years by farmers prior to the construction of the Elizabeth and Somerville Railroad, which was later to become the Central Jersey's rail line that connected the important industrial City of Elizabeth in what was then Essex County, now Union County, with the county seat of Somerset County, Somerville.

The early executives and shareholders of the railroads were often men of vision, foresight, and acumen. The original chairman of this famous line was none other than Isaac H. Williamson, the governor of the state from 1817 to 1829, who was still the councilor (senator) from Essex when the charter for the railroad was obtained. He was followed in his leadership role by the boy-wonder of New Jersey railroads, John Taylor Johnston, who is credited with revolutionizing railroads—making them more efficient, more responsive and more profitable. Today his actions would be met with a hundred stockholder's suits and a criminal investigation, but in those days the attitude toward entrepreneurship was a great deal more forgiving. The Central, like other railroad companies, had bought up huge amounts of land adjacent to its tracks. At one time it was estimated that the railroads owned as much as ten percent of all the land in the state—in some instances, the lion's share of all the land in urban centers such as Jersey City.

The Central Jersey bought 300 acres of land in 1867 in the New Market section of Piscataway. In 1868, the railroad sold it to the Central New Jersey Land Improvement Company, of which Mr. Johnston was president and Benjamin Williamson, son of the former governor, and New Jersey's vice-chancellor for twenty years, was a shareholder. Mr. Johnston's development company quickly subdivided the land. The construction of houses began within walking distance of the new station, which was promoted as having regularly scheduled service along the line. Johnston named the development after one of his favorite nieces, Ellen Betts, allegedly adding the prefix *dun* to make the station and its environs more euphonious. This explanation does not seem credible; and it may be that it was from the Scottish word for "fort" that we can ultimately attribute the final version of the station name. The Johnston family indeed needed a fort to hold all the money that was being made selling land to people who wanted easy access to the commuter depot, where they could board a train destined for Elizabeth, with its connections to Newark and New York.

Unofficial versions as to how this town became known as Dunellen also abound. One version has it that while this depot was still a *jerkwater* stop, it had also provided comfort stations for the use of passengers, prior to such facilities being built into the passenger cars. Travelers would hustle to the outhouses while the engine took on fuel and water. One regular rider was habitually tardy in returning to her carriage requiring the trainman to call out the phrase *done Ellen,* either the declarative or interrogative in nature, depending on the inflection.

The interests of the Johnston family and the interests of the railroad were coextensive. While there may have been a duty to the shareholders of the railroad to allow the company the first opportunity to exploit and develop the corporate prospects, the real estate development seemed like a fiscally responsible decision, because the more customers the railroad had, the more potential customers that the development company enjoyed as well. The inexorable conclusion to this story, to the point it has been recounted, is that Dunellen never would have grown as a community without the direct influence and impact of the railroad.

The question still remains as to why this development was not possible within the municipal context of the large Township of Piscataway? Why did not Dunellen merely become another identifiable neighborhood within the township, as did other well-known and well-recognized neighborhoods such as New Market and Stelton? What dynamics operated on this railroad suburb that induced it to create a new borough?

The answer can be found in the variance of priorities between the new commuters and the historic priorities of the older, long-established township residents. The township had three traditional priorities: roads, the poor, and schools. The residents of the commuter suburb had different priorities. They were: sidewalks, streetlighting, sanitation, and safety. The conflicts quickly arose when it came time to strike the annual budget. From Colonial times the assessments placed upon *in-town* properties were considerably higher than those placed upon farm property. The consequence was that those living within walking distance of the train station were paying more, and were unwilling to have their taxes consumed by the maintenance of roads serving only the agricultural interests. Budgeting money for road repair and snow removal based on linear feet of roadway distinctly disadvantaged those *in-town.* Moreover the widely dispersed farmers were profoundly indifferent to the issue of streetlighting and such extravagances as sewer or water connections. The farmer lit his own way to the barn, disposed of waste in the soil, and brought up water from his own well. Why should tax dollars be used for such things as streetlighting, so the late returning commuter could walk home or have water provided by a municipal water works? Tensions rose, and while most community histories attempt to gloss over it, many—including Dunellen's—are written in a manner so that it is easy to read between the lines. For the commuters, the choice between creating a new borough as opposed to being part of a larger, more agricultural, township was not a challenge. It was far better to be able to see what one was getting for one's tax dollars. It was comforting to have some influence over the budget decisions rather than pay into an amorphous pot called the township and watch while dollars that should go for sidewalk repair were diverted to the construction of some bridge over a creek that was capable of being forded most of the time.

As for the township's interests it was simpler to sacrifice a portion of the tax base than to have to respond to the constant pressure to add streetlighting or hire another constable to patrol the streets at night to insure that the rowdies at the pool-hall down the alley from the station didn't get out of hand.

Dunellen is the stereotypical railroad suburb. It developed around the passenger station; the subdivisions were undertaken by a company owned by the chief executive of the railroad; and it split off from the larger township in order that the commuters could have more influence over how their tax dollars were allocated.

The story of Dunellen can be cloned to recount the creation of the Borough of Fanwood from Scotch Plains Township, in Union County. The only real difference is in the name, which according to legend, is also the personal preference of Mr. Johnston. While Johnston restrained himself in naming the developments, other areas of Union County such as the Roselles and Cranford also were the subjects of his real estate interests and those of his inner circle of friends.

The story of Orange—and the subtext of East Orange—in Essex County, is once again a classic example of the creation of municipal entities, the genesis of which lies in the intertwining of railroad and real estate interests. Orange legitimately competes with Napierville, Illinois, for the distinction of being the first railroad suburb in America. The only factor operating to the disadvantage of

Orange is that it existed as a community prior to the laying of the first tracks by the Essex and Morris line in 1845. In that regard it has to be set apart from places, such as Napierville and Dunellen, which had been simply open areas that the track happened to traverse en route to its destination. The settlement of Orange had in fact existed to the west of Newark for almost 150 years prior to the first track being laid.

The very name tells us something of the nature and politics of its founding. William of Orange had become the king of England in 1689, following the Glorious Revolution and the ousting of James II from the British throne. Named for the native province of the new king, the designation also sent a message that this community was sympathetic to the new order and was not a group of the same intolerant followers of Robert Treat and his strict brand of Puritanism. Orange was home to the fertile farms that fed the ever-growing city of Newark, and even transported its vegetables, fruits, and livestock to the city of New York.

Newark was growing and prospering with an upsurge in the leather-goods industry. The hides of the cattle that grazed in the pastures of Orange often became the shoes that shod feet throughout the young nation. One of the leading figures in the city of Newark was the contractor Matthias Ogden Halstead. The contracting work in the city was so profitable that Mr. Halstead was able to acquire a large tract of land within Orange. With the new Essex and Morris line in operation, Halstead was able to build for himself a substantial estate in Orange, yet commute to the city easily for his construction company. Halstead was a marketer by example. His friends and colleagues followed suit, and soon he was building homes for dozens of Newarkers who wanted to get away from the city but be close enough to keep daily supervision over their mills, breweries, tanneries, and factories.

Brick Church Station may well be the first true commuter station in America. The most interesting aspect of the station is that it was constructed at Halstead's expense and presented as a gift. Today, it may seem odd that such a thing would occur, but the history of New Jersey during this time is replete with stories of either an individual or a group of public-spirited commuters building their own stations at their own expense. For example, the first wooden sidewalks in Orange. were apparently installed by a work crew under the direction of and at the expense of the women's group from the First Presbyterian Church. Once again, the issues inexorably developed along the predictable lines. Streetlighting, sidewalks, and control over taverns and shops near the station became the priorities for those who had invested in the Halstead subdivisions.

One consideration that appears time and again in stories concerning the genesis of towns along the Morris and Essex Railroad is water—a crucial element in municipal development since the construction of the first log houses in America, when the settlers were concerned with the danger presented by fire. The earliest defense and the most basic was the distance between structures. This concept was fundamental to any planned development even in the villages. Now, two more considerations were added to the constant danger inherent in the use of fire for cooking, heating, and lighting. First, commuter housing was built more compact; the houses were closer together than had been traditional and significantly closer than the scattered farms in the townships. Secondly, a steam engine now spewed sparks through this cluster of houses and other shops, stores, stables, inns, and churches. Fire protection and the requisite supply of water became essential elements for the people living in the houses clustered near the stations.

Water supply became a primary concern for reasons other than fire protection. As proximity to the train station became a desirable consideration, the effectiveness of cesspools that functioned for thousands of years in rural areas became unacceptable, because of sheer population density. A choice had to be made either to construct some arrangement for disposing of sewage other then cesspools or surrender the community's confidence as to the potability of its well water. A clean well and a septic system could be compatible on a two-acre lot. Their capacity to play their respective functions diminished when lots were reduced to half acres and smaller.

The areas that would mature into railroad boroughs routinely opted for the creation of a water system, as it had the double advantage of supplying potable water protection against destruction by fire. Orange in Essex, Summit in Union, Chatham and Madison in Morris are four communities whose histories share not only the Morris and Essex Railroad, but also the need for a reliable water supply as a catalyst for their municipal independence.

Streetlighting is the other factor that is almost universally present in the origin of railroad communities, whether they grew to city status, as did Orange and Summit, or were satisfied to settle at the borough plateau, as did Chatham and Madison.

Also a constant is the intense squabbling that went on between the residents clustered around the train station and the elected members of the township committee. It is a rare borough history that does not contain a general account describing the inequity. In his history of Chatham, John Cunningham reports how the situation became intolerable after Madison Borough separated from Chatham Township. "In 1890 the village (Chatham) represented about 7 percent of the township—and paid about 40 percent of the taxes. The township committee allocated money on the basis of all the territory; Chatham village generally received 7 percent of the tax receipts, or about one-fifth of what it paid in."

The best way for commuters to guarantee that money collected in taxes would be spent on the items that concerned them, such as sidewalks, streetlights, and a potable water supply, and not be used to subsidize rural roadway maintenance, was to incorporate as a separate municipality.

The full story of railroad boroughs would not be complete without a mention of the interim step taken by the legislature to attempt to mediate the constant disputes that arose between the commuters clustered around a train depot and the farmers spread throughout the township. The vehicle for the hoped-for accommodation was Chapter XLVII of the Public Acts of 1882.

Signed into law by Governor Ludlow on March 7, 1882, the act provided that the residents of an area of less than two square miles, containing fewer than 3,000 people, within an existing township, could petition to have a special election for the creation of a borough commission to govern *some* of the affairs of the two square miles or less. In other words, there would be an area, separate but unincorporated, within the township, very similar to a school district within the township, that would have *some issues* dealt with by the borough commission as opposed to the township committee.

Section Seven of the act spelled out exactly what those issues would be: "That it shall and may be lawful for the said board of commissioners to have the general supervision, management and control of the public streets, sidewalks and roads of said borough, to provide for the lighting of the streets and the supplying of water for extinguishing fires in said borough by the construction of cisterns or otherwise."

Section Eight provides for the residents within the borough to decide annually how much they wish to raise by way of taxes upon themselves for the specific purposes set out in Section Seven. The maximum amount could be $500, and would be collected by the township tax collector and then turned over to the borough treasurer. Section Ten specifically provides that none of this money is to be spent by the township in maintaining roads outside the borough limits.

The Borough Commission Act only served to whet the appetites of those who were elected commissioners within these areas. By 1890, the legislature passed the final act, allowing these areas to incorporate as real full-fledged boroughs. The differences in the powers of mayor and council of an incorporated borough and the limited powers of the boards of commissioners were dramatic. An incorporated borough not only could allocate their annual tax payments for street and sidewalk maintenance and streetlighting, they could borrow money and issue bonds for the construction of new roads and water systems and gas lines and sewage disposal. Moreover, an incorporated borough could have its own police to enforce local ordinances, its own magistrate to collect the fines, and on top of all that a borough could license the sale of alcohol. Finally, and best of all, the mayor and council could compensate themselves, whereas the former statute prohibited salaries for the board of borough commissioners.

Returning to the history of Orange, the initial municipal entity merely set off a wave of further reductionism. The First Ward of Orange quickly declared its independence and lobbied for separate status, becoming East Orange. In the meantime South and West Orange were getting ideas and ultimately spun off from Orange, as had Orange spun off from Newark.

It would be error to think that all of this took place in a quiet and decorous manner. The truth is that the creation of East Orange from the original First Ward of Orange, constituted as nasty a divorce as any witnessed in the matrimonial courts. Actually since at one time only the legislature granted divorces it might be appropriate to say that its was as unpleasant a fight for separation as had ever been seen in the legislature, with train loads of partisans filling the chambers to lobby for or against the proposed incorporation legislation. Legend has it that the partisans had to be physically separated both while on the trains and at the State House, and that, notwithstanding the best efforts of those empowered to keep the peace, dozens of fist-fights raged. The acrimony lingered and the strife was so active that one candidate ran on what he labeled the *Incorporation Party* ticket. This slogan would be used repeatedly throughout the state as the issue of creating a new municipality was fought and refought in different counties.

The railroad suburb was not restricted to North and Central Jersey, as evidence by the creation of Collingswood in Camden County. There, the railroad actually advertised its building lots and brought potential buyers to the subdivided plots on special home-site excursions, run out of Philadelphia on Sunday afternoons in 1888.

The dynamics involved in borough creation in Bergen County in 1894 and 1895 are unique, but occurred only because the railroads pushed through their lines by the 1850s. The pattern was distinctly different from that of the planned subdivisions of Middlesex, Union, and Camden Counties. The Paterson and Ramapo Railroad (later absorbed into the Erie system) cut through the sparsely settled townships of Bergen in 1848. Two mill owners, Cornelius Wortendyke and Garrett Lydecker, in what is now the Borough of Midland Park, fought with the railroad for over three years because the nearest depot had been situated at Ho Ho Kus. Finally, the railroad gave in and built a freight depot in what was then known as Godwinville, now Ridgewood. However, it wasn't until the residents of Godwinville chipped in enough money to erect a station at their own expense in 1858 that the railroad agreed to offer regular passenger service.

The *Paterson Guardian* carried the following editorial to mark the station's opening:

> Prosperity to Godwinville and every other station along the line! There is room enough for all to grow, and by making judicious efforts some hundreds of settlers might be induced to make this part of New Jersey their home.

Real estate developers Samuel Dayton and Christopher Stuart began acquiring farms adjacent to the new depot and selling gracious homes to buyers interested in being just a short distance from the train station. A hundred years later Ridgewood had a population of over 25,000.

The tensions between the commuters clustered around the depots of Bergen County and their more rural township residents never reached the breaking point that they did elsewhere. This may have been because Bergen was more geographically compact or because many of the larger townships had two or more depots within their borders, whereas places such as Dunellen, Fanwood, and Summit were the only railroad stations within their host townships. The Bergen County townships stayed intact until torn apart by school issues, as we shall observe, subsequently.

The other transportation alternative—the canal system—that developed in New Jersey contemporaneously with the early railroads left little or no imprint on the municipal configurations of the state. The expectations held for the Morris and Essex Canal, a true engineering marvel, and the Delaware and Raritan Canal never materialized.

There was an essential difference between the long-term impact of the canal and the railroad, and it went beyond the short-term success of each in the 1830s.

The variant impact experienced was due to the inherent nature of the two enter-prises. The canal barges needed an equal, if not greater, amount of attending. Mules and horses had to be stationed along the way. Barge-tenders were required, as were personnel to tend the animals. Lock-tenders were on regular duty along the path of the canal. The trains on the other hand were less labor-intensive, even though crews were necessary to operate the locomotives and at the stations for watering and fueling.

However, the very similar types of operations failed to produce very similar types of development. The canals did generate some modicum of community de-velopment, but nothing like the railroads. Dover and Boonton in Morris County are certainly products of the canal, as is Phillipsburg in Warren County. On the place maps of Morris County one can still see the names of places with port in the name; Port Murray for example, is a place name, but not an independent mu-nicipality. There are a dozen more places along the Morris and Essex Canal that came into existence as a result of the barge activity in the Civil War Era.

The canals failed and the towns around them fell into obscurity not merely because the railroads were the eventual winners as the preferred modality of trans-portation. The trains were the preferred modality because of their versatility as a mode of transportation for people as well as commodities. Another factor, of course, is the fact that much of the iron industry of Morris County was rendered obsolete in the latter half of the nineteenth century.

But the failure of the canals to leave a more enduring impact is more com-plex. Fundamentally it is human activity that causes a community to be formed, and not the mere trans-shipment of goods. The railroads were hauling everything from vegetables and lumber to businessmen, workers, and vacationers and tour-ists, while the barges were not well suited for passenger travel, but designed and built primarily to haul huge amounts of coal, iron, and steel. Relatively few de-pots were established along the canals, yet every stop along the rail line sported a depot and many of them grew into much more significant facilities with markets and warehouses, hotels and taverns, general stores, and stables.

The total number of railroad boroughs cannot be determined, but it would be fair to say that the number is a minimum of one hundred. The only reason a more definite number is not proposed is that many such communities fall more appropriately into other categories despite the presence of a railroad station. The railroad boroughs are definable as being geographically small, and often small in population as well. The majority of such areas can no longer support themselves on their own narrow tax base.

More important is the question of whether any of the factors that motivated their creation have any relevance in the age of the automobile. The state has to subsidize heavily not only the trains that pass through these towns, but also the schools and other public services provided in the towns created by the railroads.

To set the stage for some of the issues to be discussed in subsequent chap-ters and to demonstrate what was said earlier about personal egos and agendas, here is the wonderful story about how the City of Summit originally gained inde-pendence as a separate township from New Providence and Springfield Townships in the year 1869. The tale is from a recent history done by Edmund B. Raftis, entitled *Summit, New Jersey: From Poverty Hill to the Hill City.*

The son-in-law of the large landowner Nicholas D. E. Moller was a New York lawyer named Gus Thebaud, a Democrat. Every year he fought with the township committee over how much the area of Summit with its new train station paid in taxes and how little it received in return. The author says that "the thriving hamlet on the hilltop was the legitimate target for every form of extortionate taxation."

Thebaud drafted a bill and fought against tough odds to get it introduced and passed over the opposition of the majority of the Union County legislative delegation. He then took the bill to Governor Theodore Randolph, who was not only a fellow Democrat, but also had been the president of the Morris and Essex Railroad right up until his election as governor. Thebaud took one last look at the bill before the governor was to sign; to his shock, he found that it had been tampered with, and a clause inserted requiring a vote by the residents of New Providence and Springfield approving their loss of the goose that was laying golden eggs. The history of this period is replete with stories of bills being amended by phantoms after passage by the legislature and sometimes even after the governor had signed. The governor's outrage was said to be "unbounded," and he vetoed the bill after summoning the speaker and president of the Senate to his office. The bill in proper form was on his desk for execution the next day.

He called Thebaud into his office we are told, and told him, "Thebaud, I am signing this bill and presenting you with this pen on one condition—that you get the hell out of Trenton and don't come back. You've had this whole legislature drunk for two weeks and I haven't been able to get them to do a damn thing in all this time." Thebaud kept his word to Randolph and confined his activities to the Union County Board of Freeholders as the representative of the new Township of Summit.

CHAPTER 7

School-District Boroughs

LOCAL CONTROL AS A RELIGION

These districts aren't really rich, they only look rich.
Bergen County's legislative delegation wisdom

*I*t is no exaggeration to say that the first few pages of any work dealing with the political history of New Jersey refer to "home rule" as the driving force in the evolution of our most basic institutions. The proposition takes various pithy forms. A favorite of mine is one that states, "Home Rule is regarded as a political concept in other states, but in New Jersey it is a precept of theology." This particular version should be credited to the late Senator Fairleigh Dickinson. His comment approximates accuracy, but would be totally unassailable if he had limited the reference to local control of education.

Nowhere was the prerogative of dominion over local schools more jealously guarded, or more staunchly defended, than in his home county of Bergen. Home Rule as applied to education was a contributing factor in the creation of several towns throughout the state. However, in Bergen County it was the prime and driving force that saw the creation of 26 new boroughs in a single year.

Before exploring more fully the almost religious fervor that generated the school-boroughs of Bergen County, one should review the role taken by localities in the schooling of their young as the state developed from colonial times. New Jersey's colonial history falls somewhere between patterns of New England development and the tradition of development from Virginia southward. The diversity of the British American colonies is axiomatic. The fact that they were able to unite in a common effort to throw off European rule is, in retrospect, quite amazing. The legacy of religious dissent and nonconformity that dominated New England was at great variance from the High Church influence and its concomitant loyalty to the Crown that prevailed in the economically strong southern colony of Virginia.

The mid-Atlantic states were a buffer zone between the nonconformists of New England and the Anglican orthodoxy of the southern colonies. Maryland is indelibly identified as a colony with strong connections to the Church in Rome. New York state was, from earliest times, a melting pot, forging its liberal tradition by virtue of its multi-ethnic mix. Pennsylvania carried the stamp of Quaker influence, but that dominant allegiance was leavened by the influence of Germans and Swedes. New Jersey served as a microcosm of the colonies hugging the Atlantic Coast. The Dutch dominated what are now Bergen and Hudson Counties immediately adjacent to New York City. English Quakers spilled over from Philadelphia into South Jersey. Anglican Loyalists spread throughout Central Jersey, particularly in Essex and Monmouth Counties. The Pine Barrens were inhabited by a polyglot assemblage of persons not overly interested in being disturbed or discovered by the authorities, either religious or secular.

The British government would have continued its control for considerably longer had they followed a policy of divide and rule. King George III and many of his ministers were some of history's truly worst politicians. Their policies were so myopic and exploitative that they had the inexorable consequence of driving diverse interests together and forging alliances among unlikely allies.

However, the one common belief among the diverse religious, cultural, and political traditions was that education had some intrinsic value and that schooling the young should be provided for. America is defined by its almost religious commitment to the idea that education has a value superior to church or state.

Democratic government was in the late eighteenth century a truly radical idea. Democracy as it was understood and articulated by writers such as Montesquieu was a form of government only suitable to small, homogeneous enclaves. The only real model was the city-state of Athens in the fifth century BC, and that experiment in self government was fragile and short-lived.

The underlying subtext of the Declaration of Independence and the new Constitution was a revolutionary departure from the premises of the previous 2,000 years of the Western tradition. The idea that the general populace needed church or state, or both simultaneously, to control and direct their lives had universally prevailed for two millennia. It is difficult to conceive just how radical a break it was for a few thousand colonists to assert that they could somehow do it themselves. It was more than radical. It was heresy. It was treason.

Such an assertion could not, and would not, have been put forth except for the abiding conviction that free people, *literate and educated,* need not depend upon princes or popes to control their destiny. The schoolhouse could replace the church and the castle in the New World. Gutenberg's invention proved more influential than all the firepower of technological advances in the weapons of coercion.

The revolution was fully underway more than a hundred years before the first volley was fired in the War for Independence. There is general agreement that the first schooling that occurred outside a home or church building took place in what was then Bergen Township, now a portion of Jersey City. The year was 1662 when the Dutch schoolmaster Engelbert Stuynhuysen commenced formal instruction of his handful of students.

Each of the charters for the Province of East Jersey had contained some language exhorting the value of education and suggesting that the provision of a free education should be considered among the obligations of the community as a whole. This aspiration, which is still eluding the state more than 300 years later, has an ancient lineage in the New World and is best demonstrated by reference to the so-called Carteret Charter for the Township of Bergen granted in 1668. That charter authorized the freeholders, or the majority of them, not only to choose their own clergy, but also to make arrangements for designating land within the township for a church and a free school for the education of the youth of the township. That land which contained the church and school was to remain exempt from taxes or rents of any kind.

By 1693, the General Assembly of the Province of East Jersey was enacting laws to provide that every town had a mechanism to select a schoolmaster whose salary, once approved by a majority of the freeholders, would be paid by all of them. In the event someone failed to pay the allotted share, the law allowed for seizing of the delinquent's goods and chattels. That law also created the first school boards.

The revolutionaries of New Jersey were so dedicated to the salutary effects of education that the ink was barely dry on the new constitution when the New Jersey Legislature was addressing its attention to school matters. In 1817 a State School Fund was dedicated with an initial appropriation of $15,000 to be distributed throughout the state. Three years later the legislature allowed townships to levy taxes and encouraged the expenditure of such local funds to provide for the education of the poor, i.e., those not able to afford private or church schooling. The actual wording refers to "poor children, as are paupers." The state increased its appropriation for school funds in 1824, and in 1828 the state permitted towns to tax for the construction and repair of school buildings.

Even the State School Fund was not exempt from the predatory politicians in Trenton, who in 1832 were covetously eyeing the fund as a source of an additional investment in the stock of the Delaware and Raritan Canal Company. This created an uproar, particularly in education-sensitive Bergen County, whose citizens adopted a resolution of protest objecting strenuously to the raid on this "*Sacred Fund.*"

During the period of 1820 to 1827, there existed an embarrassing hiatus during which time the court had indicated that the Act of 1798 in regard to the common schools was improper. The legislature waited until 1827 to follow the court's admonition and adopt an act that specifically authorized both the raising and expending of funds for free public schools. The fact is that the School Act of 1827 served both as an enabling act and a validating act, as there is little evidence that the process of education was ever really interrupted.

Between 1827 and 1846 the legislature not only permitted municipalities to appropriate money for the operation of the schools, but actually ordered them to do so. It also provided that each town was to have control of its schools directly through school committees, usually of three members each. Finding members willing to serve on these boards of education was so difficult that towns offered the free dispensing of the rum jug to get people to volunteer to oversee the schools. Superintendents of school districts were approved in 1846, marking the first effort to depoliticize the educational arena. The state also provided that the local tax could raise an amount equal to the amount provided by the state. By the time

Chief Justice Joseph Hornblower wrote his opinion in the case of *State v. Albright,* a case where the citizens of Chatham wanted to overspend the approved appropriation, the law had been changed and the state was allotting funds from Trenton for the maintenance of the schools.

Prior to the Civil War tuition was still a major source of funding for the allegedly free schools, and tuition was not prohibited as a means for supporting public education until 1871. However, at the end of the Civil War, major reforms were undertaken, and the state attempted to exert more influence and control. Control of public education went to county superintendents rather than township superintendents. The pressure for Home Rule was evident even in this legislation, which was amended to give the county board of freeholders approval power over the superintendents selected by the state Board of Education, which had been created in 1841.

The history of the State School Fund begins in 1817 and progresses through to the very present. Books have been written about the impact and effect of *Robinson v. Cahill,* and its progeny. The Supreme Court hung its decision on the education clause adopted in 1875. The fact that no single issue has so dominated and controlled the public agenda demonstrates the following:

- The issue of primary and secondary education has been a central and defining issue in state politics for almost 150 years. Local control of local schools is the true precept deserving recognition as an article of faith.
- The amendments adopted in 1875 have proven to be seminal documents, despite the fact that the activities of that process are usually neglected or diminished as being mere amendments to the work done at the real Convention of 1844. There is a parallel between the amendatory process in New Jersey and the adoption of the Fourteenth Amendment to the Federal Constitution. They are both documents that have taken center stage as the central constitutional events of their respective jurisdictions. Ironically to a great extent the 14th Amendment to the U.S. Constitution lay almost dormant until the latter half of the twentieth century, as did the thorough and efficient clause of the New Jersey Constitution.
- The state saw the need to assume jurisdiction over the system of education, such as it was. The pernicious implications of the unfair and unequal system that had developed were already evident.
- A common pattern, continually present in state political history, was reflected in this amendment. The pattern consists of the state wanting to control policy, but not wanting to pay for implementing it. In 1875 the problem of disparity between the quality of education in the various districts had been recognized, but any statewide solution was resisted. If the goal was to be achieved it would have to be paid for with local taxes, although much was made of the potential of the sale of riparian rights in Jersey City as being adequate to fund the free public schools forever.

The question of taxes to support public education is a long and troublesome one. The possibility of supporting education by a broad-based tax was not even considered until well into the second half of the twentieth century. So primitive were the taxing methodologies that at one point the common schools were being supported by township poll taxes.

While the thorough-and-efficient education clause of the 1875 constitutional amendments was undoubtedly regarded as a mere platitude, other amendments would have a more immediate impact on the operation of state government. Indeed, the amendments prohibiting special laws and charters for municipalities—not the education clause—directly result in the creation of the school-boroughs of Bergen county.

The Amendments of 1875 did away with the practice of granting special charters to municipalities and also required that the legislature enact only general laws affecting municipalities. Under no circumstances was the legislature to meddle with the internal governance of any community.

Regrettably the impetus for the adoption of these particular amendments is long forgotten. They were the response to one of the most notable scandals in the long history of a state that is all too often noted for the dimensions of its questionable political environment. The scandal that prompted general laws and prohibited legislative interference in municipal affairs was of gargantuan proportions. Moreover, it included such humorous vignettes that it should be cited more often as an extraordinary example of the colorful history of New Jersey politics.

Republicans, buoyed by the dominance of their national party, and attempting to emulate the practices condoned by their revered leader, Ulysses S. Grant, set about systematically to plunder Jersey City. To accomplish this they had to emasculate the indigenous political strength of the immigrant vote that had been won over by the city's Democratic leaders. Gerrymandering had been a useful but not fully effective device. The Republicans simply stripped the population of any voice in the city's operation and by special legislation provided that its internal affairs would be controlled by legislative appointees. It was not too long before a full revolt was at hand. In the interim the Trenton-appointed treasurer of Jersey City, Alexander Hamilton, was found absent from his post. Over $100,000, a small fortune in those days, was equally unaccounted for, as was his mistress. The tale of the hapless treasurer, his fortune, and his mistress is the stuff of legend.

Statewide the voters clamored for reform. The reaction to the misdeeds of the municipal looters was reflected in the constitutional reforms of 1875 regarding special laws. The consequence of eliminating the mechanism by which new municipalities had been theretofore established, i.e., special charters granted by the legislature, required the adoption of legislation that would be general, as required by the constitution, yet address localized political and economic pressures for establishing new municipalities.

To describe the political climate of 1877 as unsettled would be to understate the situation. New Jersey was still in the throes of the economic hangover precipitated by the nationwide panic of 1873. Compounding the economic depression were the excesses of the Republican's grab of power and money. The slowly seething acrimony between the immigrant Catholic Democrats, who were already concentrated in the urban centers, and the native-born Protestant Republicans in their suburban and rural enclaves exacerbated the situation. The Democrats sensed the potential for a victory that would have a strong flavor of vindication. Republicans relied on the prestige and power of their national party to carry them to another victory at least in the legislative contests.

Out of this milieu of factions emerged the Borough Act of 1878, enacted by the legislature on April 5. This statute embodied a new and radical departure from the previous tradition. Entitled *An Act for the Formation of Borough Governments,* this law became Chapter CCIX of that year's General Laws.

The most controversial section of the act was Section 2, which read as follows:

> that it shall be the duty of the chosen freeholder, or if more than one, then of one of the chosen freeholders of any township in which it is proposed to constitute a borough under this act, upon presentation to him of a petition for that purpose, setting forth the name and the boundaries of the proposed borough, signed by persons owning *at least one-tenth in value of the taxable real estate in the limits of the proposed borough, as the same appears upon the assessor's duplicate of the township, to call a special election* to be held at some convenient place within the said borough. . . . Notice shall be set up *at least ten days previous to the proposed election.*

It is easy to understand why this particular section became so controversial. Any group of citizens owning the requisite taxable property could trigger a special election, on very short notice, on the issue of incorporating a borough that would be officially recognized by the state. What had been the exclusive power of the legislature was now delegated to the voters themselves. It is truly amazing that the law, as written, permitted the process to be set in motion by as few as two landowners.

The other aspect of this particular section that must grate upon the sensibilities of the modern reader is the priority given to property over population. The idea that somehow the value of the real estate involved took precedent over the number of people affected reflects a political orientation that one associates with the eighteenth century rather than the twentieth.

The first section of the act is almost as bizarre. Legislation normally establishes thresholds that must be crossed, sets a hurdle that must be cleared. This act turned that rule of bill drafting on its head. This act established maximum parameters for the creation of a borough. In essence it was setting a hurdle that had to be crawled under rather than jumped over. The pertinent language of Section 1 read as follows:

> that the inhabitants of any township or part of a township in this state, *embracing an area not to exceed four square miles, and containing a population not to exceed five thousand,* may become a body politic and corporate, in fact and in law, whenever at a special election. . . . it may be so decided by a majority of votes of the electors of said proposed borough.

Between the period of 1878 and 1894 a number of areas took advantage of the new law and new boroughs were created. Initially these new laws that had transferred so much power to the electorate were used primarily to create three basic types of municipalities:

- The so-called holes in the donuts that dot the political map of the state.
- The railroad suburbs.
- The Atlantic shore boroughs spreading from Sandy Hook to the tip of Cape May.

Each of these types has been discussed at length elsewhere in this book, and the operative dynamics fully examined.

In 1894, the legislature passed two bills that were to serve as the extraordinary catalysts for the creation of new boroughs. In their own particular way these new laws served as stronger stimuli to proposed incorporating referenda than the railroads' interests or the protection afforded by the legislature to land speculators along the shore. The response has been described, quite accurately, as a *fever* that ran through the political life of the entire state, but most virulently in Bergen County. Unlike a fever that rises to a critical point only to be broken and leaves the patient on his way to recovery, the school-district borough fever that afflicted Bergen County was to have ill effects, which linger to the present.

The Republican legislature that assembled in Trenton in January of 1894 was a credit, not so much to its own brilliant campaign, as to the excesses of the Democrats who had controlled that branch of the state's government in the previous session. The bad light in which voters saw New Jersey Democrats intensified to a glare by the national financial panic of 1893. Democratic President Grover Cleveland became the scapegoat for the country's fiscal woes. Cleveland, it might be said, was merely at the wrong place at the wrong time. The Democrats who controlled the New Jersey Legislature were constantly appearing in the wrong places, at the wrong times, accompanied by the wrong people and doing the wrong things. In short they were not only corrupt, but flaunted their corruption. The voters threw the rascals out, and Democratic Governor George T. Werts, who personally disapproved of the conduct of his fellow Democrats in many regards, but who also needed their support for his agenda, found himself without many of the legislators who had ridden into office with him in 1892.

Those who today wring their hands and bemoan the precipitous decline in the ethical and moral tone of the political world would find it both gratifying and reassuring to spend some time reviewing the conduct of the legislature a century ago. By comparison even the most controversial actions of the last twenty years must be considered paradigms of good government held up against the proceedings of 1893 and the first months of 1894. Recognizing that they had been abjectly repudiated at the polls in November of 1893, the Democrats devised an outrageous scheme to prevent surrendering control of the Senate to the new Republican majority. With the aid of both Governor Werts and his Attorney General John Stockton, the Democrats who had not been faced with answering to the voters in the past election refused to recognize the credentials of three Republicans who had been elected in November. When the matter was finally forced into court the issue was quickly resolved in favor of the Republicans. The actual maneuvering is a story that is both long and sordid, including as it does the most incredible manufacturing of charges and distortion of evidence. The Democrats accused Senator James A. Bradley of having bribed voters by distributing scrub-brushes as the symbol of his campaign.

The very first order of business for this new legislature, which boasted such reformers as Bradley of Monmouth County and Foster M. Voorhees of Union as members of the Senate, having needed a court order to be officially seated, set about undoing much of the Democrats' scandalous work. The very first voting session, delayed until late March, saw the repeal of the law that had allowed local licensing of racetracks. Another act canceled and annulled all racetrack permits issued under the year-old law. Adding insult to injury, the act of the previous year decriminalizing bookmaking was repealed. March 21, 1894, was a banner day for the anti-sin lobby—the prohibitionists, the America-Firsters, the Know-Nothings—and their Republican-reformer allies who had ridden to power on the promise to stamp out vice and other enjoyable pastimes.

May 25, 1894, on the other hand was not such a good day in the state's history. The law of unintended consequences was the dominant principle for which that particular day must be remembered. The same spirit of reform was still operative, and now addressed the glaring inequalities that existed between the poor and wealthy school districts in the state. Often these inequalities were most startling and dramatic in districts located within the same township. The high-minded motivation of those voting for education reform cannot be questioned. Chapter CCCXXXV of the Public Laws of 1894 was apparently enacted with the best and purest of intentions. At least the purity of purpose can be ascribed to Section 13 of the act, which provides that "several school districts in each township shall be consolidated into one school district." If the legislature had left it at that, New Jersey might have had fewer than 500 municipalities today. However, they proceeded to include Section 24 of that act, which provided "that each city, *borough* and incorporated town shall be a school district, separate and distinct from the township school district."

The reaction in Bergen County was particularly noticeable with the immediate creation of 26 new boroughs, each asserting jurisdiction and the prerogative to establish its own school board simultaneously with the passage of the incorporation referendum.

Benjamin C. Wooster, the author of the chapter on public education in the *History of Bergen County,* provides the following account:

In 1894 the Act of the Legislature known as the *Township School Law* was passed. This act was intended to consolidate all the districts in any township into one district under one Board of Education. Its main purpose was to equalize educational opportunity so that children in a poor section might get some of the advantages given to children in richer districts of a township, but in Bergen county the attempt was a failure. The richer districts were unwilling to share their funds with their neighbors, and advantage was taken of the *Borough Act, which permitted portions of a township to become separate municipalities with municipal and school governments of their own. In the same year(1894) that the Township Act was passed twenty-six boroughs were formed in Bergen county alone, and scarcely a year has failed to add to the number.*

Census figures applicable to this period indicate a population in New Jersey of approximately one and a half million—divided into over one thousand separate school districts. The data for 1866, when the office of County Superintendents of Education was created, indicates that the student count in all of Bergen County totaled 6883, and that their educational needs were addressed by 64 school districts. The Township of Franklin in the northwest corner of the county had 774 students and 11 separate school districts, or roughly one district for each 75 students. Even the county average showed one district for each 106 students. These figures were a substantial improvement over those assembled in a survey of 1851 that had shown the existence of 70 school districts for the 2599 pupils in attendance that year.

The alphabetical listing of Bergen's communities begins with Allendale, and the genesis of its existence sets the tone for stories repeated over and over as we review the history of the individual communities:

The residents of Allendale, fearing that the neighboring towns would incorporate under the Borough Act, and, by including a portion or the whole of Allendale, would thus divert its taxes to the improvement and maintenance of the other towns, determined, in order to protect themselves, to also incorporate. (The population included in the survey was about 650).

Looking back a hundred years later, one may be incredulous that a community of only 650 would have the temerity to set out on its own, but by the standards of 1894, Allendale was one of the larger boroughs. The majority of new school-district boroughs had populations of under 500.

The borough fever epidemic of 1894 caused some very strange behavior. Take for example the creation of the Borough of Bogota. This *settlement* had taken its name, not, as many suppose, from some historic connection with the South American capital, but from the Bogert family, who were earlier Dutch settlers. Judge Peter F. Bogert was the sixth generation of his family when he was elected to serve on the Ridgefield Township Committee from 1880 to 1887. He, for one, saw absolutely no reason to change the system despite the honor to his family that would be inherent in the formation of a new borough bearing the name Bogota. Lined up against such conservative positions was Frederick W. Cane, who would become the first mayor. He argued, apparently persuasively, that the residents of the *settlement* should not sit still and run the risk of being responsible for the past or future extravagances of the Ridgefield Township School Board. Cane persuaded 36 of the 57 people voting that incorporation was the best course for them and their 150 or so neighbors. The following year Cane won election as mayor, thus marking the final shift of political power from the farmers to the new commuters. The new progressive element controlling the town oversaw its doubling in size in the course of a decade. The growth was prompted by the extension of the Hudson River Trolley Line on Main Street from Leonia to River Road. By 1930, the population had grown to 7300. Lest anyone feel badly for the old order presided over by the Bogert clan, they did very well in selling off their lands for residential development.

The old guard and the new commuters were also locked in combat in the ancient Huguenot settlement of Schraalenburgh, which was destined to become the Borough of Bergenfield. Not only was there competition within the proposed town, but there was competition from a group in the adjacent settlement of Dumont. The duel involved conflicting surveys which were attached to the respective petitions that were circulating simultaneously. The petition of the prospective Dumontites extended their land grab about half a dozen blocks south so that the proposed Borough of Dumont would have its southerly border at Church Street. This would have meant that the major industry and tax ratable, the Cooper Chair Factory, and the pond upon which it was situated would go on the tax rolls of Dumont. The prospective Bergenfieldians countered with a petition and survey that pushed the Dumontites north to the center line of Columbia Avenue, thereby placing the Cooper factory on their ratable list. The race to the court house was on, and Bergenfield won by fifteen minutes.

The competing forces in Bergenfield agreed on two things.

- They were not going to pay for the past or future extravagances of the schools in Palisades Township other than those incurred by Schraalenburgh's School District No. 11.
- The chair factory of Tunis R. Cooper should help pay the extravagances of only District No. 11.

The people in and around what was to be the Borough of Wood-Ridge provide what I believe is the very best story of how out of hand the municipal multiplication became. The *Citizens' Ticket,* headed by Anton Molinari, strongly favored incorporation, while the *Workmen's Ticket,* headed by Frederick H. P. Imbert, was staunchly opposed. Molinari knew how to count and how to draw lines. The four voters in the Schoonmaker family were allied with the Imbert faction, as were most of the voters on the east side of Berger Street. The boundaries of the new proposed borough reflected Molinari's mathematical skills. The new borough would include the Schoonmakers' farmland but exclude the farmhouse itself, as it would exclude the east side of Berger Street. The inclusion of these areas would have made the vote much closer than the 56 in favor and 40 opposed that was the vote tally creating the Borough of Wood-Ridge. Once the Molinari faction felt themselves in firmer control, they relinquished and annexed by ordinance the Schoonmaker farmhouse, but the east side of Berger Street remained in Lodi Township until Moonachie claimed it as part of their borough when it was formed in 1910.

It would be wrong to think that the legislature's emergency measures of 1896 and 1897 ended the great school-district battles of Bergen County. The fight to control local schools continued, but at a pace now controlled by the ability of the local promoters to muster enough political influence to have the Bergen legislative delegation sponsor the necessary bills to permit incorporation. The borough-forming phenomena culminated in the early 1920s with the creation of new boroughs at the greatest rate since 1894.

The story of Paramus and Rochelle Park is illustrative of the lingering school-district battles. The Township of Midland once contained six *settlements,* four of which decided to participate in the borough fever of 1894. They were Maywood, New Milford, Delford (now Oradell), and Riverside (now River Edge). This left Midland Township with two remaining *settlements,* both rural in nature, but with Rochelle Park closer geographically to the urbanized county seat of Hackensack than was the sparsely populated area of Paramus. The population in New Rochelle was greater than that of Paramus. In 1921 there were four schools serving all of what was left of Midland Township, and in that year a proposal was advanced to eliminate all four schools and consolidate the system into one new building to serve everyone in the district. Where to locate the new structure? The southern end of the township had the majority of voters and students, and therefore argued that it made sense to place the new school in that area. Bearing in mind that this was occurring in an era that predated the school bus, the parents in the area of Paramus, who would be required daily to drive their children to the new school and retrieve them later in the day, took exception to having the new school in the *backyard* of those living in the southern end of the township. The farmers of Paramus were mobilized by its leading corporate citizens and some of the area's oldest residents. The opinion to break away from Midland Township and form the Borough of Paramus was almost unanimous, a vote of 160 to 1.

New Rochelle incorporated at the same time, and Midland Township ceased to exist. Each of these new boroughs set about running their own schools and governing themselves. Rochelle Park continued to enjoy its suburban status. However, the construction of the George Washington Bridge in the latter half of the decade, the widening of State Highway 4, and finally the construction of the Garden State Parkway made the name Paramus synonymous with shopping malls.

While most of the attention was focused on Bergen County, it is equally clear that other municipalities that had flirted with the idea of creating an independent borough were inspired to take the plunge by the enactment of the Borough Act of 1894. In Chapter Three, which was the case study of the division and re-division of the southern section of Middlesex County, the Borough of Jamesburg received some close attention. The ongoing tension caused by the allocation of funds for road maintenance and repair was the most public aspect of the split between Jamesburg and Monroe, but clearly the officials in Jamesburg were equally encouraged to take the final step when they realized that full borough status would also give them total control of their schools as well.

Careful examination of the dates when a number of boroughs were finally incorporated provides compelling evidence that the majority can be viewed as school-district boroughs with equal justification for viewing them as railroad suburbs or street-fight boroughs. Road money and school expenditures are two constants that appear throughout the history of municipal formation in New Jersey.

Mountainside and Roselle Boroughs in Union County, along with a host of others outside of Bergen County, are true school-district boroughs. All tolled, the number of boroughs incorporated in 1894 to 1895 was 40, but the story does not end there. Even with the new law requiring legislative action to incorporate a new borough, the creation of new municipalities was merely rendered slightly more difficult and time-consuming. Fifty or more years later, we still find that schools are the driving force in the legislative enactments creating the last boroughs ever to be formed in the state, such as Raritan Borough in Somerset County, Victory Gardens in Morris County, and Roosevelt in Monmouth County.

The perverse effects of the legislature's acts are best reflected in the story of the little Borough of Allentown in Monmouth County. This community was really only a crossroad on the way from Mount Holly, Burlington County, to Freehold. It had been bypassed by the original railroad alignment, and to this day is one of the smaller boroughs in the state, with a population under 2,000. It was one of the smarter boroughs in that it saw early that the law was counterproductive to its best interests. The official history of the borough tells the story this way: "In 1895 came the Township School Act consolidating all of the township into the larger township district and then Allentown no longer was District No. 14 of the county of Monmouth, but School No. 1 of the Upper Freehold Township District."

The township and the borough worked out an arrangement whereby Allentown got two members on the nine-member Board of Education. Everybody was happy. In fact, we are told: "This was a most successful arrangement for several years when new troubles appeared." According to the November 19, 1903, issue of the *Allentown Messenger,* Allentown, because it was a borough (a fact since April 2, 1889), "must become a separate school district and have its school district apart from the township. This unhappy state of affairs was brought about because of a decision of the state Supreme Court."

Both political entities showed great wisdom and tenacity, working diligently to put back together what the legislature and the court were trying to break up. They "knew that each could not possibly make out on their own. They had to become one to save unnecessary expense and to provide better educational facilities." The story continues on, regaling the reader with the details of the problems that ensued, and how they were overcome so that a consolidated school district could operate. Regrettably, there are very few stories such as this one.

The exponential increase in the number of incorporated boroughs that the state witnessed after passage of the School Act of 1894 prompted a swift reaction. The pendulum that in 1878 had swung so dramatically in toward placing municipal creation in the hands of the voters was now grasped firmly by the legislators and swung back firmly into their exclusive province. Within two years of the enactment of the School Act, a new law was adopted on March 26, 1896, prohibiting the creation of any further boroughs by the means of a special election. That was just a stop-gap measure to stem the tide.

Chapter 161 of the Laws of 1897, commonly referred to as the Borough Act was adopted on April 24th, and began with this prohibition:

> Hereafter no borough shall be incorporated or dissolved, nor shall its territory be increased or diminished, or its lines altered, except by special act of the Legislature.

The short experiment in incorporation by special election or referendum had lasted only eighteen years, but had resulted in the doubling of municipal corporations in the state. The proverbial straw that had broken the camel's back was the wholesale creation of school-district boroughs in Bergen County.

The ultimate cost to the state's taxpayers over the subsequent decade, directly attributable to the Republican reforms of 1894, is incalculable. One need only take an afternoon drive through Bergen County. The only evidence that you have traversed one borough in the past five minutes and are now entering another, which may take only three minutes to cross, is a sign. Otherwise it is virtually impossible to tell one fungible borough from the other. Yet each has its own most prized possession, and prized it should be considering its cost: its own school district.

Bergen County now has 70 separate municipal governments to be divided into its land mass of 234 square miles. The otherwise simple mathematics is somewhat distorted by the fact that communities still exist in Bergen County, such as Mahwah and Franklin Lakes, that may be described as sizable. In fact the removal of these two townships from the equation drops the land area of the remaining 68 towns to under 200 square miles. The fact is that the vast majority of Bergen municipalities are under three square miles in size, with many less than a mile square. However, it is not simply the geographic size of these communities that carries significance; it is the composition of the tax ratables within each town that is important. North of Route 3, it is difficult to find a community in the entire county that does not fit the cookie-cutter profile of the bedroom community, with anywhere from a low of 85 percent to a high of over 95 percent of all taxable real estate classified as residential.

Few, if any, even among the wealthiest of communities, could today afford the luxury of their independent school system, given present economic realities. However, with the type of perversity that has come to identify state policy toward municipal multiplication, the residential enclaves of Bergen have been rewarded rather than punished by the state for their exclusivity. Since the inception of modern concepts of state school aid, every formula has been driven by some notion of the equalized real estate valuations per pupil. At no time over the past forty years has any formula been used that took into account the median or average income per household. The result has been that the suburbs of Bergen, free from the pollution of industry and the congestion of commerce, have actually benefited from their diminutive size and absence of ratables.

In retrospect, the decisions made back in 1894 proved to have been politically astute from the vantage point of the local officials who led the incorporation fever. From a different perspective—one that measures the cost of duplication, replication, redundancy of offices, overlapping of jurisdictions, unneeded services, and just plain simple waste—the experience of Bergen County has been egregious and shameful.

This chapter began by referring to matters that are accorded reverence for things held sacred. Only a religious impulse can raise a cathedral such as Chartres; only spiritual conviction can gild altars in gold, and commitment to a belief can explain the incredible sacrifices of wealth that are necessary to accomplish such things. The Bergen County school districts have cost billions, justifying the proposition that the neighborhood school is a matter of religious principle in this state and most particularly in that county.

CHAPTER 8

Dry Towns versus Wet Towns

DRAWING THE LINE AT ABSTINENCE

There is nothing which has yet been . . . contrived by man by which so much . . .
happiness is produced as by a good tavern or inn.
Samuel Johnson

*H*istory is never the simple recitation of facts and dates. History is always written from a vantage point subsequent to the actual events. It includes an extra-factual perspective—a prejudice, a context in which the author collects the facts and then molds them into a coordinated presentation that tends to support the argument the author intends to advance.

The history of New Jersey can be told using a panoply of vantage points. One may start with the earliest and most basic division of East and West Jersey and tell the story of how the actual line was considerably off the mark and had to be recalculated. The parallel histories of East and West Jersey, presented chronologically, provide fascinating and amusing reading.

The North/South variation on the theme is equally as interesting and historically valid. This frame of reference is readily grasped with the North developing a commercial orientation to New York City, while the South gravitated both economically and culturally to the nearer metropolis of Philadelphia.

Perhaps the proper introduction to an appreciation of the state's colorful history is to view it as the continuing struggle of the industrial centers whose builders viewed a future forged by iron and steel versus the abiding and enduring agricultural interests of those that preferred a more bucolic existence. Another variation on this theme is one that positions the centers of wealth and population against the institutionalized political power of more rural counties. These are just some of the possible approaches, but each of these traces the tensions that existed between the conflicting interests with alternate, if not opposite, priorities.

Another possible theme to follow is one that was played out in a minor key, but included a great deal of percussion in its orchestration. It is the fugue that demonstrated the counterpoint of the puritanical, prohibitionist interests, *dry* in their drinking habits, against a central coda that was predominantly liberal and tolerant in religious matters and *wet* in its preferences for liquid refreshments.

Teetotalers were an object of humor, unless they were someone who had *taken the pledge*, in which case they were to be commended. Inebriates, on the other hand, were the subject of derision and were to be avoided because they wasted one's time. Drinking had its place and was to be tolerated and controlled, both by the family and the law.

During my apprenticeship for what might be an attempt to secure political office, my father gave me some very practical advice. He said: "Never vote for anything or take a position against barbers, hairdressers or dentists—they all have captive audiences—and never offend the tavern owners—their audience might be voluntary, but it tends to listen longer." This was very sound advice, especially for anyone interested in New Jersey politics, where the interests of the tavern owners have been treated with deference.

The reasons underlying this exalted status include the personal predilections of most citizens, as well as the continuing debt of gratitude owed to the liquor industry for their role in the War for Independence. During my political life, the liquor-selling business was trying to improve its image, an effort that eventually resulted in its becoming the "hospitality industry." Even before the tourism boom associated with the advent of legalized gambling, the neighborhood tavern enjoyed a legacy of good will that was a reaction to Prohibition's excesses and to the contribution tavern keepers had made to home-front morale during the Second World War. While drinking and driving don't mix, drinking and politics have always mixed in New Jersey.

The first Dutch settlers in the Hudson and Bergen County area regarded strong spirits as a natural blessing. The same was true for the early Swedish and German enclaves in South Jersey.

The early settlement of Newark, however, was a totally different picture. The pastor of a congregation that brought an entire community from its original location in the state of Connecticut to the banks of the Passaic River presided over a group that held strong religious convictions—an affinity for hard work and an abiding belief that alcohol was of the devil. It was not until the massive influx of Germans and Irish into that city in the middle of the nineteenth century that the lingering vestiges of its *dry* founders were eradicated. The majority of Newark's early blue laws were forgotten, repealed, or ignored, but its pulpits hosted some of the most active Prohibitionists well into the twentieth century. The city became as well known for its breweries as it was for its tanneries. They both produced an amber liquid in huge quantities. One industry placed it in barrels for consumption. The tanneries dumped their brownish, toxic effluent into the river—for pollution. Ironically many religious leaders of the time crusaded against the product of the breweries while finding the work of the tanneries to be nothing more than the advancement of God's work on earth.

That liquor and its production fueled the Revolution is not disputed. Resentment against the original Molasses Tax of 1733 served as the foundation upon which the Revolution was built. With the ever-growing antitax sentiment, the Molasses and Sugar Taxes and then the Stamp Act triggered the War for Independence. The taxes imposed on sugar and molasses by King George II and King George III were designed to replenish the royal coffers—not to provide the colonies with protection or services. The Crown thought it had a perfect closed system of production, commerce, and taxation. The sugar was grown in Caribbean colonies, was being shipped into the Continental colonies, including New Jersey, for the manufacture of rum, and was sold in the colonies or shipped to Africa for trade for more slaves to be brought to the colonies to grow more sugar, completing this sinister cycle of commerce.

Always creative and self-reliant, New Jerseyans knew they had enough raw material to produce an ample supply of intoxicating beverages—particularly from their apple orchards. Cider mills were indigenous to virtually every section of the state, and the distilling of apple jack was a home-spun art that enhanced the alcohol content and preserved the product far longer than the simple fermentation of the cider. Hard cider had a short life span between its first refreshing sparkle and its resolution into vinegar. Distilling the mash gave it potent qualities. The natural sugar content of the apples rendered the molasses from the British West Indies superfluous.

Taverns and inns existed throughout the state and the books of Arthur D. Pierce, such as *Smuggler's Woods,* are simply excellent in emphasizing the important role played by the taverns in our Revolution. However, taverns and inns were not welcome everywhere, and long before the advent of Prohibition there were communities being formed for the specific purpose of creating enclaves where *demon rum* and the ubiquitous products of the cider mills of New Jersey would not be welcomed.

Vestiges of the efforts to create entire alcohol-free communities free still dot the New Jersey's municipal map. Ocean Grove in Monmouth County is the clearest example and perhaps the best known. Originally organized as a camp meeting, Ocean Grove was so observant of religious principles that it once attempted to prohibit the Pennsylvania Railroad from servicing its station and even passing through its borders on the Sabbath. If one had the courage and temerity to fight the power of the Pennsylvania Railroad in its heyday, one also enjoyed the firm conviction that God was on one's side, as that was the only possible entity with more political clout than the railroads.

The camp meeting in Ocean Grove inspired the creation of a substantial number of similar communities—some with an enduring legacy, and others with a legacy that literally and figuratively drowned out. The best example of the abiding influence of the camp-meeting code of conduct can be found in Ocean City—the city that can trace its lineage directly to the camp meeting of Ocean Grove. The Reverend William B. Wood and the Reverend S. Wesley Lake attended services at Ocean Grove on August 22, 1879. Within three weeks the Reverend Lake was out scouting a place known as Peck's Beach to determine if the successful camp meeting in Monmouth County could be replicated in Cape May County to provide the same environment, but easier access, for the devout Christians of Philadelphia, Wilmington, Baltimore, and Washington, D.C. He persuaded his father,

Simon Lake, to mortgage his farm and put up the ten thousand dollars he realized from that transaction to buy up the island. Working with his colleague the Reverend Wood and his father and two brothers, Ezra and James, the Reverend Lake commenced construction of what is now Ocean City, a community with a year-round population of 15,000, which swells to three times that size during the summer. It remains a community wherein the temperance traditions of its founders are still publicly observed, although rumor has it that private consumption within one's own residence is now tolerated. Those interested in a family resort—where the streets are safe, the noise level minimal, and the evening diversions wholesome—flock to Ocean City. While it has been relatively secularized over the years, the principles of its founders have left an indelible mark upon the cultural climate of this city that stands in such stark contrast to its neighbor to the north, Atlantic City.

The other communities along the shore that were clones of Ocean Grove have experienced a much different fate. Belmar, which started as somewhat of an annex to Ocean Grove, was originally called Ocean Beach. The early camp meeting enthusiasts did not demonstrate much imagination when it came to names, but by the turn of the century the community was operating as a successful summer resort under its present name, Belmar, where secularization has taken a definite hold. The same is true for the town of Avon-By-The-Sea, founded by Baptist ministers under the extremely perplexing title of Key East. As with Ocean Grove, it was originally a camp meeting within the jurisdiction of Neptune Township, but was incorporated as a borough, with its present name, at the turn of the century. It has, of course, changed its drinking laws as dramatically as it changed its name.

Further north along the coast we arrive at the Borough of Bradley Beach, a community whose origin is inextricably entwined with both Ocean Grove and Asbury Park. The existence of Bradley Beach south of Ocean Grove and Asbury Park testifies to the influence of the Ocean Grove phenomenon and the impact that camp meeting had on one individual, James A. Bradley. In a state that is proud of a great many people who left unique marks upon its landscape, a place must be reserved in New Jersey's pantheon of uniqueness for the irrepressible James A. Bradley.

Bradley was a visionary, who mixed the conservatism of his religious beliefs with a progressive and innovative approach to urban planning. With no formal training in either theology or architecture (urban planning as an academic discipline had not been contemplated), in a stunning tour de force of energy and enterprise over only one decade, Bradley converted the extended thicket north of Ocean Grove into a thriving community. For the three decades between Bradley's first exploratory hike in the woods and his sale of his holdings to the city itself, the names Asbury Park and Bradley were virtually synonymous. He was *the founder.*

He named the City of Asbury Park in honor of the first Methodist Bishop to be ordained in America and a man who had ministered to many within the state of New Jersey, Francis Asbury. (Pitman Township, in Gloucester County, similarly pays homage to a remarkable and well-respected Methodist clergyman.) Asbury instituted a code of conduct that reflected the strict moral tenets to which Bradley subscribed. These included abstinence from all alcohol and a dress code that makes the Ayatollah Khomeni appear a libertine. Women were allowed to bathe upon his beaches only if they submitted to wearing straw hats and stockings under ankle-length pants that were worn under ankle-length skirts. These were affectionately called *Bradley bags*.

On the other hand, his innovations in city planning rivaled Baron Hausmann's and L'Enfant's, with spacious boulevards, large lots, parks, and playgrounds interspersed throughout the city. The diversions placed along the beach front were interesting and engaging—a free amusement park in many ways. He even demonstrated a very modern sensitivity to animal welfare, providing shady shelters for the horses who drew carriages from one place to another in his burgeoning city.

As he grew older he became a curmudgeon. After seeing his life's work in Asbury Park slowly but surely become ever more secularized and his standards more often honored only in the breach, he founded a new community south of Ocean Grove, modestly called Bradley Beach. Before his death in 1921 he could take solace in the fact that national Prohibition enforced abstinence in both the communities he had founded. However, with national repeal came a new code for both communities.

Sadly both towns fell into serious decay. And while the one that carries his name has made strides to recover, the once-proud city of Asbury Park has proven almost immune to rehabilitation efforts, no matter how vigorous or well-intentioned. Myopic state policy has encouraged the *dumping* of mentally ill patients into the city's old hotels that have been converted to boarding houses, and today one observes with sadness and frustration that Thorazine is probably consumed in greater amounts than alcohol within Asbury Park.

The notorious blue laws were prevalent and enduring, despite the separation of church and state articulated in the First Amendment of the Bill of Rights. Blue laws have a history that stretches back to the earliest of colonial days and predates the adoption of the First Amendment by a minimum of a hundred years. The comfort level of New Jersey's diverse and multicultural society would be raised undoubtedly if the citizens could see that such laws were limited in scope, intention, time, and locale. However, the exact opposite was true. New Jersey was no bastion of tolerance standing strong against a tide of religious bias. The prevailing sentiment of deference being accorded to religious practices and traditions was common throughout the state well into the twentieth century. If it were not for the close association that the religiously inspired blue laws had in the public's mind with the excesses of Prohibition, many of these laws would still be on the books today.

As Prohibition was swept away by a consensus that the measure was an utter failure, so too were the majority of other laws that attempted to dictate how the public was to spend its Sunday afternoons. New Jersey must admit to a legacy that includes the attempted criminal prosecution of a young man for having been sighted surf bathing on the Sabbath within the distant view of some serious churchgoers in 1884, as well as the condemnation of Sunday baseball right through the 1930s. However, the state successfully shed the vast majority of its blue laws by the end of the Second World War, even though such laws left their mark upon the state and upon its geography.

The mark left by the abstinence movement is indelible. But before going into a serious analysis of how abstinence affected the state, it is relevant to understand how liquor actually helped create some of the most famous towns in the state, such as Tavistock.

The Borough of Tavistock in Camden County, a bona fide entity with perhaps the smallest population of any recognized municipal corporation in the entire United States, is—from the perspective of public policy and regional planning— a joke. It came into being as a result of the type of political maneuvering that helps provide New Jersey with its reputation for colorful politics.

Center Township was a fair sized municipality occupying a good portion of the center of Camden County. It was removed from the bustle of the waterfront and the industrial complex that spread along the Delaware River adjacent to the shipyards and docks of the city. Center included within its borders a fine golf course, where many of the executives, who oversaw the manufacturing and shipping along the waterfront, spent time when they were not canning tomato soup, building ships, or cranking out radio parts. There were two problems that the very exclusive members of the country club wished to solve, and they both involved *blue laws*. The first was the local ordinance that prohibited the playing of golf on Sunday; and the other was the recently enacted Amendment to the U.S. Constitution that frowned upon indulging in alcoholic beverages after a long round of golf, or worse still with Saturday night dinner at the *club*.

The way to insure that the local constabulary would not be overly diligent was to provide that the club would be a municipal entity unto itself. The wheels were set in motion, and a compliant legislature passed an act providing that the Borough of Tavistock be created with all of the same dignity as the city of Newark or Jersey City. By last report the population of Tavistock is under double digits. The newspapers howled, the town fathers of Center Township fulminated, every one who saw this legislation for what it was screamed their outrage in unison. A concerted effort was launched, led by the elected officers of Center to persuade the Governor to do the only right and proper thing by exercising his veto power and sending this abomination back to the legislature.

In politics it is often beneficial to know the governor personally. It is even better if you have shared a drink once or twice. It is also very helpful if (s)he returns your phone calls promptly. All of these categories seemed to have been amply filled by the secretary of one of the state's largest and most powerful companies— Victor Talking Machine Company (later part of RCA Victor). The secretary was by all reports an avid golfer, but fond of putting in a little overtime on Saturdays. Apparently this was also true of many of his fellow executives who filled out the membership of the country club. Being able to get in a round on Sunday would help morale and assist their companies to grow, prosper, and create more jobs.

The governor at the time was Edward I. Edwards, who had taken office after the election of 1919; the Constitution of 1844 prohibited him from running for another successive term. This provision of the constitution had been inserted so that the incumbent governor would not be tempted to make decisions with one eye on his reelection prospects and would do what was best for the state without consideration of fear or favor. Edwards was also a governor who enjoyed the exercise of playing eighteen holes, as well as the traditional and accustomed bonhomie of the nineteenth. Legend has it that the governor was prevailed upon by his friend Frank B. Middleton, president of the club, the avid golfer and secretary of the Victor Talking Machine Company. Supposedly, the governor acted swiftly in bringing about the creation of the Borough of Tavistock in February of 1921, so that citizens would have a safe haven to enjoy the peace and tranquillity of a few hours of leisure, free from those who would interfere with either their friendly and healthful sport, or their imbibing a few social drinks.

One might think this was a unique situation brought about by the impending ratification of the Eighteenth Amendment, universally known as Prohibition. But in fact, Tavistock was not the first nor the last municipality whose very creation was the by-product of the blue laws. And the creativity of evasion turned out to inspire others. The final state needed to ratify the amendment did so in March of 1922, and it became the law of the land one year later. But the handwriting was on the wall long before. If anything, this story gives credit to the planning capabilities of the corporate executives, and also gives credence to the adage that money talks. But Edwards, although a bank executive, was not an elitist. He was just as aggressive and protective of everyone else's right to drink. After leaving the governor's chair, he successfully ran for the U.S. Senate, using the attractive slogan that he would "make New Jersey as wet as the Atlantic."

In Chapter 6, the railroads and their pervasive and dominant influence were explored, with the observation that these had a greater effect upon the formation of communities than any other factors. Hightstown in Mercer County was the indirect product of the railroads' advent, but, the real story here is the combination of the railroads and the liquor laws.

A ride on the original Camden Amboy Line was long, hot, dusty, dangerous, and brutish. The line opened early in railroad history, with the first cars being pulled by horses along the iron rails. The steam locomotive's arrival was a technological advance, but at a severe price in comfort and safety. The steam, dust, and cinders commonly sprinkled passengers with a layer of grime and worse. Stories abound concerning passengers' clothing being ruined and even ignited by sparks from the boiler or flames spewing from the smokestack. Travel under these conditions could build a mighty thirst. The locomotives also had the bad habit of derailing or otherwise malfunctioning in transit, so the well-equipped traveler never wanted to be without provision for what could amount to a serious delay of several hours.

The early engines needed refueling along the route, short as it was. Water had to be added, and the wood-fired boiler needed a guaranteed steady supply. Moreover, farmers wanted railroads to deliver goods to the cities of the farmers' choice so they in turn could be carried for ultimate sale in New York or Philadelphia.

One of the first depots designed to satisfy the needs of watering and refueling was the area known as Hightstown. The folks in this neighborhood quickly realized that the passengers also needed to be watered and refueled. The traditional licensing mechanism at the time for anyone wishing to purvey alcohol was the Court of Common Pleas. It seems strange now that such an obviously administrative function would have been placed in the hands of the judicial branch of government, but we are still dealing with a period when the judiciary was independently recognized, but existed under the auspices of the legislative branch. Various regulations had existed, of course, since colonial times, and the licensing by the Court of Common Pleas was one of the distinct vestiges of earlier customs.

However, the legislature also had the power to confer upon a group of inhabitants the status of borough. This could be done by a special charter that would delegate powers and duties to the council of the chartered borough. Such a special charter was granted creating the Borough of Hightstown in 1853. This special charter, pursuant to Section Nineteen, specifically gave to the Common Council of the Borough of Hightstown the power to license taverns and inns within the borough limits. The significance of this section was still being fought over fifty years later. All the while the thirsty passengers waiting for the their engine to be watered and the wood supply to be replenished could avail themselves of the local tavern, where they could dust off their cinder-laden outerwear, answer calls of nature, and get a reinforcing drink or two to sustain them for the balance of the journey. A little something *to go* was also available.

Hightstown's charter was the subject of great debate and remained so until 1876. At this time the legislature passed legislation making it clear that they had not intended the council of this small town to control the granting of licenses for taverns, but that those seeking such licenses must apply to the Court of Common Pleas.

In contrast, the history of South Jersey is replete with efforts to create towns that would be totally *dry*. Such towns as Millville, Bridgeton, and Vineland, the three major towns of Cumberland County, as well as the Borough of Haddonfield in Camden County, were created under what were known as Prohibition Charters. These special charters were granted prior to the Constitutional Amendments of 1875 and specifically prohibited the sale of alcohol within defined township borders. Thus, they were communities whose very existence was the product of abstinence.

The irony of their boundaries was exposed during the gubernatorial administration of John Franklin Fort, 1908–1912. Fort was a churchgoer, a reformer, a justice of the Supreme Court, where he had spoken out vigorously against gambling interests—and a winner.

At the governor's request the legislature created a blue-ribbon commission to investigate the observance and enforcement of the liquor laws. The governor appointed such men as: Charles J. Fisk, a Wall Street lawyer and mayor of Plainfield; the attorney for the Roman Catholic Church in Trenton, Peter Backes, the man who had drafted the most recent Jersey blue laws, commonly called the *Bishop's Laws;* the declared Prohibitionist, T. Frank Appleby, mayor of Asbury Park; and the crusading editor of the *Hackensack Record,* Caleb Van Husen

Whitbeck. The activities of the commission made sensational headlines, more sensational as a result of the commission being granted subpoena powers. What they did expose was a system riddled with monopolistic abuse by the major breweries. However, the testimony in South Jersey revealed that liquor and beer were dispensed from more outlets in the so-called *dry* communities than virtually anywhere else in the state—and dispensed without observance of the niceties of excise taxes or licensing fees.

The point must be emphasized that the very rationale of these towns' borders had been rendered moot. There may have been something very devious going on in South Jersey, i.e., the towns were incorporated as *dry* communities to avoid the attention of the Federal Revenue authorities. On the other hand, puritanical zeal may have been the motivation behind the towns' creation, particularly in Cumberland County. Or, perhaps, it might have been a little bit of both—a strange symbiotic relationship between the moonshiners and the Prohibitionists, with each getting something they wanted. The churchgoers got their legitimacy, and the bootleggers got their tax-exempt status.

The Fisk Commission, focusing on North Jersey activities, pointed out the comfort and protection provide by a number of locales for hard-working men set upon enjoying their Sunday while their womenfolk tended to church obligations. The commission would send out investigators for a week or two prior to their scheduled hearings in certain counties. The detectives would then report back to the commission that they had personally witnessed the fact that dozens of saloons had been open and doing brisk business on the previous Sunday in direct contravention of the state edict, known as the Bishop's Law. Fisk and his fellow commissioners would then call the police chiefs to testify under oath and inquire if the chiefs were aware that a number of saloons had been observed openly doing business on the previous Sunday. The screen writer of the movie *Casablanca* must have read the transcripts of these interrogations, and borrowed the composite answer for the famous reply of the police chief when advised that gambling was taking place at Rick's. Each expressed the same shock and surprise. The police chief of Perth Amboy went a step beyond being shocked at the 68 Sunday-opened saloons—he was *horrified.*

The extensive report filed by the Fisk Commission also falls squarely within New Jersey tradition. It was warmly received by the governor, who profusely thanked the members for their invaluable contribution to the betterment of the state and assured them that their personal sacrifice of time, effort, energy, enterprise, and attention would never be forgotten. The governor then sent a special message to the legislature. They in turn accepted the report and the governor's accompanying admonitions and exhortations with the diligence that was warranted by such an important undertaking. Then everyone proceeded to do nothing.

The Temperance Movement was alive and well in New Jersey. In fact, the movement had made such a strong showing in the governor's race of 1887 that the Republican candidate who was strongly favored had been denied the victory by General Fisk, who led the Prohibition Party ticket and garnered almost 20,000 votes, primarily from Republican strongholds in the south.

Taking control of both houses of the legislature in 1888, the Republicans made a brilliant tactical move to win back the affections of the Prohibitionists. After some shrewd back-room negotiations with the powers of the Prohibition Party, the Republicans brought to the floor of the legislature a bill that would be far-reaching in its consequences and controversial in its immediate effect. The bill provided that municipalities set the excise or licensing fee for saloons at a minimum of $100 and a maximum of $500 per license. The fee was a sliding one, with licenses within cities of the first class being most expensive. The second provision of the bill allowed for a referendum, county by county, on the issue of banning alcohol altogether. Special elections could be scheduled after presentation of a petition bearing a minimum number of signatures to the circuit court of each county.

The liquor interests were so offended by the new licensing fee and so confident of the people's support for their enterprise that they ignored the referendum provision and concentrated their lobbying efforts on persuading the Republicans to lower the fees. They were successful in having the fee schedule cut in half, but even that reduced tariff was five times what the prevailing rate was in most cities, with the $50 per year fee charged in Jersey City and Newark being typical. The bill passed both houses only to be vetoed by Governor Green. It may have stayed in that condition, but for the heavy lobbying efforts of the Anti-Saloon Movement, who insisted that a united Republican Party effort at override be mounted or the Republicans would face another three-party race in the election of 1889. The Republicans, convinced that the passage of the legislation known as the High Fee–Local Option Act would buy them peace and support from the Prohibitionists, overrode the governor's veto and this act went into effect.

Efforts for its repeal began immediately with the liquor interests swearing undying fealty to the Democrats if they would just get back the majority and repeal this bill before it wreaked havoc on their industry. The effort intensified as Cumberland County voted to go dry while the ink on the bill was still wet. Warren County was next and Cape May County, despite its tourist trade, was not far behind. Even some larger counties with a heavier population of immigrants and working class were seriously considering the referendum. Only Essex and Hudson seemed immune to the effort, and even within their borders there were clergy and crusaders at work gathering signatures. When Hunterdon County voted dry, in a special election, near panic set in.

The Democrats, funded with liquor money, outpolled the Republicans, funded with dry money, at the election in November of 1888, but not by much. The Senate organized with eleven Democrats and ten Republicans, in January 1889. The key to overturning the act of the previous year was the newly elected Democrat from the dry county of Cumberland. The story of how the Democrat caucus ultimately prevailed on Senator Philip K. Baker is a long and fascinating tale, but the final compromise was even more important in its impact.

The bill repealing the Local Option Act and negating the Prohibition referendums that had already been conducted also included a municipal option. By special election, town by town, the price of each license could be established. A rather strange piece of legislation in retrospect, it was certainly within the mainstream of Prohibition strategy as articulated by the Women's Christian Temperance Union (WCTU) and the Prohibitionist Party.

So while no county could elect to turn dry, each individual town had the right to allow its voters to set the fees for the right to purvey alcohol. In the meantime the section of the law setting out the new excise rates at the higher figures established in 1888 remained untouched, and cities such as Newark and Jersey City had little difficulty closing their budget gaps that year. The increase in the fee from $50 to $250 caused a great deal of grousing, but most licensees anteed up the money. Considering inflation, the new fee was the equivalent of asking each saloon keeper to come up with an amount equal to three month's wages for the ordinary laborer, or in today's values approximately eight to ten thousand dollars.

The battle had really just begun; the Prohibition Party felt themselves betrayed by the Republicans and fielded a candidate for governor notwithstanding protestations from the Republicans that they had kept their end of the bargain. The Democrats chose Leon Abbett, who had served previously and had helped the Democrats forge their alliance with the liquor dealers whom he represented. It was Abbett who had crafted the strategy for undoing the Local Option Act and kept the liquor dealers from doing anything rash, such as carrying out their threat to start a political party of their own.

In 1893 the Anti-Saloon League was founded in the state of Ohio. Its goals were clear, and its strategy of starting from the grass roots and working upward was no secret. In this regard it had learned from the prior mistakes of its allies, the WCTU and the Prohibition Party. Local action was needed. First the small towns would vote out demon rum, then larger towns, then counties, then the entire state, and in the end there would be no need for action on the national level, because little by little everything underneath would have already been dried up. The Anti-Saloon League gave new hope to those in New Jersey who still wanted to ban the sale and manufacture of beer and liquor. The momentum built for years and in 1906 the climate seemed right for another run at the legislature. This time it was with the same type of legislation that had succeeded in other states—legislation that not only would permit the local voters to set the fee for a license, but also would allow them to vote to have their town dry.

Despite the sentiment for reform, generated by numerous exposés of abuses by the liquor interests, the state as a whole was not ready for a new wholesale referendum procedure by which town after town could be picked off by the drys. While the efforts to adopt a local-option law were quickly and easily turned back, it was defeated only at the price of the legislature adopting the draconian Bishop's Law of the same year.

It is critical to understand from all this political maneuvering and posturing on the state level that with the advent of municipal control over the wet/dry destiny, a new dynamic took hold in drawing town lines. From the promise of some municipal input that was contained in the Repeal Bill of 1889 right through to the final Armageddon of the passage of the Volstead Act, one could surmise that no new municipality came into existence during this thirty-year period, without wary eyes being cast to ascertain and project how the new configuration would react to the possible question of dry or wet. This was an important, if not the dominant, consideration of voters and politicians whose actions in those years brought onto the political map of New Jersey 100 new municipalities.

As relevant and driving a rationale as it may have been to New Jersey voters at the turn of the century, it is totally irrelevant today—as irrelevant as the "dry" plaque on the water fountain that once stood in the South Amboy train station. The fountain and the plaque are now gone, but the city still has innumerable taverns. South Amboy ranked second only to Hoboken in the number of liquor licenses per capita after the repeal of Prohibition, a ratio of one license for every one hundred and fifty residents. The plaque read that the water fountain was a gift to the city from the Women's Christian Temperance Union.

This is the only entrance to Tavistock: both the borough and the country club. They are, of course, one and the same.

At the rear of the country club there is a sign forbidding trespass on the grounds, thereby rendering Tavistock the only town in America where permission is needed to enter. This gives new meaning to the phrase "get out of town."

The slogan on this Bergen County schoolhouse (circa 1894) reads "Children First." It is silent as to the proposition of "Taxpayers Last."

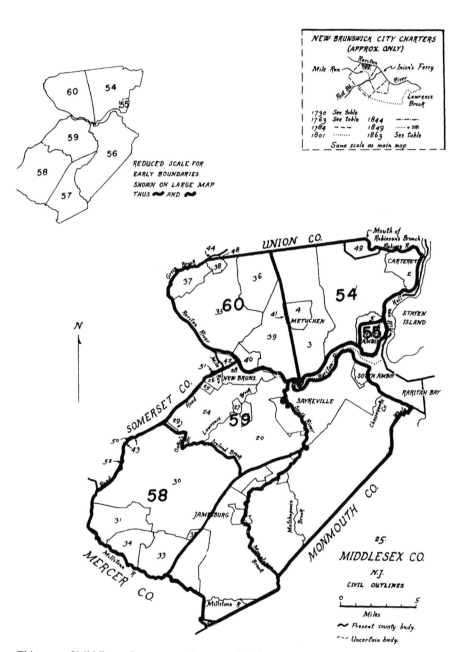

This map of Middlesex County provides a wonderful opportunity to see how all of the various present-day towns of South Amboy, Sayreville, Old Bridge, Monroe, Jamesburg, Spotswood, and Helmetta, as well as portions of East Brunswick, Cranbury, and South River were all generated from what was basically a rectangle of a hundred square miles running from the Raritan River to the county lines of Mercer and Monmouth. John P. Snyder, *The Story of New Jersey's Civil Boundaries, 1601–1968* (Trenton: Bureau of Geology and Topography, Department of Conservation and Economic Development, 1969).

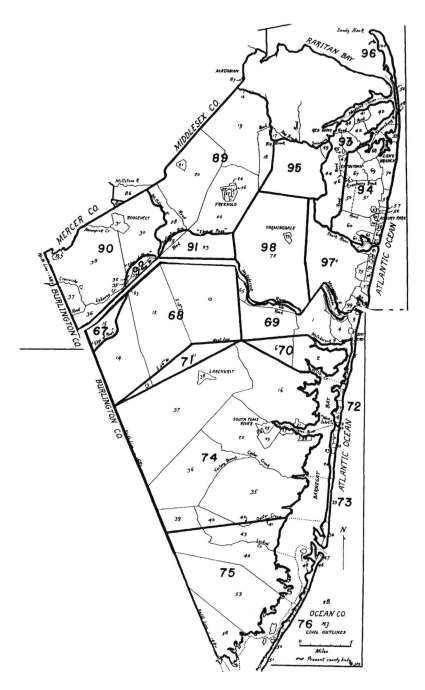

This is a composite map that includes all of what was once Shrewsbury Township. At the top of the map is an area between the Raritan River and the Navesink River wherein the numbers have been whited out. This is the only area of all of Monmouth and Ocean counties that was not originally part of Shrewsbury Township. After reading Chapter 4, see if you can pick out what is left of this once enormous township. John P. Snyder, *The Story of New Jersey's Civil Boundaries, 1601–1968* (Trenton: Bureau of Geology and Topography, Department of Conservation and Economic Development, 1969).

Fanwood and Dunellen owe their existence to the clever real estate manipulation of the early railroad executives. Having discretion as to where to locate stations, the executives would first buy control of and then subdivide all the adjacent land. The old Fanwood station, in beautiful and elegant Victorian style, stands behind the newer, utilitarian one. The Dunellen station bears the architectural stamp of Stalinist neo-hideousness.

Here are two of the early temples erected as part of the religious fervor for local schools that brought about the great borough fever of 1894 in Bergen County. These buildings have been recycled and are still in use. The balance of the legacy of 1894 endures only in the outrageously redundant school costs of New Jersey's 611 separate school districts.

James Bradley, the "founder" of Asbury Park (named for America's first Methodist bishop, Francis Asbury) and adjacent Bradley Beach was the state's most famous and powerful tee-totaler. At the time of the creation of these communities the existence of a store called Bradley Liquors would have been both scandalous and impossible. Now it is merely ironic. A wall around the entire borough is not needed for the message of exclusivity to be adequately and forcefully conveyed. The gates on the north side of Spring Lake send a clear message that the community is unlike other places.

$\mathcal{T}$ O THE HONORABLE, THE LEGISLATURE OF THE STATE OF NEW JERSEY. The Memorial of the subscribers, inhabitants of the Town of Princeton and its vicinity respectfully therewith.

That the Town as appears by the late census contains a population exceeding seven hundred persons. That it is situated on the line dividing the counties of Somerset and Middlesex and so far from Somerville and New Brunswick their county towns, that much inconvenience arises hence to the inhabitants of the place in the transaction of all business connected with the administration of justice.

That great difficulty is often experienced in executing those laws for the security of persons and property and more especially those intended to prevent acts of vice and immorality- that at the Annual Commencement of the College and on other occasions there are large assemblages of persons of various descriptions many who on these occasions, indulge in acts of intemperance, and in consequence of these, in acts of riot and disorder, disgraceful to the State and greatly to the annoyance of the peaceable inhabitants of this place. That on occasions there are unlawful meeting of black people at improper hours for the purpose of drinking and carousing, to the manifest injury of the blacks themselves, their masters and employers- for the preventing further continuance and checking the growth of these vices- which you memorialists subscribe principally to the want of an efficient police- as well as to promote the due execution of the law.

Your Memorialists pray this honorable legislature to grant an act of incorporation to this town with such powers, privileges, and limitation as to their wisdom may appear most conductive to the public good.

And your Memorialist as in duty bound shall ever pray, Princeton January 25 1813.

This instrument contained thirty-six signers, most of whom were later to take an active part in the future government of the Borough.

The Council and General Assembly being in session, received this petition from the inhabitants of Princeton and feeling that same was just and reasonable, enacted that their prayer should be granted, so therefore on the 11th day of February 1813 passed an Act incorporating the town of Princeton as a political subdivision of the State to be known as a Borough and the limits therein to be known as "The Borough of Princeton."

You will not find any mention in our State Constitution where the authority is granted to incorporate municipalities; the legislature no doubt took their authority from Article 60 of the Concessions of 1664.

Princeton was the first town incorporated as a borough in New Jersey. This does not mean that the Borough is the oldest municipality, as most municipalities at this early date were incorporated as townships.

Many residents of Princeton Borough firmly believe that the origins of the town are cloaked in nobility, and that this demi-Eden was designed by mystical forces. The unvarnished truth is reflected in a petition sent by the townsfolk to the Legislature in 1813. Princetonians are usually shocked to discover that the borough was formed for easier control of alcohol consumption and for repression of African-Americans.

CHAPTER 9

Exclusive Enclaves

THE PRE-ZONING PROPHYLACTIC

In a borough, you can do things as you please.
Mahlon Pitney, senator from Morris County and later associate
justice of the United States Supreme Court

*U*pon the completion of his first term as chief executive, Governor A. Harry Moore reported that the most significant achievement of his term was passage of the constitutional amendment allowing municipalities to zone, and therefore to control their fate without incorporating as a new municipality. Moore had in fact proposed a number of other amendments that had made their way to the ballot in November 1927, but the zoning amendment was the only one to pass.

The new Constitution of 1947 included the zoning provision in a form only slightly different from what the voters had considered and approved twenty years earlier. The present constitutional provision is contained in Article IV, Section VI, paragraph 2. It reads as follows:

> The Legislature may enact general laws under which municipalities, other than counties, may adopt zoning ordinances limiting and restricting to specified districts and regulating therein, buildings and structures, according to their construction, and the nature and extent of their use, and the nature and extent of the uses of the land, and the exercise of such authority shall be deemed to be within the police power of the State. Such laws shall be subject to repeal or alteration by the Legislature.

Zoning by municipalities has an extremely interesting and strange history in New Jersey. This chapter will investigate how certain municipalities were formed as an exercise in de facto zoning prior to adoption of the constitutional amendment referred to above. However, first it is useful to review briefly the history of zoning both in New Jersey and in a broader context.

The idea of geographically separating functions and labor in a city or town, the world-renowned urban scholar Lewis Mumford tells us, predates the money economy. Ancient city ruins tell specific tales of how various sections within the walls were dedicated to the religious function, while the market occupied another specific place. In some instances special areas were reserved for travelers and other strangers who, while being lodged and entertained, were quarantined from the general populace and from the armory, which was also housed in a specific area.

The city of Venice, divided as it was by canals, became the first modern city that demonstrates a segregation of manufacturing from commercial enterprises. It had a definable industrial area separated in large measure from other activities by order of the Grand City Council as early as the twelfth century. Proposals for establishing zones within the city of London were being discussed as early as 1661 by a man named John Evelyn, best known as a diarist, who realized that something must be done about the air quality. Within the Anglo-Saxon tradition, credit must go to Sir Thomas More as the first advocate of zoning. His *Utopia,* published in 1516, spells out the benefits of city planning.

Lewis Mumford discusses house types as "class envelopes"—a visible and tangible method of conveying a clear message as to what one will find inside. Indeed, entire communities became envelopes. Some envelopes were left unsealed and had a message on the outside such as "open immediately," while others were double sealed and read "personal and confidential."

In New Jersey the legislature had enacted permissive legislation as early as 1920, allowing municipalities to enact ordinances regulating construction and types of activity within certain areas. In 1923 the New Jersey Supreme Court had ruled that this attempt by the legislature to authorize the enactment of zoning ordinances was unconstitutional. The court held that it was beyond the legislature's power to allow towns to interfere with the rights of private property owners under the guise of exercising municipal police powers. The decision, written by Justice Frank S. Katzenbach, Jr., a former candidate for governor and a very highly regarded jurist, came in the case of *Ignaciunas v. Risley,* 98 N.J.L. 712. The plaintiff in this case was certain that the Township of Nutley could not properly restrain him from building a store at street level with the family living quarters above it.

The town fathers of Nutley were obviously disappointed by this outcome, and they appealed to the highest court. Chief Justice William S. Gummere wrote the opinion affirming unanimously the lower court's ruling. Both decisions indicated that communities could exercise their police powers to protect the general welfare from real dangers to the health, welfare, and safety of their residents. These courts, however, were not persuaded that anyone in Nutley was being placed in jeopardy by having a store in a residential zone.

Hope rose in the hearts of all those interested in controlling unpatterned growth when the United States Supreme Court agreed to hear a zoning case in 1925. Hope turned to jubilation when that court ruled in the *Euclid* case, referred to in Chapter One, that zoning ordinances were a legitimate exercise of municipal police powers.

Given the pronouncement of the nation's highest court, there were those who thought that an amendment to the state's constitution was superfluous. However, Governor A. Harry Moore was not one to take any chances when it came to matters close to the heart. In this instance, the New Jersey Court of Errors and Appeals had struck at the heart of Moore's power base in ruling against the interests of his patron Frank Hague in the 1925 decision in the case of *Krumgold and Sons v. The Mayor and Aldermen of Jersey City,* 102 N.J.L. 170. The power of the Democratic organization had been challenged, and the highest court in New Jersey, Justice Katzenbach writing the opinion, had sided with the Krumgolds. Their assault on the powers of Mayor Hague and his Council, of which Moore was a member, had come in the form of a decision concerning the construction of a project that included six stores on the ground floor of a four-story apartment building on the city's busiest street. Apparently the city had contended that the presence of the stores might endanger the students attending the nearby high school. The court was unable to see this potential danger as clearly as it was viewed by the Hague administration. Under the circumstances, Moore had little alternative but to put the issue to rest once and for all. That is why New Jersey amended its constitution in 1927.

Our new Supreme Court was created by the 1947 constitution. At the same convention that so radically redefined the judicial branch of government, a significant, but futile, battle was waged to repose zoning powers in the counties rather than in the municipalities. Nine years later the court had the opportunity to reflect on the constitutional aspects of zoning, and with vivid hindsight decided that the constitutional amendment had not been needed after all. It was clear to these new justices that the courts of the 1920s had just been misguided and had missed the mark by only a fraction. However, their opinion categorically indicates that the constitutional amendment had not been necessary.

In the case of *Roselle v. Wright,* 21 N.J. 400, the court, speaking through the very highly regarded Justice Harry Heher, had this comment to offer:

> The police power does not have its genesis in a written Constitution. It is an essential element of the social compact, an attribute of sovereignty itself, possessed by the states before the adoption of the federal Constitution.
>
> These constitutional provisions relating to zoning were designed to remedy the judicial denials of the fullness of the power and to regulate its use so as to accommodate essential common and individual rights in the fulfillment of the principle.

Some communities already inoculated themselves from the type of threat that was posed to Nutley by Mr. Ignaciunas. These communities had already constituted themselves in such a manner that zoning ordinances would serve only as a third wall of fortification—a fail-safe defense—for the impregnable fortress of privilege that they had already engineered for themselves.

The first two walls of defense were:

- A community development scheme—designed, planned, laid out on a map filed with the county clerk. All lots on said development plat were to be sold by deeds containing restrictive covenants running with the land usually guaranteeing one or more of the following: that the houses would have a minimal construction cost; that they would conform in style and appearance; that no commercial activity would be permitted on the land; that no liquor would ever be sold on the property; that the original buyer and all subsequent owners would never resell the property to members of certain races, religions etc.

• The planned community had developed to a point where it had incorporated itself as a borough. With this municipal corporate status other activities could be controlled such as the stabling of horses; the maintenance of sidewalks and streets; the lighting of the streets; the providing of an adequate domestic water supply; the hours of operation for the village stores if indeed any shops at all had been allowed in the community; and of course the borough could decide if any alcohol would be sold. Even more important was the fact that the borough government could regulate even the mere presence of undesirables; passing local ordinances to protect the residents from peddlers, drifters, vagrants who might find themselves incarcerated for the simple failure to give a good account of themselves.

This last prerogative of borough incorporation cannot be overemphasized. The majority of the statutes defined disorderly persons, including "tramps," as persons who simply were not in the place where they belonged. And providing the punishment for the disorderly persons were statutes adopted contemporaneously in the sessions of 1876, (Chapter Law CXXVI, an Act to Define and Suppress Tramps) 1877, 1878, 1880, 1881, 1882, and 1884, all being acts supplementing the disorderly persons laws and spelling out how and by whom they were to be enforced.

The borough was protected from intrusion or disruption through the strict enforcement of these draconian measures. This all makes perfectly good sense if we recall the economic condition of the country immediately after the Panic of 1873. The ensuing depression lasted for five to seven years, depending on whose estimate is being used. The immediate impact of the panic was to shut down such enterprises as the Morris and Essex Canal for a considerable period, and reports indicate that a minimum of 25 percent of the work forces in Newark, Paterson, and Jersey City were thrown out of work. "Tramps" became a considerable segment of the population in these years. The legislature defined them in the act of 1876 as persons who "Have no legal settlement in the places in which they may be found, and live idly without employment, . . . or shall be found going from door to door, or placing themselves in the streets, highways or roads to beg or gather alms, and can give no reasonable account of themselves or their business in such place."

Almost every one of the more egregious disorderly persons laws have been struck down by the U.S. Supreme Court as being so-called "status crimes." Today no longer is it an offense, punishable by incarceration in the county workhouse, simply to be poor, but such laws existed and were vigorously enforced in the years between 1876 and 1931. During the Great Depression, so many tramps and vagrants existed that it was impossible to enforce the laws as a practical matter.

The legislature, prior to 1875, had been the principal source of corporate charters. A list of private laws, under the heading of "Land and Improvement Companies," shows almost two hundred entries between the 1804 issuance of the charter to the famous "Associates of the Jersey Company," who would control so much of the Jersey City waterfront, and the final Private Law Charter in 1875. Many of the names will be familiar to anyone who has traveled the state: Absecon Beach Wharf and Building Association, chartered 1854; Belleville Land Improvement Company, 1868; Ridgewood Land and Improvement Company, 1866; Roselle Land and Improvement Company, 1866; Sea Girt Land Improvement Company, 1869; and Spring Lake Beach Improvement Company, 1875.

Denied by this 1875 constitutional amendment the prerogative of passing special laws or awarding special grants or charters to corporations, the legislature simply found another way to help their friends. If the reforms in the constitution prohibited the passage of special charters for towns, there was certainly nothing that could stop the legislature from adopting an act that would permit the creation of towns by private corporations.

It took the legislature only two sessions to figure out the best manner to circumvent the restriction granting special municipal charters. Enacted by the legislature on April 5, 1878, the new borough statute embodied a novel and radical departure from the previous tradition. Entitled An Act for the Formation of Borough Governments this law became Chapter CCIX of that year's general laws.

We are already somewhat familiar with this unique and infamous statute, having spent some time exploring its consequences in chapter seven. To briefly refresh our recollection, this law allowed for a new borough to be created any time voters who owned 10 percent or more of the taxable real estate within a township petitioned the Freeholders for a special election for the creation of a new borough. Of course there was the additional requirement that the question receive an affirmative vote at the special election, but affirmation was usually a foregone conclusion. My research fails to reveal a single instance where the public question of the creation of a new borough was defeated at the polls.

Imagine the horrendous economic tensions that would confront the state and its major townships if this law were still in effect today. Study the zoning and development patterns in our populous townships and you will notice that the heavy tax-paying industries and commercial ratables are normally clustered together, while the tax-consuming residential districts are located in separate areas of the township. Now imagine if the industries and shopping malls had a law on the books that allowed them to break away from the rest of the township provided only that they took with them a block or two of their nearest voting neighbors.

How long could anyone expect townships such as Livingston and Millburn in Essex County to stay intact? Why would owners of the office parks in Parsippany want to continue to pay for the expenses of the balance of the township if such taxes could be avoided? Obviously, residential neighbors nearest a valuable office park would willingly join forces to form a new borough so that they could divide the tax revenue among a few dozen households rather than share it with several thousand others. The same pressures would exist throughout Middlesex County in Woodbridge, Edison, and Piscataway Townships. The same could be predicted for Hamilton in Mercer County and Cherry Hill in Camden County. These are just the most obvious examples. Not only would there be fiscal chaos, but New Jersey would have 2,000 municipalities instead of a mere 566.

Does the idea seem ludicrous? Of course it does. But one is forced to ask again, if it doesn't make sense to allow such a situation today, why do we so willingly pay for the acknowledged mistakes of yesterday?

One hundred and twenty years may have almost passed since the enactment of this statute, and much of the original and actual intent of the legislature may be obscured by the elapse of time, but it still is evident that this was very special and unique legislation.

The legislature revisited it in 1890, and actually dropped the area requirement to a minimum of two square miles, provided the value of the real estate was a minimum of $100,000, and the population was no lower than 200, even if that number could be reached only by including summer residents.

The wretched excesses of Bergen County in the creation of school-district boroughs prompted the repeal of these liberal borough incorporation laws, but between the period of 1878 and 1896 a number of areas took advantage of the new law and new boroughs were created. Even after the law had changed in 1896, reality did not change. Enclaves that were small, exclusive, wealthy, and privileged tended to contain residents with more than the usual amount of political influence. Thus, the legislature allowed incorporation referendums in the privileged areas up to the time that zoning had really taken hold and gained credibility as a tool that would protect exclusive neighborhoods from intrusion without the necessity for creating a new municipality.

An examination of some of these communities should begin with the prototype of the small, highly residential, wealthy community. The creation of Merchantville by the legislature in 1874 was the genesis of the borough acts. Had the constitution not been amended, it is safe to say that the other boroughs which were self-generated under the borough act, would have simply been established by legislative fiat. The communities share certain characteristics with Merchantville: diminutive physical size; very little if any vacant land; 95 percent or more of all assessment entries residential; income levels in the top quadrant.

Merchantville Borough is only about 400 acres or six-tenths of a square mile in size. While many of its beautiful older homes have seen better days, it is a community with an extraordinary past. It contains no industry, and only one in twelve of the over 1250 items on the tax rolls is listed as commercial. The residents in 1874 who appealed to the legislature for their separation from Stockton Township were proud of their status as business people and wanted a community that would identify itself with their success. These were members of the nouveau riche who would not be accepted in the hallowed confines of Haddonfield, so they responded by creating a community that in every detail would rival or surpass their older neighbor. They also wanted to be separated from the encampments in Jordantown, where their African-American servants retreated to every evening. The surest way to protect their way of life and to exert control over the conduct of their community was to be set off as an independent borough.

By pushing its incorporation as a borough under the rubric of a "Special Public Law," Merchantville got a three-page list of ordinances that the new council would be allowed to adopt and enforce, as set forth in Section 8 of the law. The local officials could do everything, including build parks, hire policemen, regulate privies and the cleaning of chimneys, and suppress vice and disorderly conduct. They also had the full powers necessary to restrain vagrants, mendicants, and beggars. Moreover they could impose fines for the violations of these ordinances up to the amount of fifty dollars, a handsome sum in those days. The real prize however came in Section 9, which authorized the borough to license the sale of alcohol, to collect a fee for the license, and to keep all said fees for borough purposes.

On the opposite end of the state the Borough of Rutherford was one of the first to exercise its prerogative to become a borough, doing so by a referendum that created it as distinct from Bergen County's old Union Township in September 1881. The Rutherford Land Company had been chartered by a special law of the legislature in 1871, and that development company was quickly followed by the formation of five or six other land development companies, such as Home Land Company, Mount Rutherford Land Company, Rutherford Heights Association, Park Land Associates, and Rutherford Park Association. All of these appear to have been controlled by New York businessmen who had taken up residence in Rutherford. The Rutherford of today contains 18,000 people within its 2.81 square miles. It would be an error to confuse the community we see today, as pleasant and charming as it is, with the Rutherford of 1881. Even today industry is minimal and Rutherford's 200 commercial enterprises are minor compared to the 5,000 residential entries on its tax list.

An argument could be raised that Rutherford does not belong in this category—that it is really a railroad borough. Even though the railroad station played a large part in its growth, Rutherford's development was of a special kind. It set itself apart, not because of the railroad, but because by 1881 it was already the most desirable of Bergen's suburbs, offering the best of country living while affording its residents a high level of urban amenities. Businessmen from nearby Paterson found it an extremely easy commute, while others who earned their livings in Newark, Jersey City, and even New York were happy to be able to return to this distinctive retreat.

What made this otherwise upper-middle-class community slightly different, and what qualifies it as an enclave rather than a railroad town, was its focus from the start on exclusivity in the sense of personal protection. The land companies controlled the style, value, and conformity of the housing units. The "Rutherford Protective and Detective Association" ensured that no vagrants, tramps, or other miscreants saw the sun set in Rutherford. This organization was basically a vigilante operation formed in 1879 to fill what was obviously a perceived void in law enforcement in Union Township, where all these burgeoning real estate develop-ments were located. That the new borough took law enforcement seriously is evidenced by the fact that the community had four justices of the peace, and the mayor and council were authorized to hire as many police officers as necessary.

If Merchantville and Rutherford are not quite what they once were, neither are some of the other boroughs that fall into this exclusive category—with some being more, and some less than they were at the time of their creation. The homogeneity that once prevailed in some of the shore communities disappeared, but it was impossible to maintain the rigidity of social classification that motivated their initial creation. Bay Head, Beach Haven, Point Pleasant Beach, and Island Heights Boroughs were all products of the 1880s. Harvey Cedars held its referendum in 1894, but clearly it was not a school-district borough. Island Heights does not fit with the others, as religion was what motivated its creation. The railroads spurred Point Pleasant and Bay Head, but the facts speak for themselves. At the time of their incorporation, these were summer colonies from which no one entertained any idea of commuting to work.

Despite its commercialization over the past fifty years, Point Pleasant Beach still has ten residential entries on the tax roll for each commercial enterprise within its 1.44 square miles. Bay Head, even with all its hotels and bed and breakfasts, has over twenty residential entries for every commercial establishment in its .59 square miles. The same twenty-to-one ratio of residential to commercial is evident within Beach Haven's 0.98 square mile.

The statistics tell the same story about boroughs along the coast in Monmouth County: Manasquan, Brielle, and Spring Lake were still too far removed from the urban centers to be considered railroad boroughs at the time of incorporation. Spring Lake, founded as a colony by the Spring Lake Beach Improvement Company, is a quintessential class-homogenic community. Within its 1.31 square miles are almost 2,000 residential units, with the majority of its 96 commercial ratables located along three or four blocks in the "village." The median value of these homes in 1990 was $412,000, and almost two-thirds of them were built prior to 1950.

Why is the year 1950 so important? Houses are classified by the New Jersey Department of Community Affairs as to whether they were built before or after 1950. This arbitrary date would be much more accurate if it were 1930. There was precious little housing stock added during the Great Depression. In fact the overall figures probably indicate a decline in single-family homes during those difficult years. The decade of the 1940s was much the same, but for different reasons. Building materials were at a premium, as was skilled construction labor. That takes us back nearly to 1927—the year that zoning made municipal creation a moot point when it came to protecting the quality and class of the area.

The majority of the houses in this category were built before 1950—most before the Great Depression, before zoning was widely used. In Rutherford for instance, basically 5 out of 7 houses were built prior to 1950. In Merchantville the ratio is even higher, with 1300 of its 1600 houses dating to the pre-zoning period.

Elmer, which is the place to live in Salem County, was created as a borough in January 1893—too early to be a school borough. It consists of about 550 acres or .86 square miles. There are about ten times more residential than commercial entries on the tax rolls. Almost 70 percent of the residential units date from before 1950, i.e., pre-zoning.

The hurried passage of the legislation in 1896 that concluded New Jersey's period of borough creation by self-initiative did not stop the ill-considered creation of new municipalities. What it did was interpose a small obstacle, what was more than likely a toll gate in the form of a legislative delegation. Anyone who was "connected," who had political access, who was willing to do what was necessary, or was simply powerful enough to dictate terms could get legislation passed to create a borough.

The Borough of Florham Park in Morris County somewhat deviates from the typical borough-establishment characteristics—it is large by nineteenth-century borough standards, containing almost 7.5 square miles, and 80 percent of its housing units have been built since 1950. However, Florham Park was created as the grandest enclave the state ever witnessed. Dr. Leslie Ward and the Twomblys virtually owned the entire area. The former owned an enormous estate known as Brooklake Park, with a driveway two miles long. Florence and Hamilton Twombly kept a modest home of approximately 120 rooms on their multiple-square-mile estate. Florence was the daughter of William Vanderbilt. Hamilton knew something about politics, having served in the Massachusetts Senate, and of course he also knew how to marry well.

Annoyed that the taxes that they paid to Chatham Township in 1898 seemed a bit excessive, they visited their friend the state senator from Morris County, Mahlon Pitney. He advised them that they really did not wish to create their own township, and that what they really wanted was a borough of their own. He explained that, "In a borough you can do things as you please." The Ward-Twombly contingent suggested that the senator prepare the legislation. The bill, introduced in 1899, passed in both houses and went to the governor's desk on March 6 of that year. Governor Foster Voorhees let it sit for two weeks and then, being the good Republican that he was and recognizing it was always helpful in those days to have a Vanderbilt owe you a favor, took a deep breath and signed the act. The name of the new borough was taken from the first syllable of Florence and Hamilton, to which was added Park in deference to Doctor Ward. Eleanor Weis, who wrote *Saga of a Crossroads: Florham Park,* said, "The new borough became known as the wealthiest town with the lowest tax rate in America." It still needed to be approved by the voters at a referendum. The Twomblys did not even vote in New Jersey. Fortunately 90 percent of the people living in the proposed borough were employed as household staff or gardeners on these two estates.

The wisdom of Senator, soon to be Mr. Justice, Pitney reverberated in every wealthy village throughout the state. The residents of "Millionaires Row" in Deal had been ahead of the curve, acquiring corporate status in 1898. Their fellow millionaires in Rumson had legislation passed in 1907. The *History of Rumson* contains wonderful vintage photos of yachting regattas and legendary polo matches that were played in the borough. It also has pictures of the municipal building given as a gift to the borough by one of its early mayors. That same mayor is reported to have commented that the adoption of the rigid zoning ordinance in 1927 would preserve the unique character of Rumson and was the single most important event in the borough's history. Alpine in Bergen County and Essex Fells in Essex County followed the suit played by Deal in Monmouth and Florham Park in Morris.

These five communities would have been on any list of the twenty wealthiest communities in the state at this time. They had the highest family incomes and the greatest real estate values per capita. A number of other communities that would be on the list delayed action until after World War I.

What did these communities do? As the constitutionality of zoning wended its tortured path through the state and federal courts, the communities panicked. The initial statutes were challenged successfully in the state courts, and the fate of zoning before the federal courts was very uncertain. The richest enclaves that had not already adopted the prophylactic of municipal incorporation rushed to do so. This is most evident in the counties of Bergen, Somerset, and Morris. The towns are on any list of Who's Who—Franklin Lakes, Far Hills, Bernardsville, Harding Township, and Mountain Lakes—each of them rushing to incorporate to protect against the prospect that zoning would fail in court. Mountain Lakes, the smallest of the group, makes no pretense as to its origins; it readily admits that it was created to enforce exclusivity in a pre-zoning age. The other four are sizable, but virtually free of any industry whatsoever.

One additional statistic may be of interest. African Americans constitute approximately 14 percent of the total population of the state. However, in the aggregate of all populations, African Americans represent less than 1 percent within all the enclaves mentioned so far in this chapter.

This statistic would be radically altered if Montclair Township had been included. Montclair was rated in 1922 as the third wealthiest town in the entire country, but it has an extremely diverse community with a third of its population constituted by minorities. Its history is so variegated that it does not fall neatly into a specific category.

In summary, the wide-scale use of zoning ordinances that followed the adoption of the amendment to the New Jersey Constitution in 1927 signaled the end of municipal multiplication. Since ratification by the voters, the number of new towns created represents less than 3 percent of the total. Zoning protected the status quo of housing patterns. The zoning ordinances preserved the local "way of life" in a manner that was significantly superior to the prior methodologies of restrictive covenants, municipal incorporation, and aggressive enforcement of local ordinances aimed at controlling public conduct.

*B*y the onset of the Great Depression, each of the five major dynamics in the creation of municipalities diminished significantly in relevance.

• Local altercations generated by budget appropriations for road construction and maintenance diminished as the state and county governments assumed a far greater role in planning, designing, enlarging, paving, and supervising the network of roads that became necessary to accommodate a public ever more attached to automobiles. After the twenty-five-year hiatus of residential construction that resulted from the Great Depression, World War II and the Korean conflict, municipalities resolved potential conflicts over the cost of street construction by imposing the obligation on developers.

- Thanks to the automobile, the rationale justifying the creation of the dozens of railroad towns is now as outdated and obsolete as the steam locomotive. The towns that had been formed to assure that the rail commuters had lighted sidewalks to assist them in their walk to and from the depot now found that the residents of the townships from which they had separated shared the same priorities and expectations. The reasons for the independent incorporation of railroad towns began to shrink as rapidly as the number of trains on the printed schedule. The number of new train stations built in the past sixty years has been a fraction of the number of those closed. Metro Park on the Edison/Woodbridge border and the Princeton Junction station in West Windsor are gigantic car parks with no aspirations of independent municipal status.

- Just as the automobile altered the underpinnings that had supported the creation of so many municipalities, the school bus has rendered the rationale behind the creation of school-district boroughs irrelevant. It is regrettable that tolerance and open-mindedness failed to increase at the same pace as transportation technology.

- In a society whose very fabric is torn by drug abuse, it is difficult to believe that dozens of New Jersey municipalities owe their creation and configuration to the question of whether alcohol might be sold within their corporate limits. The incredible irony is that some of those very towns, whose genesis is traced to protection from "demon rum," are the same communities that suffer most acutely from the ravages of the drug trade.

- The protection of exclusive enclaves by means of municipal incorporation has no longer been used, since zoning has been implemented as the modality of choice for preserving the status quo.

It is impossible to explain the present existence or configuration of most New Jersey municipalities without reference to the five major categories of municipal origins—which no longer bear any relevance to today's realities. However, as illustrated by the stories in the next chapter about a number of towns around the state, some municipal origins defy categorization. The novelty of their births is matched only by the irrelevance of the factors leading to their conception.

CHAPTER 10

Happy, Sad, and
Interesting Origins

"The time has come," the Walrus said,
"To talk of many things."
Lewis Carroll

$\mathcal{E}$very line on the geopolitical map of New Jersey tells a story. As we have already seen, most of the stories fit neatly into the five categories that have been examined in detail: street fights, railroad suburbs, school-district boroughs, dry towns, and exclusive low-taxed pre-zoning enclaves. Some towns fit perfectly into one of these categories, while others qualify for multiple categories. Still other municipalities have such unique and fascinating origins that they deserve additional attention. Finally, some communities that can be classified as one or the other of the above, have stories that are so novel that they warrant closer examination.

There is a common theme that connects all of the following stories. The tale of their origins is now relevant only to history and folklore. The motivations that led to their existence have become simple curiosities, but the consequences of their independent municipal status is a reality, and that affects policy considerations and hampers constructive resolution of current problems.

What follows is a random medley of tales. It goes without saying that each of the 566 towns in New Jersey has some story to tell, but these towns have been chosen because their particular stories help to demonstrate the incredibly diverse genesis of New Jersey towns.

Merchants of Dennis and the End of the Diaspora

Cape May County contains two communities of special interest for the fact that neither one realized the full potential of its founders' dreams. These are Dennis Township, whose population hovers in the range of 4,000, and the Borough of Woodbine, which struggles to stay in the vicinity of 3,000 residents.

The dream of Dennis was that it would become the county seat, and thereby serve as the principal town of the county. The entire county had been created, as mentioned previously, by an act of the colonial legislature, and it was provided with the unimaginative but descriptive precinct names of Upper, Middle, and Lower. In 1789 the term *Precinct* was changed to *Township*.

At the tip of the island there had existed, since approximately 1690, a whaling colony, which had migrated from New England. The whalers set out to sea from the west side of the peninsula in pursuit of their prey, whose oil, extracted from blubber, was perhaps the most prized and valuable commodity, pound for pound, of anything grown, manufactured, or mined in the new world.

The Township of Dennis was created in 1826 from a portion of Upper Township. What existed there at the time was a community that viewed itself as dominating the county because of its strategic position astride the major roadway from the cape to the mainland. The road led toward the capital at Trenton and branched off to the major markets of Woodbury and Salem. This important artery from Cape May County had a definite westerly vector, and the idea that anything constructive could be achieved by heading from Cape May directly north would have to be considered ludicrous. Going north would mean traveling through endless pine barrens before arriving at the nearest community worth discussing, which was Tuckerton. Beyond that to the north there was not much until Shrewsbury. The orientation of the county seemed clear, and the dominant force in its future seemed to be the Delaware Bay and the ports along that bay. To get to those trading centers on the Delaware one had to go through Dennis either by road, or by way of its port facility, which was thriving. Dennis already served as a major supplier of cord wood to Philadelphia, with cargoes leaving at least weekly to move up the bay to the big city. The actual community of Dennis sat on Dennis Creek, inland from the Delaware Bay by a number of miles. This was necessary as the tides of the bay often rose to such a degree as to inundate the entire coastline and the low-lying areas along the entire bay. The most difficult task was getting boats up and down the creek; however, this obstacle did not prevent Dennis from being a major shipbuilding center in the nineteenth century.

The notion that anyone would wish to visit the coastline of the Atlantic Ocean for recreation or on holiday was not taken very seriously. The ocean had been of interest until about 1800, when the whales had become scarce—the beach had only been useful as a place to set up a rendering operation to reduce the whale blubber to oil for the lamps of Philadelphia and Trenton. Certainly some visitors were going to Cape Island in Lower Township, but that was probably just a passing fad, or so thought the people who were concentrating on increasing the influence of Dennis.

The citizens of the new Township of Dennis must have been shocked to discover the popularity that Cape May was developing as a vacation destination. More startling still was the possibility that the small colony of hotel- and innkeepers could presume their tiny resort should rival Dennis for the center of gravity in the county's economic life. It could be said the merchants of Dennis bet on the bay.

When the resorts on the Cape Island began to be served by steamships, thereby making it unnecessary for travelers to pass through Dennis, the leaders thought it was time to bring the matter to a head before they lost further ground to Cape May; but the battle was already lost. The sun and sand would prevail over the commercial interests of what was really nothing more than a shipyard and a tavern with high hopes.

However, the battle raged on for what must now seem an interminable length of time, twenty-four years to be exact. It started in 1824 when the freeholders determined that the existing court house in Middle Township needed repairs. At the time the freeholder board consisted of six members, two each from the three existing townships. The creation of Dennis Township increased the membership to eight, and a stand-off ensued about the construction of the new facility. The freeholders from Dennis persuaded their fellow board members from Upper and Middle to side with them on the vast majority of issues—so much so that it is estimated that eighty cents of every county dollar spent during the period of 1826 to 1848 was dedicated to some improvement in Dennis Township. The same operating majority could not be mustered to resolve the court house issue, as it was a four-four tie with Lower and Middle voting to retain the existing site and Upper and Dennis supporting the relocation. The question languished until 1848, when a countywide referendum was finally held.

It seems that the electorate of Cape May took the proposition seriously, as 1003 of the 1005 eligible voters cast their ballots. By a margin of 89 votes the new court house would be built on the site of the existing court house in the central area of the county. The battle over relocating the court house was the highwater mark for the political ascendancy of Dennis. Flushed with victory, the residents of Cape Island petitioned the legislature to be recognized as an independent community. The legislature complied and in 1848 a new entity emerged known as Cape Island Borough, which became a full city in 1851, and ultimately adopted the name Cape May City in 1869. The freeholder board was enlarged to ten with the two new members from the city, and the hegemony of Dennis was overthrown. Actually the merchants of Dennis were quick to see that their bet on the bay was misplaced and many shifted their commercial interests to Cape May City (see Jeffrey M. Dorwart, *Cape May County, N.J., the Making of an American Resort Community* [New Brunswick, NJ: Rutgers University Press, 1992]).

Another section of Upper Township broke away eighty years later, shortly after the turn of the century. Woodbine became a borough in 1905, and was unique as the first municipality in the state, and probably in the nation, to have every public official, elected or appointed, a Jewish refugee. More remarkable is the fact that all of these officials had only been in America for a short time. Not since the seventeenth century had any municipal government been entirely run by people who were exclusively foreign born. However, it was merely by happenstance that this group was founding a municipality in New Jersey, and not in Argentina, where a number of such colonies were also launched.

The wealthy French banker Baron de Hirsch had created a fund to establish a community that could be developed in America by Jews escaping persecution at the hands of the Cossacks in southern Russia. The trustees of the fund appropriated $50,000 to buy the acreage in Upper Township and to pay for the transport of the refugees. The experiment was called Woodbine, and it benefited from the experience of other Jewish settlements in South Jersey that had begun in 1881 in Cumberland and Salem Counties. The most famous of these settlements, known as Alliance, was located in the Township of Pittsgrove in Salem County.

The track record of the Jewish settlements was checkered to say the least, but the Baron de Hirsch fund trustees studied the other settlements carefully and adopted a modified approach. Where all of the previous settlements of Alliance, Norma, Brotmanville, Rosenhayn, and Carmel had been dedicated exclusively to agriculture, Woodbine was planned around a mix of both agriculture and light industry. The addition of the manufacturing component is credited with the durability of Woodbine and its ability to evolve and grow into a full-fledged municipality, whereas the other settlements dissolved or were slowly reabsorbed into their host communities. The settlements did not disintegrate but rather dissolved with their inhabitants moving out and often up in a society that permitted social mobility. Many of the original settlers bought their own farms in Vineland, then Landis Township, or moved to the towns of Vineland and Bridgetown, where they became artisans and merchants; their children in turn became doctors, dentists, lawyers, engineers, and professors (see Ellen Eisenberg, *Jewish Agricultural Colonies in New Jersey 1882–1920* [Syracuse, N.Y.: Syracuse University Press, 1995]).

Perhaps the most famous son of Woodbine, at least for those with an attachment to Rutgers University, was Professor Jacob G. Lipman, the noted dean of the University's internationally acclaimed agricultural school, now Cook College. Doctor Lipman was not only a credit to his university, but was a man of enormous compassion and sensitivity. As the community at Woodbine began to lose its vitality he recognized that what appeared to others as a serious problem was really a wonderful opportunity. He negotiated the transfer of the building and schools at Woodbine to the state of New Jersey, and they were immediately put to humanitarian use. The colony became the state's Developmental Center for the Profoundly Retarded, and the majority of the present residents of the Borough of Woodbine are involved in some manner in the direct or indirect operation of this major state institution.

As a side note, some of the original inhabitants of the settlement of Alliance were expelled from that settlement and were relocated to an extremely infertile piece of real estate in Atlantic County. The former glass-making center, known as Estelville, in the Township of Weymouth, served as the location of this resettlement. In 1925 Estell Manor City, whose present population is about 1,000, was created by many of the second generation of these immigrants who were twice exiled.

Acres of Diamonds in Bergen County

Attorneys are required as officers of the court to maintain a high level of civility in what they say and write. This rule of etiquette is often honored in the breach, but only once did I experience having an adversary ask the court to strike wording from a complaint I had filed. If memory serves, the matter involved a suit to which the Borough of Teterboro was a party defendant, and I referred to that borough as being a tax haven—New Jersey's own Cayman Island—so small and wealthy as to be the equivalent of Kuwait or the United Arab Emirates. The attorney for Teterboro took umbrage at this reference, and invoked the Rules of Court to ask that the references be struck as being scandalous and defamatory.

Teterboro did not set out to be a tax haven, and it certainly was not the site of an exclusive and elitist country club when it was formed in 1917. The census takers had an easy day of it in 1920 when there were a grand total of twenty-four residents. That number has been about the average population over the last seventy years of its existence. The best that can be said is that Teterboro started out as a failed real estate development. Most important, its existence demonstrated that indeed a municipality can be extremely well off if it contains a great deal of industry and very few people.

At its birth Teterboro contained less than one square mile. It was only 540 acres and was formed by taking a portion of three communities, Lodi Township, Little Ferry, and Moonachie. In 1919 it secured an additional 175 acres from the Borough of Hasbrouck Heights, thereby giving it additional status as being over the one-square-mile threshold.

In the year after its creation, Mr. Walter Teter was still exerting his best efforts to get the residential development back on course, but in the meantime everybody was still caught up in the war fever and Teterboro became the temporary site of what might have been the single largest Victory Garden in the greater New York area. The never-ending war fought by the Salvation Army turned to Teterboro for assistance in replenishing their arsenal—in this case the soup kitchen in Jersey City. The land had been cleared for development so there were no trees or underbrush to remove. Cultivation seemed to everyone involved as a reasonable alternative, and so daily a platoon of Salvation Army leaders and their recruits would arrive to till the fields of the real estate investment gone sour.

The war ended, of course, and some of those flat level fields that had previously yielded beans and vegetables for the urban soup kitchens were converted for the extremely novel use of airplanes by the Wittemann-Lewis Aircraft Company, who also built an immense factory and hangar to manufacture these newfangled machines. Seventy-five men were working at the plant in the mid-twenties.

Then came the Bendix Corporation, which took over the airplane business and even the name of the community, which became Bendix Borough in 1937, honoring the corporation that played such a large part in the community. Eventually the voters of the borough changed the name back to Teterboro in 1943. One must remember that the number of voters involved in these decisions never reached twenty. While its population was never very large, its taxable ratables assumed enormous proportions. Even after the Port Authority of New York and New Jersey took over the airport, rendering it exempt from local taxation, the industrial and warehouse uses surrounding the airfield that remained made Teterboro New Jersey's wealthiest town in the category of ratables per resident.

Teterboro must be viewed as an anomaly even by Bergen County standards. Its very existence was a measure of the laissez-faire attitude of the legislature, who was more than willing to allow a town to exist with two dozen residents. Of course no one foresaw the emergence of the airplane industry, and the town officials, who subsequently served on the governing bodies of the four towns from which Teterboro had been taken, must have spent many a sleepless night around budget time wondering not only how to resolve their annual problem but ruing the day that their predecessors had blithely given away the acres of tax diamonds that lay in their backyards.

I was in my second year in law school when I was fortunate enough to be selected by Senator John Lynch, Sr., the first Democrat in fifty years to serve as the president of the Senate, to serve as his secretary. It was a very exciting experience for me at twenty-two to be standing alongside the second most powerful elected official in the state, and I truly never imagined that one day I would be a presiding officer of a house of the legislature. In that year of 1966, a member of the General Assembly from Bergen County named Vito Albanese made it his personal crusade to abolish Teterboro and actually held hearings on the subject. Notwithstanding his party's control of the legislature and the outrage of allowing this tax haven to exist, the Albanese measure never gained enough momentum to be taken seriously. At this writing, the question of Teterboro's existence is pending in a federal court case, which challenges the actions taken by the citizens of Teterboro to preserve their status quo.

The fate of another Bergen County area is almost as interesting and ironic. The people in the now extinct Township of Ridgefield did not even wait until the famous School Act of 1894 to start dividing up their community. Ridgefield Township had been a sizable community when it was created in 1871. It was divided and separated time and again over the course of the next thirty-three years until what was left changed its name to the Borough of Fort Lee in 1904.

Ridgefield Township consisted of a major drainage basin receiving groundwater that ran westerly from the Palisades. The major waterway through the township was Overpeck Creek, a major tributary of the Hackensack River. Overpeck Creek runs from north to south until it turns sharply to the west on a line that is about parallel with Yankee Stadium in the Bronx. It moves then from east to west until it empties into the Hackensack. The land on what is at that point the south bank of the river was, to express it mildly, undesirable, consisting of meadows and swamp. This area on the south bank of the Overpeck adjoined what had been ceded to Hudson County in 1840. Even in modern times the area was famous for its pig farms, where the garbage from New York City's restaurants was part of an ecological cycle, fattening pigs to be slaughtered and butchered and served at the finest restaurants in New York.

By 1892, the Bergen County residents on the north side of Overpeck Creek were certain that the creek should have been the dividing line between the counties instead of Bellman Creek. Since it was not to be, the next best thing was to be set off from the south side of the creek and let the south-siders fend for themselves. Actually the creation of the borough can be attributed to the power and industry of one man, W. B. Pugh, who had bought the store belonging to Christie and Ackerman, and founded the Ridgefield Building and Loan Association in 1891. He opened a real estate business and started subdividing the property he had acquired. Pugh served on the council when the borough was formed and later as the mayor for two terms. He was also a Bergen County freeholder from 1896 to 1899, by which time the population was approaching 600. In the next twenty years Mr. Pugh, as a real estate broker, banker, and building contractor, pushed the population to almost 1600. One other significant enterprise was steadily expanding in the borough. That was the coal yards of the Banta family. The ease with which coal from Pennsylvania could be brought to the yards along the south bank of the creek via both barge and the rail lines of the Erie Railroad would ultimately make Ridgefield Borough the logical site for the construction of a coal-fired (now oil) power plant, constructed by Public Service Electric and Gas (PSE&G) in 1960.

Ridgefield became a borough in May 1892, and the Township of Overpeck was created less than a month later. The trustees of the new Township of Overpeck could not agree on anything, and the community was virtually torn apart by fights of every nature. The trustees' meetings became the major source of public entertainment, with such high levels of rancor and acrimony that insults and mutual indignities led to threats of physical violence. Whereas Ridgefield was able to employ the permissive statute to incorporate itself as a borough, Overpeck wanted to be a township, and therefore had to apply to the legislature for special consideration. With what one writer described as *a little earnest work in the right direction*, the legislature created the new township. Overpeck could have incorporated as a borough without the state's consent as the law stood, but they apparently insisted on doing it the hard way. The fights within the township became legendary, and only quieted down after the township opted to reincorporate under the Walsh Act in 1912.

Between 1910 and 1920, the population of Overpeck soared, growing from about 4,000 to over 8,500. Among the new residents were the members of an artists' colony, who found the new political peace conducive to their creative work. Among those pursuing their muses on the ridge was Man Ray, who would remove himself to Paris after the war and gain an international reputation, becoming as controversial as an Overpeck Township trustee's meeting.

In what remained of Ridgefield Township, the quarreling centered around the usual problem, taxes and how they would be spent. There were the expected fights about road maintenance and school costs, and they were ultimately resolved in the traditional fashion. By the end of the century Bogota, Leonia, Cliffside Park, Palisades Park, and Fairview had all become boroughs, breaking off from Ridgefield Township, which also made contributions along its northern border to Englewood and Teaneck.

A year after Teterboro changed its name to Bendix the citizens of Overpeck, nestled between the creek and the Hackensack River, decided to eliminate the reference to the creek and become known as the Village of Ridgefield Park. The creek is not really very wide, and many a resident of the village, having just received a property tax bill, must have gazed enviously across the creek to where PSE&G had constructed an enormous generating station—a facility of such gargantuan proportions that it dominated the life of both communities. But the utility paid huge amounts of gross receipts taxes only to the municipality on the south bank—the one near the old pig farms—the one that for decades had one of the ten lowest tax rates in the entire state, based on the Gross Receipts and Franchise Act, originally passed in 1900. Once again there had been acres of diamonds in the backyard of Ridgefield Township, but the other communities threw them away, never imagining that an electric generating station would be built there or be so extraordinarily valuable.

A Rose by Any Other Name in Essex County

The word *village* has a special cachet. It has developed a poetic aura ever since Oliver Goldsmith lamented the passing of "sweet Auburn, loveliest village of the plain." Henry Wadsworth Longfellow evoked associations with the virtues of honesty and hard work in his references to the village smithy. Summer residents in upscale Spring Lake and Sea Girt never say they are going shopping or going downtown—they are "going into the village."

The term is of exceptionally ancient origin—traceable to the rural administration of the Roman Empire, which divided farmers into hundreds for administrative purposes. The practice continued in France and after the Norman Conquest became the standard in England—the center of the vills became the village.

In New Jersey the first Village Act was adopted by the legislature in 1891, and it stayed on the books for ninety-eight years. The Village Act predates the City Act and the Borough Act, and of course was consolidated into the Home Rule Act of 1917. Under the terms of the Village Act, a municipality could choose to be governed by a five-member board of trustees who would be elected for three-year staggered terms. The five trustees would annually select one of their members to be the president and another to serve as treasurer. No such office as mayor existed. In 1961 the legislature prevented any additional chance for villages to incorporate, and in 1989 the law was changed to effectively make the remaining villages operate precisely as township forms of government do. Presently only the tiny Monmouth County community of Loch Arbor, population 350, is a bona fide village. (In 1997 a referendum appeared on the ballot in Loch Arbor to ascertain whether or not the residents wished to have discussions with potential merger partners. The question was rejected, and Loch Arbor voted to remain independent and expensive.)

The cachet of the term however was irresistible to a few places throughout the northern section of the state. Ridgefield Park, as we saw above, thought the term provided a wonderful distinction as did the toney Bergen community of Ridgewood. During the division of the Oranges in the 1860s, there was one community that thought of itself differently, and after a brief period of being a township, changed to become a village in 1869. South Orange was content, if not smugly pleased with its unique status for the next one hundred and twelve years.

Wealthy and exclusive, South Orange was the right address for the upper social and economic class of Newark business and professional people. However times changed, and by the 1970s even the wealthy enclave of South Orange was anxious to get its fair share of the new federal program known as revenue sharing. The official name of the bill was the State and Local Fiscal Assistance Act of 1972. The federal government allocated lump sums to each state, and the state got to keep a third of the total, with the balance being divided by formula among the local units of government.

The states were eliminated from the program in 1981 by which time Washington was distributing billions of dollars nationwide, but under their particular bureaucratic rubrics. The formula designed in Washington was the product obviously of code writers who did not grow up in New Jersey, and therefore were not familiar with the entire spectrum of municipal entities available such as boroughs and villages. The regulations were geared to the most common form of local government in America—the township.

Fairfield was slightly ahead of the curve, and as early as 1979 dropped the title borough and became known as a township. In 1980 West Orange eschewed its town title and became a township as well. The towns of Nutley, Montclair, Bloomfield, and Belleville followed suit in 1981, all becoming townships. In 1982 the Town of Irvington and the Borough of Verona joined the list of townships, and were rewarded appropriately by the federal government for doing so. Essex Fells, North Caldwell, and West Caldwell decided to retain their borough forms of government but call themselves townships in order to get a better deal from Washington.

If that was not sufficiently bizarre, four additional municipalities in Essex joined in the movement to confuse the federal check writers. These last four, however, refused to abandon their historic names and thought it sufficient to merely append the title of township to their existing corporate name. Caldwell, which as a township had provided the birthplace of President Grover Cleveland, could not surrender the title of borough it had acquired in 1892, and so became the Township of the Borough of Caldwell. Tiny Glen Ridge, a school-district borough class of 1895, became the Township of Glen Ridge Borough. America's first legitimate railroad suburb, which by 1982 desperately needed all the additional money it could get, adopted the confusing title of City of Orange Township.

The still affluent community of South Orange, not to be left out of the rewards to be achieved by playing the Washington word game, altered its corporate title to become South Orange Village Township, and promptly received a higher allocation of the nearly four and half billion dollars that Washington was distributing at the height of the program. The irony of all this is found in the fact that by 1986 the federal government changed its policy and eliminated the revenue sharing program, and so the rationale for all the name changes was eliminated.

A variation on this name-change theme reemerged in the consolidation efforts of the two Princetons in 1996. Believing that if either name were used by the consolidated community the municipality required to surrender its corporate identity would consider itself to have been annexed, the Consolidation Commission opted for the neutrality of a totally new name—the Town of Princeton. The issue was diplomatically worded so that neither the voters in the borough nor those in the township could find fault.

Those wanting to preserve the historic Borough of Princeton in both name and corporate existence challenged the subterfuge in court, claiming that the wording of the ballot was confusing, since the new entity would be called a town, but actually be governed as a borough. I found myself in the unique position of being asked to represent the interests of the Preserve Our Historic Borough organization in their court fight. I explained to the members of the executive committee who gathered at my home that I was in the odd position of writing this book, and that furthermore I thought New Jersey had about twice as many or more towns than were necessary. In fact I was so candid as to admit that I thought the solution might be forced consolidation of all municipalities with populations under 10,000.

On the other hand I explained that I opposed the consolidation effort under way, as it had all the earmarks of becoming a disaster for future consolidation efforts. If it passed in the borough it would only be the result of the abnormally high participation of the Princeton University students who ignore all other elections but vote in large numbers in presidential elections. This would be, I thought, a pernicious precedent and result in lingering animosity among the full time taxpaying residents who would always resent that their destiny had been decided by transient non-tax-paying students from other states.

We made our challenge in court on a whole array of issues, but we concentrated on the fact that the ballot proposition was misleading and inherently confusing. I argued that the word *town* was a term of art in New Jersey, since there still existed nine communities that were towns, and that a municipality should have a name coextensive with its form of government. The experience of Essex County municipalities playing word games with their status undercut the viability of this argument—technically, it could be done. Therefore I advanced the argument that since it was confusing to ordinary voters, it would be extremely confusing to the student voters, the majority of whom had grown up in states that did not have the niceties of borough forms of government. The solution would be, I suggested, that an interpretive statement be included on the ballot. The court ruled that it was not arbitrary or unreasonable for the commission to have eschewed an interpretive statement on the ballot, as the statute only required that the commission prepare and have published in the newspaper an abstract of their decision.

We lost and the ballot proposition was allowed to be on the ballot as worded and without an interpretive statement. An appeal was filed, but the Appellate Division refused to hear the matter until after the election. In a final effort to avoid the appeal, I offered the other side the settlement proposals of either including an interpretive statement but keeping the ballot question the same, or keeping every thing as proposed but delaying its submission to the voters until the non-presidential election year of 1997. Both settlement suggestions were rejected, as was the ballot question by the residents of Princeton Borough. A majority of students voted for it, but many others simply had the good grace to realize it was not their business to decide on this issue for their temporary home.

Mending and Building Political Fences

New Jersey has a well-deserved reputation for taking its politics seriously. It is difficult if not impossible to point to one specific area of the state and, with conviction, assert that this is where the game is played the hardest. However, it can be pointed out with some authority that Galloway Township in Atlantic County was the site of some of the most famous and disorderly elections in the state's history.

Since the advent of casino gaming in Atlantic City, Galloway has been identified with rapid growth and significant population increases, but when the township was first recognized in 1774, it was merely a sprawling area of tidal creeks, salt marshes, and pine barrens. The township contained one recognized settlement, the historic village of Smithville. Now restored, the village has long been an attraction for tourists interested in a good meal and some sense of how things were back in the old days.

One of the things not highlighted these days in a walk through the village is the colorful political tradition associated with the township. For elections in the early nineteenth century, an entire day might be consumed—along with much else. Legend has it that partisanship ran as high as the top of the drinking cups— perhaps in a direct ratio. In order to avoid physical combat the election officials built a fence at the polling place to segregate those asking for the respective ballots of their parties. This fence had no other purpose but to keep the partisans from wreaking havoc on one another.

As one might expect, the fence was not maintained carefully between elections, but as the fateful day approached, the election officers were diligent in going out *to mend their fences*. The care and repair of the Smithville fence allegedly gave rise to this political idiom.

Only a few miles north of Galloway is a community historically so partisan that it was expelled from a county. Little Egg Harbor Township appeared on the famous list of municipalities confirmed in their corporate existence in 1798 by the legislature. It appeared then as a part of Burlington County, and remained so through almost a hundred additional years. It was of course the most easterly section of Burlington, which stretched across the pine barrens to the Delaware River. Needless to say, not only the great majority of the population, but also the greater part of the county's political power was concentrated in the river towns of Burlington and Bordentown, Beverly and Florence. In the period following the Civil War much of that political power was wielded by Democrats. Little Egg Harbor was totally opposed to the powers in the court house over in Mount Holly, and the distance that they were forced to travel through the pine barrens to the county seat was a matter of contention.

The geographical distance from the Atlantic coast to Mount Holly served as a convenient rationale for the action taken by the legislature in 1891. While much was said about the bill's purpose being to accommodate Little Egg Harbor Township citizens, by virtue of the fact that Toms River was more accessible than Mount Holly, most commerce that the area enjoyed was indeed with Toms River and Freehold, which was served by stage coach three times a week; but the real reason for giving the township to Ocean County was purely political. The voters of Little Egg Harbor were ornery and contentious as far as the Democrats in Burlington were concerned. By the same token, so were the Republicans over in Ocean County.

Leon Abbett, the Democratic governor from Jersey City, was satisfied that the Republicans in Little Egg Harbor and in Ocean County deserved each other, and so he happily inked the legislation by which the entire township was annexed to Ocean County.

A few years later a section of the township was surrendered for the formation of Long Beach Township, and the Borough of Tuckerton was created in 1901. Tuckerton is one of the state's oldest and most honored pre-Revolutionary sites. The Quakers who settled the area were the hosts of a meeting that gathered Friends from throughout south Jersey. The early settlers took their religion seriously, and the Friends Meeting House in Smithville was only started because so many Quakers had drowned over the years in journeys to attend meetings in Tuckerton, which had required the dangerous crossing of the Mullica River. The Quakers took their allegiance to Lincoln and his efforts to abolish slavery as seriously as they took their other religious convictions. The names may have changed, but the allegiance to the Republican cause remained a hallmark of the area right down to the present time.

Back north in Hudson County we find evidence of political fences in Harrison being in such poor condition that they were totally beyond repair. Harrison had been set off from Union Township in 1851 at around the same time a portion of the township was being returned to Bergen County. Among the issues dividing the residents of Harrison was the Civil War. Democrats throughout New Jersey were not enthusiastic about the war, nor about President Lincoln, who failed to carry the state in either 1860 or 1864. However, Lincoln and the Republican Party did have their adherents even in Hudson County.

Partisan emotion and the recriminations visited upon the Republican enclave within Harrison Township prompted efforts for some relief following the war. The daylight appeared for the oppressed Republicans when they succeeded in electing Governor Marcus Ward in 1865. The petition of the Hudson Republicans was viewed with sympathy in Trenton, and in 1867 the Township of Kearney was created, thereby separating the political factions with the Democrats safe and secure in Harrison and the Republicans in control of a new township bearing the name of the Civil War hero. Brigadier General Philip Kearney was a bona fide hero, ultimately sacrificing his life in battle. Even prior to his personal selection by Lincoln, he had enjoyed a legendary military career. The town named in his honor eventually grew to be a sizable community, aided by its location and extremely favorable tax base in the twentieth century as the result of a power plant being built in the meadows by PSE&G. Despite the enormous changes that the area witnessed, Kearney remained true to its historical allegiance and historically was the one place in all of Hudson County where the Republicans could turn for some small solace. Had it not been for the brief window of opportunity provided by the election of Governor Ward, it is unlikely that Kearney would have come into existence notwithstanding the fame of the general for which it was named.

Was Gibt?

Three other municipalities in Hudson County, one in Bergen and one in Atlantic County, warrant special comment as the by-products of the revolutions that convulsed Europe in 1848. Prince Metternich of Austria, whose name had become synonymous with conservative political perspectives, fled Vienna for England in that year, as did his counterweight in political philosophy, Karl Marx, who in fleeing Germany sought refuge in the same country. The turmoil associated with that revolutionary year saw tens of thousands of German-speaking refugees, the majority of whom leaned more to the Marxian side of the argument, leaving Europe. Only a few hundred settled with Metternich and Marx in England. The vast multitude that composed the exodus did not stop moving westward until they reached New York City. Still thousands more ventured even farther, not stopping until they arrived on the west side of the Hudson River.

Hoboken absorbed thousands, and still more kept coming. Finally the German-American Steamship Company made Hoboken its terminal rather than New York City because of the traffic destined for that community. Hoboken had been recognized as a village within Bergen Township as early as 1840. With the influx of immigrants it rose to township stature in 1849, and by 1855 it was a full-blown city.

Gutenberg and Weehawken claimed independence in the course of a single week in March 1859. Both were nothing more than real estate developments promoted by the growing German population. In fact, the impetus for the development came from German-American building societies with headquarters in New York City. The Germans bought 1,000 acres of Weehawken in 1852. Until then it had been a rather sparsely settled locale most noteworthy as the site of the infamous duel between Aaron Burr and Alexander Hamilton. Now with control of over one and half square miles along the river the German Americans began rapidly to terrace development up the sides of the Palisades. (We shall be examining more closely the entire question of the development of the northern section of Hudson County when we focus attention on the reasons why Jersey City was frustrated in attempting to consolidate itself and develop into a rival to New York City.)

The German influx spilled over into Newark, but the numbers of new arrivals were not sufficient to have a dramatic or rapid impact. Not so in Bergen County, where the German Democratic Land Association purchased 140 acres in 1854 and founded the settlement of Carlstadt (Carl's city) in honor of the president of the association, Carl Klein. Six years later this small German-American colony was governing its own affairs as a village, and it jumped on the school-district borough bandwagon in 1894.

Perhaps the New Jersey community that most reflected the phenomenon of 1848 was the Atlantic County community of Egg Harbor City. This community was sponsored by the German-American community in Philadelphia. One could make a study of events related to Independence Day that had an impact on New Jersey history. It was on July 4, 1854, that the first regular train service from Philadelphia to Atlantic City was inaugurated. The train was carrying a varied assortment of politicians and businessmen. Even considering the higher echelon of dignitaries being transported, the train still had to make some refueling stops. Legend has it that among the passengers on that historic trip were a group of German businessmen from Philadelphia. Included in the distinguished group were Doctor William Schmoele, Henry Schmoele, P. William Wolsieffer, and J. H. Schoemacher, all leaders in the German-American community. As was the custom, the passengers pitched in with refueling the tender car. While disembarked, these gentleman took the opportunity to survey the land surrounding the fuel depot, which had been placed at Cedar Ridge. Whether it was the heat, the sun, the libations, or just the festiveness of the occasion, they were all struck by the vision of a new ideal city to be built by their landsmen on these level plains in the valley of the Mullica River. It was to be a city where German would be the spoken language and the customs and traditions of the Fatherland would be preserved and honored.

From their dream sprung the Gloucester Farm and Town Association, which bought 40,000 acres in Galloway and Mullica Townships before the year's end and immediately started selling subdivided lots. The project catapulted to city status by 1858, a fact that for good measure was reconfirmed in 1868 by the legislature. It is interesting to note how much farther a dollar traveled in Atlantic County with the association able to purchase such a huge tract for about the same as what was being spent for much smaller parcels in the Hudson, Essex, and Bergen County region.

The most telling aspect of the Egg Harbor City story, however, are the names given to the wide, right-angled streets that were laid out in this planned community. The street names are not confined to the expected, although Heidelberg, Cologne and Leipzig are represented on the north-south arteries. Alongside these reminders of the homeland are streets that bear the names of prominent American cities as well. The selection of these street names reminds one that the failed revolutions of 1848 had as their principal aim the establishment of a German republic to be modeled on the American experience and following the United States Constitution. The love of learning and the respect for the attainments in the arts and sciences that marked the often highly educated immigrants is reflected in the fact that the cross-streets running east and west are named for artists, scientists, and scholars.

Finally, a few words should be said about the Township of Washington in Morris County, the first new township created after the famous legislative promulgation of 1798. Running through the heart of the township from north to south, past Schooley's Mountain, once a world-famous health spa in the nineteenth century, is a beautiful valley that for a hundred years carried the name German Valley. The legend is that many of the Hessian troops routed in Trenton, as well as other Hessians who simply deserted the British cause in the Revolution, sought refuge and a new life in this fertile, remote valley, among their countrymen who had long since relocated here from Long Island. A deserting Hessian would blend into this valley of farmers without raising any questions, and the extra hands to clear the woodlands and bring additional lands under cultivation was apparently welcomed warmly. The German influence was unquestionably great no matter where or how the original inhabitants had come to settle there. However the strong anti-German sentiment generated during World War I caused the name to be changed to Long Valley around 1917. The township in which Long Valley is located has not been affected in any way by diminution of its borders since 1798, and the governing body of the township seems content to see no change of any kind now or in the future. In 1996, Washington Township was in the news, suggesting that they would zone out all commercial establishments of any size, shape, or description, leaving this geographically large township, consisting of almost 45 square miles, exclusively residential. The task is not overly daunting, because of the 6200 tax-assessment parcels carried on their rolls, fewer than 175 are considered commercial or industrial. With its large area the township averages only about one person for every two acres.

Orphans of the War

Since its Revolutionary War history as the refuge of George Washington and his beleaguered troops, Morris County has had a distinguished record of contributing to the military efforts of the country. From the time that cannons were cast to the modern manufacture of armor-piercing explosives, the area has a rich tradition as an arsenal. Picatinny still serves as one of the country's largest arms depots.

The armament and ordinance manufacturers of Morris County had their mettle tested by the advent of World War II. Dover, the industrial center of the county, lacked sufficient housing for the influx of new workers who were called upon to work in the round-the-clock war effort.

The federal government was not about to allow the niceties of local zoning laws to interfere with the production of essential weaponry; it simply condemned a 91+acre tract in Randolph Township and began construction of a 300+unit housing project. Ground was broken for the barracks-like units just fifteen days after the Japanese bombed Pearl Harbor.

The three-member board governing Randolph Township failed to reach unanimous agreement on cooperating with the federal government, and it was only by a split vote of two to one that Randolph agreed to provide education for the children of the war workers, even though Washington agreed to make quarterly payments to the township. The federal government paid for the entire construction of the project, including all streets and sewers. Likewise, they agreed to pay for all utility charges.

Within six months families were moving into the new federal project, called Victory Gardens. By the time the war had ended over a thousand people lived there. This created two separate problems, one for the federal government and one for the adjoining towns of Dover and Randolph. Victory Gardens was no longer essential to the war effort, and so Washington returned Victory Gardens with its school-aged children to Randolph Township. For good measure it also canceled its subsidy to the township.

Victory Gardens made a pitch to be taken in by Dover, but the proposal was spurned by Mayor John W. Roach, Jr., who did not want the heavily Democratic vote of Victory Gardens diluting his steady and reliable Republican base in Dover. One would have hoped that Trenton would step into the vacuum left by Washington, D.C., and assure an equitable resolution to the status of Victory Gardens. In one of the sadder moments of the state's history, the legislature responded to the petition of Randolph Township and orphaned the community, forcing it to become the Borough of Victory Gardens. Ever since Governor Alfred Driscoll signed the legislation in 1951, Victory Gardens has been a challenged community, enjoying no industrial, and very little commercial, tax base, and having to support its school obligations from its moderate residential ratable base. Consisting of only 0.15 square miles, and with only 4 percent of that land vacant, this war orphan's future is bleak.

Sad to report, Victory Gardens has siblings. Other municipalities were conceived as the result of the patriotic efforts to mobilize and support our fighting men and women. What municipal officials considered above and beyond the call of duty was paying for the education of the children whose fathers and mothers routinely worked twelve- and eighteen-hour shifts in the emergency war industries. While the Victory Gardens situation was not resolved until six years after the global conflict had ended, Winfield Park was a 100+acre war-effort development whose status had to be resolved even before war was declared. Situated in Union County at the juncture of Linden, Clark, and Cranford, this development carried the historic name of one of Union County's most honored heroes. That was not sufficient to find it a proper host.

President Franklin D. Roosevelt had already committed the country to serve as the armory for the beleaguered Allies. The Lend-Lease Program was England's only hope of maintaining any type of naval parity with Germany's fleet. The importance of the program was heightened by the fact that England was totally dependent not only on shipping that could supply needed goods, but also on military vessels that could break through the attempted blockade by Hitler. The shipyards at Kearney in Hudson County were retooled and geared up to produce the ships that were to fulfill America's pledge to the Allied Forces. Thousands of workers were added to the shipyard's workforce. Housing all these emergency workers was virtually impossible. Washington responded to this crisis with the creation of the housing units that would become Winfield Park.

Regrettably, the patriotic fervor that swept the legislature at that time manifested itself in a willingness to cut shameless tax deals for the railroads, and not in any action to help house and school families of the workers at the Kearney shipyards. Intense negotiations were undertaken to find a suitable host community, with the federal government offering proposal after proposal to all three towns that abutted Winfield. The pleas from Washington fell on deaf ears, and the legislature passed a bill setting up Winfield Park as an independent township. Charles Edison, governor at the time, vetoed the bill, believing it not to be in the best interests of the county or state to create another municipality just because of the emergency brought on by the war in Europe and America's promise to help England. The legislature bowed to the importuning of the Union County delegation and proceeded to override Edison's veto.

Shipbuilding was also the priority of the Camden and Gloucester City ship-yards, which spread down the east side of the Delaware. The emergency federal housing units constructed to serve the workers at those yards wound up as Audubon Park Borough, a community consisting of approximately 90 acres, being one apartment complex housing over a thousand residents.

World War II was not the first conflict to have created municipal war orphans. The precedent had been set back at the end of World War I. The extensive construction efforts involved in the creation of the Naval Air Station at Lakehurst in Ocean County and the Army Training Center that was Fort Dix, in Burlington County, had required the War Department to scour the countryside for workers. Not enough indigenous labor could be induced to surrender their accustomed life styles in the pines, so laborers from New York and Philadelphia were recruited. These civilians, often to the dismay of the local Townships of Manchester and New Hanover, remained in their little villages after the war. In order that these outsiders not become drains on the local schools and voting blocs to disturb the historic power structures, the Boroughs of Lakehurst, consisting of 0.92 square miles and 3,000 residents, and Wrightstown, the largest of the group with 1.75 square miles and 4,000 population, were formed.

Roosevelt Borough, consisting of almost 2 square miles in Monmouth County, is a war orphan of a slightly different kind. In the battle against prejudice and intolerance, this community lost; and therein lies the story of its existence as a borough.

Conceived as an American kibbutz for Jewish and Polish refugees displaced by the European conflicts, Jersey Farmsteads was a project sponsored by the U.S. Department of the Interior. Originally intended to be simply a housing development within the large expanse of Millstone Township, the settlement and its new residents were viewed with great suspicion and occasionally open hostility by their neighbors, who considered the Jewish settlers' politics radical, their ideas un-American, and their children unacceptable in the local school system. Millstone Township forced the creation of the borough as the only available option to the resolution of the fight regarding the school issues.

The War to Make the State Safe for Teetotalers

Please refer back for a moment to Chapter 3, the case study of the divisions of the Township of South Amboy. That chapter ended with the legislature allowing the Township of Sayreville to reincorporate itself as a borough. The drive for boroughhood was led by my great-uncle John J. Quaid, who, according to family lore, was a man of extraordinary learning who had read widely and wisely. He would be elected the first mayor of the new borough, as he had been the first assemblyman ever elected from that town. Despite his learning, I am more than willing to wager that he had never heard of Frederic William Maitland, nor seen a copy of any of his writings on the origins of English boroughs in the eleventh century.

In fact, I am certain that the primary thing my great-uncle John knew about the distinction between a township and a borough was that the Department of War in Washington, D.C., had ordered, in May 1918, that all saloons be closed in townships near military bases, but had allowed them to stay open in boroughs. In the best of the family tradition of service to his constituents, he set to work to save local enterprise and satisfy the huge thirsts that working in the brickyards and the ammunition plants caused.

Sayreville became a borough, thereby sharing in an ancient and honored line of Anglo-Saxon jurisprudential tradition, not for some selfish purpose such as preserving the exclusivity of its school districts. Nor did it become a borough to satisfy the desires of its commuters, who wanted greater amenities in the proximate vicinity of the train station; in fact, Sayreville had no passenger station. No, Sayreville became a borough in order that its taverns could reopen legally. (Legend has it that they never actually closed for either the order of the War Department or in observance of the prohibitions of the subsequent Volstead Act.)

Sayreville acted because it was losing the licensing fees paid by the taverns, and because its residents either had to drink in an illegal establishment or bear the expense and nuisance of traveling to South Amboy or South River to get a drink.

All this may appear today as simply funny, and that would be the case if Sayreville had been some singular aberration where the native ingenuity of the home-spun townsfolk had trumped the bureaucrats in the nation's capital. However, Sayreville was not alone in exercising this gambit; nor was it the first township to resort to this name-changing maneuver.

Go back and check the incorporation dates of Lakehurst and Wrightstown, and particularly notice that they are boroughs and not townships. Visit these towns and you will notice that what is now known as the hospitality industry is flourishing there as it has been since the construction of the military installations.

The lovely resort of Sea Girt in Monmouth County faced the choice of having its hotels go dry while it remained a portion of Wall Township or incorporate as a borough. Oceanport a few miles to the north made the same choice.

All in all, a dozen or more municipalities throughout the state were incorporated as boroughs or as cities (such as Clifton) during the time between 1917 (when the action by the War Department was first threatened) and 1921. A quick check of whether the town fell within the proscribed radius gives an almost instant indication of whether or not the town was doing the very same thing that Sayreville did to protect its vendors and consumers.

PART III

*Factors Thwarting
Consolidation and
Case Studies of the
Largest Cities*

Chapter 11

The Effects of New Jersey's cAnti-Urban Bias

We have met the enemy and he is us.
Pogo (Walt Kelly)

cAs was noted in Chapter 1, the A-words—avarice, ambition, altercation, abstinence, and agenda—spurred municipal balkanization in New Jersey. The A-words, however, are balanced by the U-words that have thwarted efforts of any city to emerge into national prominence. They are:

1. *Undersizing.* Critical land mass was absent from the inception of every New Jersey city. The largest was Newark, which at one time had shrunk to under 20 square miles. The two smallest, Trenton and Camden, were, at their most contracted, less than 3 square miles.
2. *Unequal representation.* The cities were grossly under- represented and the rural counties unfairly overrepresented in the legislature until 1966, by which time it was too late.
3. *Unfair tax policies.* Exempting the railroads from taxation virtually robbed the cities. Even after the reforms of the Railroad Tax Act, the state kept too much, and effectively crippled the urban ratable base.
4. *Unwillingness to share riparian proceeds.* The legislature refused to share the proceeds of riparian grant income with the cities that contained the riparian lands.
5. *Unimaginative corporate tax policies.* As the host state from 1880 to 1910 of the national holding companies (great trusts that were unwelcome in virtually every other state), New Jersey could have extracted enormous benefits from these malefactors of great wealth. Instead, the state sold its "safe harbor" for less than a mess of pottage.
6. *Undercapitalization of the banks.* The provincial and myopic prohibition on intercounty banking that lasted until 1977 purposely restrained the growth of state banking institutions.

133

7. *Underfunding of urban mass transportation infrastructures.* The corollary to this was the expenditure of massive funds on suburban highway construction.

Each of these issues operated to a degree in every effort by any city to strengthen itself. Obviously, the effect of one issue was more critical than another, depending on the particular location, as illustrated by the upcoming case studies of New Jersey's major cities. Each city had unique factors and events that frustrated its growth, but these seven items just outlined played a role in every one.

Undersizing

As of 1798, all the land within the state was contained within a recognized political subdivision, i.e., one of the existing 104 incorporated municipalities. The deed by Charles II to his brother James in 1664 established title, i.e., ownership of the soil. This pattern is distinctly different from other parts of the country, and even from the original thirteen colonies, where substantial parcels of land lay unclaimed and "unincorporated."

Municipal maps of other states demonstrate huge areas designated as "unincorporated," often adjacent to emerging cities. In other states, as cities recognized the need to expand, the cities simply extended their borders. New Jersey never presented this alternative to its cities. The opposite phenomenon occurred here. Cities often started as larger entities and then purposely contracted by either intentionally jettisoning surrounding areas or acquiescing in their separation. Trenton, Camden, Newark, and Jersey City woefully undersized themselves; when it became essential to expand in order to survive, the state's policy on annexation altered dramatically. The history of the laws governing annexation and consolidation will receive closer scrutiny in the chapter on Newark. The handicaps imposed by under-sizing and weak annexation laws are obvious. If Newark and Jersey City were combined they would barely equal the land encompassed by the island of Manhattan, New York City's smallest borough. Even if all of New Jersey's largest cities were contiguous and merged, their population and area would barely be equivalent to the land mass and population of a small American city such as Boston.

Unequal Representation

The land always voted in New Jersey and this state suffered enormously from the variance between population and voting strength. The origin of this practice that so dominated the political tradition of the state can be traced to the negotiations leading up to the surrender of the Proprietors to Queen Anne on April 15, 1702. The principal architect of the compromise that made New Jersey a crown colony under the governance of the British monarchs was Lewis Morris, later the first royal governor to govern only the colony of New Jersey, not the combined provinces of New York and New Jersey. Morris brokered the agreement through the London Board of Trade, which in turn presented the arrangement to the royal court. Under the agreement the monarchy assumed dominion over the entire province, both East and West. It is a reasonable assumption that Morris had persuaded the Proprietors to concentrate their efforts on exploiting their land holdings, and to let the politicians worry about nuisances and nuances of governing. He had himself in mind for the position of royal governor as early as 1702, although he was not to attain the position until 35 years later. However, having succeeded in becoming royal governor, he then discovered, as many another subsequent aspirant to power in New Jersey has learned, that wielding power is harder than it appears. Under any circumstances, it seems to have been Morris who negotiated the arrangement under which the Assembly would meet alternately at Burlington and Perth Amboy.

More critical to the fate of the state, the bargain also provided that in elected members of the General Assembly both East and West Jersey would be equally represented, despite their disparate populations. Equal representation in appointments to the Governor's Council was also an aspirational objective. The overarching rationale for this provision was that the alternative was worse. The alternative was annexation of the provinces—East Jersey to New York and West Jersey to Pennsylvania. Therefore a doomsday scenario of separation, annexation, and obliteration hung as the sword of Damocles over the deliberations and strategy discussions of the Proprietors. The East Jersey Proprietors thought it better to share power equally with their peers from West Jersey than to be swallowed whole by the powers of New York. The West Jersey Proprietors likewise realized that they were getting the better end of the bargain while also protecting themselves from being annexed to the west bank of the Delaware. A marriage of convenience, and an unequal match at that, but far superior to the alternative of becoming small fish in large ponds.

At the time this deal was struck, the estimated population of East Jersey, already divided into five counties, was more than twice the population of West Jersey, with its great plantations, small settlements, and vast wildernesses. This arrangement was also a substantial departure from the procedures in place in the other colonies at the time, and radically different from the traditional system utilized for the composition of the English Parliament.

The original political arrangements of both East and West Jersey were more sensitive to democratic principles than were the terms of the agreement by which the Proprietors yielded their power to the Crown. The Jersey Agreement provided for a large assembly of 100 members to be freely elected without regard to political subdivisions. Young Philip Carteret, governor in 1665, summoned the first assembly in 1668, and its composition reflected the traditional English Parliament; the seven recognized settlements each sent two burgesses, and the Delaware settlements sent two representative to the first convening of the General Assembly in Elizabethtown.

The concept of pure geography having inherent political viability, as contained in the terms of the Agreement of 1702, stuck. As the system evolved through the eighteenth century, the principle continued to be honored in the modified form that each county would be entitled to have a member of the Governor's Council, notwithstanding its population, or lack thereof. This was an understanding often honored in the breach.

Despite the total lack of any historical or philosophical foundation of legitimacy, the pragmatic principle that real estate had political rights was alive and flourishing when the Provincial Congress met in Burlington to craft a document that would serve both as a written Constitution and Declaration of Independence. Article Three of the 1776 document left its indelible mark on the politics of the state and constituted New Jersey's equivalent to England's "Rotten Boroughs."

Article Three provided for equal representation by county in the upper house known then as the Legislative Council, and, after the Constitution of 1844, known as the Senate of New Jersey. The reasons for equal representation regardless of population can be analyzed as follows:

1. Equality of representation was not a matter of overwhelming concern, given the facts of population dispersal in 1776. Only Cape May County, of the original 13 counties, had an aberrantly low population; the other 12 counties had estimated populations ranging between Cumberland's 10,000 and Hunterdon's 20,000, with the other 10 falling in the middle range. By 1800 Sussex County had become the most populous, pulling slightly ahead of the three nearest challengers: Essex, Hunterdon, and Burlington.

2. The precedent for New Jersey's structure was established in 1702, and the problems arising under that system were few.

3. The framers of the 1776 constitution had to make a decision defining what the basic political unit of the state would be. The ten days between the formation of the drafting committee and the final vote on the document left little time to weigh the comparative benefits and deficits between making the county the basic unit or opting for an alternative arrangement, as some of the New England colonies had done, with the municipality or township as the basic unit. Sending members to the legislature from the township or borough was a tradition of the mother country. However, the society of New Jersey, even in 1776, was much more heterogeneous than the homogenous cultures of New England.

4. Other alternatives were always available, such as guaranteeing representation to the six charter cities of New Brunswick, Perth Amboy, Mount Holly, Burlington, Elizabeth, and Trenton, but given the time constraints it was obviously easier to follow the path of least resistance and use the county as the fundamental political unit for representation. No one, not even the most prescient among them, could envision the growth patterns that lay ahead. To them, George Washington was their general and not the name of a bridge that would cause the quadrupling of Bergen County's population within 25 years of its opening.

In 1844, the new constitution, despite some heated debate, retained this provision, and the issue was revisited in 1875, with the outcome remaining the same. As recently as the Constitutional Convention of 1947, the system was still held as having some kind of blessing from Divine Providence, elevating it to a status that was beyond debate or question. This fundamentally undemocratic system held until it was successfully challenged in the case known as *Jackman v. Bodine,* and the apportionment of the Senate was finally struck down by the state's Supreme Court in 1965.

The effect of the historical malapportionment of the Senate resulted in the domination of land, not people, for almost 200 years. Thomas More in *Utopia* satirized the fencing of the English commons by describing it as a system by which sheep ate people. The structure of the Senate perhaps was not so drastic in its outcome, but nevertheless it could be described as a system under which the land owned the people. The pine trees of the barrens stretching across Ocean, Burlington, Atlantic, Cape May, and Cumberland Counties had more influence in Trenton than any county in the north, no matter how densely populated.

At the height of the great railroad wars in 1870, a coalition of eleven senators representing the least populated counties were in a position to control the fate of New Jersey—despite the fact that their aggregate constituencies amounted to less than 20 percent of the state's population.

By 1960, the hypothetical coalition of eleven senators from the least populated counties were being sent to the state house by about 10 percent of the state's population. Even worse, it only took a majority of the Republican Senate Caucus to control the fate of any legislation; thus, a coalition representing about 5 percent of the state had a stranglehold on the other 95 percent.

While the state enjoyed a legion of big-city newspaper editors who fulminated and Jeremiahed, it lacked a Lord Russell or Professor Attwood, whose combined efforts had reformed the worst aspects of British Parliament representation in the 1830s. Ultimately, New Jersey had Christopher Jackman, later to rise to be an extraordinary speaker of the Assembly. Jackman, a man who epitomized the best in New Jersey's political traditions, had brought the challenge even before being elected to the General Assembly, represented by his counsel, David Friedland. Later a senator himself, Friedland sustained another of the state's long traditions, that of the freebooters and privateers, ingenious but undisciplined, who helped to launch this state in its infancy.

The decision to repose political power in the counties irrespective of population had enormous and unforeseen consequences, which mirror and reinforce the thesis of this book. *Political decisions driven by socioeconomic-political considerations of times long past have paralyzed and frustrated the ability of future generations to make intelligent or even rational policy choices.*

The political map of New Jersey would look very different today had the Provincial Congress decided that townships would serve as the political unit, rather than counties, and/or that both houses of the legislature would have membership determined by population and not geography.

The states of Connecticut and Rhode Island made the choice early to leave the township as the basic political unit. The development of political power in those state legislative bodies was clearly distinguishable from the track taken by New Jersey.

The New Jersey idea or provincial experience, however, was not totally without benefit. The New Jersey experience allowed its delegates to the Constitutional

Convention of 1787 to propose the compromise that ushered in the creation of the United States. For its part, New Jersey was among the most anxious of jurisdictions to see a new nation founded on constitutional principles that might protect smaller states such as itself from the bullying of larger states. No state's economy had suffered more from the predatory practices of New York and Pennsylvania than had New Jersey's.

Even though New Jersey's suggestion of two senators per state regardless of size broke the constitutional log-jam in Philadelphia, the principle that land had rights was a pernicious influence in New Jersey politics for 200 years. This concept is directly responsible for the fact that no urban area of the state ever emerged as a major national center.

The insistence upon the voting power of mere land invests a material object with attributes that should be reserved for the dignity of humans. It reflects fear and distrust, and must be viewed as an attempt to build into the system some guaranty against abuse by the majority. Locke and Montesquieu confronted the same type of challenge and resolved the problem by dividing the functions of government in such a manner as to provide checks and balances.

The anti-urban bias and antidemocratic prejudice—inherent in the structure of the Legislative Council and later the New Jersey Senate—expressed itself in many ways. New Jersey's blind adherence to the proposition that cows and pine trees deserved the same political power as people not only tainted legislative policy, lasting from 1776 through the latter half of this century, but also doomed any chance that New Jersey might have had to foster a city of national stature. By the time the Supreme Court abolished the system, the fate of the cities was no longer a speculation on the limits of their potential, but already a question of triage.

Unfair Tax Policies

New Jersey has managed to carry an agrarian mind set about taxation right through major social and economic revolutions of the nineteenth and twentieth centuries. The first revolution that altered the political environment of New Jersey was the transportation revolution, which began with the first railroads in the 1830s and has continued through the emergence of Newark Airport as one of the five busiest commercial flight centers in the country. The second revolution was the Industrial Revolution, which came into full force in the late 1850s and resulted in New Jersey's becoming the first state in the nation to employ more nonfarm workers than agricultural workers. The final revolution was the technology or information revolution, with New Jersey once again leading the trend of shifting from manufacturing to service-enterprise employment.

The legislature's response to these dramatic changes was an ever-increasing reliance on property taxes. It would be beyond the scope of this study to debate the superiority of progressive taxation, or the common sense of hooking revenue requirements to the real source of wealth. However, this study does explore how and why the state's cities were denied the opportunity to have the resources necessary to emerge into national prominence.

In twelfth- and thirteenth-century England, towns would be required to petition the sovereign for grants of murage (to repair the city's walls), pontage (to
repair the town's bridges) and pavage (to repair streets), according to Professor
William Maitland. These were not grants in the sense of the king's sending money
for the work to be done, but rather grants allowing the towns to withhold sums
otherwise due the Crown so that necessary capital construction or maintenance
might be done. In the eighteenth century, New Jersey towns were still being required to petition for legislative approval to borrow money for the construction of
roads, bridges, and other necessary improvements. The same is true today, with
state law limiting the amount of borrowing allowed rather than leaving it to the
bond markets to determine the credit-worthiness of an individual municipal
applicant.

The worst historical abuse of the taxing power came about during the transportation revolution of the 1830s. The state, dominated by rural interests, not only
gave itself the exclusive benefit of the railroad franchise revenue, but also compounded the affront to the cities serving as major railroad hubs in two other ways:
1. granting the powers of eminent domain to the railroad companies; and 2. allowing the railroads to use their enormous new wealth to buy up incredible amounts
of real estate, which was thereafter considered to be exempt from local taxes.

No city suffered more than did Jersey City, which was victimized by this
and other legislative policies for decades. The state gave the railroad companies—
who were pouring money into the state's treasury at such a rate as to allow New
Jersey to eschew all other revenue raising for over twenty years—permission to
fill in the entire waterfront of Jersey City with New York City's refuse. This allowed the railroads to claim riparian rights, and effectively blocked all other would-
be competitors from access to the docks and wharves, over which the railroads
could now assert a monopoly. The environmental affront to the health and well
being of the city's residents was incalculable. Moreover, the tracks of the railroad
companies were laid down in such a manner as to frustrate the orderly and rational development of the city.

The state adamantly refused to allow Jersey City (or for that matter any other
municipality in the state) to realize any meaningful revenue from the presence of
a railroad until the General Railroad Act of 1873. The railroads had escaped any
local tax and had paid precious little state tax from the granting of the original
charters in 1830 to the adoption of the first meaningful reform forty-three years
later. By the time the first Railroad Tax Act was imposed the railroads owned between one-quarter and one-third of the total usable land in Jersey City.

Considering the handicap, it is truly remarkable that Jersey City sustained
itself. The passage of the General Railroad Act of 1873 was the most hotly contested legislative matter in the history of the state up to that point. An entire book
could be written on the legislative efforts to break the railroad monopolies. Such
a work could have chapters listed in alphabetical order—from avarice and betrayal
to xenophobia, yeggery and zones of influence. Thirteen years later the democratic
governor, Joel Parker of Monmouth County, reflected upon those turbulent events
and put the bravest and most tactful front on it by explaining that

as time progressed, these corporations extended their business operations and acquired additional property, often of great value, until in some sections of the state, especially in the cities, the exemptions from local taxation, became so great, as to encumber the property of citizens liable to be taxed with a heavy burden. To prevent injustice arising from inequality of taxation, and to equalize, as far as possible, the public burdens, the Legislature, on the 2nd of April, 1873, passed an act the avowed object of which was to establish just rules for the taxation of railroad property. This act made a radical change in the system.

He put a remarkable spin upon the tumultuous events of the legislative session of 1873. This radical change, adopted as it was during the administration of a Democratic governor who presided over a state whose legislature was dominated by Republican majorities of two to one in both houses, embraced one nasty little fact—never mentioned in the historical accounts. The act resulted from a conspiracy, the object of which was to plunder Jersey City. The secondary purpose was to save other New Jersey cities such as Elizabeth and Rahway from remaining wards of the state.

The original act of 1873 had been declared constitutionally defective, a problem that required correction. Such a correction probably never would have come to pass had not that infamous treasurer of Jersey City, Alexander Hamilton, absconded to Mexico in January of 1874 with all the spare cash contained in the city's vaults. The defalcation of one of their own inspired the Republicans in the legislature to adopt the Tax Act of 1876. The stench of the ill wind wafting from the treasurer's office in Jersey City blew benefits into the city coffers of a number of needful cities, such as Newark and Paterson, and dozens of others.

The General Railroad Act of 1873 was unequivocally a major tax-reform act. The enormous wealth of the railroads went from being totally exempt at the local level to being taxed at 1 percent of cost, and after the constitutional amendments of 1875, this formula was altered to require taxation at 1 percent of true value. The railroads fought this legislation and did so successfully, but the door had been opened and there was no turning back to the good old days for the railroads. Many of the railroads contended they were paying double taxation, and worse still, they were paying 1 percent in towns that had general tax rates substantially below 1 percent. They never mentioned that their tax liability was capped at 1 percent even in communities where all other taxpayers were paying rates higher than the 1 percent guaranteed to the railroads.

The railroad tax battles moved back and forth from the legislature to the courts to study commissions to ultimate passage of the Railroad Tax Act of 1884, which is a seminal document in the history of taxation in New Jersey. This legislation legitimized the concept of classification of property for tax purposes. All railroad property was divided into four classes, which has remained the basis for the taxation of railroad property through to the present time:

• Class one: the value of the main stem of the rail line.

- Class two: all of the remaining property owned by the railroad outside of the main stem.
- Class three: the rolling stock of the railroad company.
- Class four: the value of the franchise of the railroad to operate across the state and particularly across other public rights of way such as roads and highways.

The inevitable litigation followed in the wake of the adoption of this new Railroad Tax Act. Round one went to the railroads with the Supreme Court declaring that the act was unconstitutional. A month later the highest court in New Jersey, the Court of Errors and Appeals, reversed the Supreme Court, and upheld the constitutionality of the tax. The decision takes up over two hundred pages of the forty-eighth volume of the New Jersey Law Reports and is the landmark decision in the legal history of the state, providing an insight into the public policy of that era. The attorneys representing the railroads advanced—in good conscience—arguments that revealed the mind set of these attorneys. Those same arguments would send shudders through the body politic today even if they were whispered.

For example, Thomas N. McCarter, representing the Lehigh Valley Railroad and others, thought that the additional revenue made available to the municipalities might be squandered on such "extravagances" as parks, and that the state might spend their new revenue on equally extravagant projects, such as improving the state prison or building a new facility for the insane. Heaven forfend that such items should be paid for by the railroad barons. Former Governor Joseph D. Bedle, employed by the Morris and Essex Railroad, feared that taxes on business interest would lead to tyranny—turning town against country, farmer against manufacturer, rich against poor, with no one to protect the railroads from the unbridled will of the legislature. Both of these gentlemen were extremely able advocates, and demonstrating that he was way ahead of his time, McCarter invoked the recently adopted U.S. Constitutional Amendment and claimed that any tax on the railroad violated his client's rights to equal protection under the 14th Amendment.

After resolving the titanic battle over the tax's constitutionality, thereby saving many a city from bankruptcy, the cities and the railroads settled down to 50 years of quibbling over what was Class one property taxable only by the state and what was Class two property subject to local taxation. The railroads contended, often to very sympathetic state officials, that every inch of track and siding was either main stem or ancillary to main stem and therefore exempt from local taxes. The major battles took place in reference to Jersey City and Newark, where the railroads owned so much property that it was measured in square miles as opposed to acreage. The other ploy of the railroads followed the example of the state. If the government could classify and divide property, then the railroads could split up their holdings, and create hundreds of subsidiaries who owned only a few miles of siding that they said was their "main stem." Regrettably the state's public policy sided with the railroads and was adverse to the cities' receiving their appropriate share of the modest taxes imposed on the richest enterprises in America.

Unwillingness to Share Riparian Proceeds

The history of riparian rights is sad and sordid. High-minded but prejudiced politicians rescued the state's riparian rights from being stolen by the railroads, but diverted the income from the sale of such rights to lessen the costs of education in wealthy counties such as Morris, Somerset, and Hunterdon, at the expense of primarily Hudson County. The story is long and complex, and moreover deserves more time and attention than can be provided in this brief review.

Suffice it to say that against their inclination the legislature was forced during the period of 1864 to 1871 to forgo any additional sweetheart deals with the railroads. Thereafter valuable riparian grants were only sold or leased by the state for market value. For our present purposes it is only important to recognize that the state exercised full sovereign powers over all riparian properties, and laid claim to all of the income. Never was any thought given to sharing the revenues with the municipality wherein the riparian lands were situated, nor did the state use the riparian income to make improvements to harbors, channels, or other commercially beneficial projects.

The riparian rights issue in New Jersey left an indelible mark of further victimization on Hudson County and to a lesser degree on Essex and Union. Most notably damaged were the major cities who had significant waterfronts, Jersey City, Newark, Elizabeth, Trenton, and Camden. Because of the political power of New York City and Philadelphia, the states in which they are located, despite asserting their legitimate sovereign rights to riparian lands, were never able to exploit these cities. The pattern of cooperation by the respective legislatures of New York and Pennsylvania in assisting their cities to develop their waterfronts were examples totally ignored by the rurally controlled New Jersey legislature, which viewed the state's riparian lands as just one more city asset to be exploited rather than nurtured.

Unimaginative Corporate Tax Policies

New Jersey's liberal policy in the late nineteenth century toward the monopolies and corporate trusts—reviled and prohibited by the vast majority of her sister states—provided a safe haven for the holding companies of the Rockefellers and other corporate barons. Labeled the *traitor state* by the famous muckraker Lincoln Steffens, New Jersey shrugged off the criticism and prided itself on its role as the protector of the economic exploiters. The interests of the farmers who controlled the elections of the New Jersey Senate were not sufficiently compromised by the excesses of big business to motivate them to direct their senators to reject harboring these predators. Moreover the corporate taxes paid by the trusts as tribute to the state eliminated the need for other taxes.

The Trust Company of New Jersey was formed to aid and abet corporations and holding companies in violating the laws of virtually all the other states. The business of the Trust Company was to house the corporate records, and provide a New Jersey address for the home office of the companies whose interests were actually far flung across the country. The production of corporate charters became a major manufacturing enterprise in New Jersey. In return for this prostitution, New Jersey received taxes in the amount of twenty cents per thousand dollars of corporate capitalization.

This pittance went to the state treasury and was not shared in any formal manner with the cities that served as the locations for the home offices of these corporations. The home office status was a subterfuge, but it need not have been. Having made the policy decision that the state would permit holding companies and trusts, the state could have insisted that the trusts maintain an actual home office as opposed to a mere mail drop in the state. The trusts having found a safe haven would have been more than willing to do more, particularly in view of the fact that they were considered pariahs in every other civilized jurisdiction. Foolishly, New Jersey allowed the trusts to maintain their real operational offices on Wall Street or in Cleveland or Chicago, requiring only that the directors send in their tax money and come to New Jersey once a year for lunch on the day of their annual meeting.

The senators from the rural counties obviously thought they were doing enough for Newark and Jersey City by boosting their lunch trade. Had they even defined "home office" in terms of a skeleton staff it would have promoted the construction of office buildings and provided employment within these cities to thousands of clerical workers. New Jersey got street-walker compensation when it could have demanded that of a high-priced courtesan.

Undercapitalization of the Banks

New Jersey's provincial attitudes were nowhere more evident than in its restrictive banking laws, which continued almost to the present time. The rural senators, fearful of big city competition for local deposits, constructed a banking system that prevented the accumulation of capital within the major cities.

The roots of this myopic banking policy can be traced to the colonial days when the major danger was that New Jersey farmers' earnings would quickly vanish into the pockets of New York and Philadelphia manufacturers. In order to ease the continuing problem the colonial legislature authorized the printing of more money. The new money would circulate within New Jersey's economy for only a short time before finding its way across either the Hudson or the Delaware.

The fear of big city banks resulted in legislation reflecting how the senators totally misunderstood the threat to the state. They confused the danger posed by out-of-state banks with the threat of having the banks of New Jersey's cities compete for deposits in the underserved areas of the state. The prohibition against out-of-state banks opening offices within the state might have at one time made some sense, but forbidding a bank headquartered in Newark from opening an office in Union or Morris County was absolutely counter to the interests of urban growth.

The fear, of course, arose from the farmers' distrust of urban institutions of any type. This was coupled with the concern that funds would be unavailable to farmers when they needed them most. Better to have the money in the hands of people who would make credit decisions on personal factors. As a result of the prohibition against intercounty banking, the big money poured out of New Jersey and into the banks of New York and Philadelphia.

The severity of the problem struck home only when the state proposed the construction of the Meadowlands racetrack and Giants Stadium in the mid 1970s. New Jersey's banking community was unable to finance this project because the capital available was so paltry; New York banks were not anxious to finance a project that would compete with their city's facilities. Only with a consortium of New Jersey banks and the moral equivalent by the legislature of a pledge of the state's full faith and credit was the project able to proceed.

The lesson of the Meadowlands was a strong wake-up call to the state that it had better allow its larger banks to grow and expand or the state would always be at the financial mercy of Wall Street. The opportunities already had been lost for the major banks of Jersey City or Newark to grow to a size where they could have played a fundamental role in the development of urban New Jersey.

In 1975 the legislature finally granted permission to maintain branches in other counties than the county of the home office, and since that time the state's banking institutions have grown exponentially. However, given the handicap with which they started many were easy targets for acquisition by out-of-state banks when interstate banking was permitted.

Underfunding of Urban Infrastructures

The highly touted progress of highway and bridge projects has destroyed New Jersey's major cities. The American romance with the automobile reflects a level of passion in New Jersey that is difficult to adequately summarize. New Jersey remains the state with the lowest taxes on motor fuels, the most miles of paved highway per square mile, the largest complex of super highways per square mile and per capita, and the highest number of registered vehicles per capita. These statistics tell the tale.

When I was in the legislature it was a standing joke that New Jersey taxed gasoline the way Virginia and Kentucky taxed tobacco. My congressman for many years, Edward Patten, would brag how there was more oil in his Middlesex-Union district than in any district in Texas. He of course was referring to the refineries, which were forced to work overtime to satisfy the demands of New Jersey drivers.

The public policies just outlined have brought New Jersey to the wreckage: the tawdry strip malls; the ticky-tacky suburban subdivisions; the abandoned factories, surrounded by battle-scarred ghettos; the pervasive ugliness of blight that has crept from city to suburb, disrespectful of municipal boundaries. The phrase that comes to mind is, in the immortal words of the cartoon character Pogo, "We have met the enemy and he is us."

CHAPTER 12

Perth Amboy
and Burlington

CAPITAL CITIES THAT DID NOT CAPITALIZE

They are all Pryvatyrs and Pyrates.
Governor Jeremiah Basse, referring to settlers
of Perth Amboy in 1694

When I was very young, a trip to the city meant that my parents were taking me to Perth Amboy. Some of my very early recollections were of visiting my pediatrician, who maintained his offices there, and I can still recall eating my first restaurant meal, and having the meaning of a menu explained to me, at the famous Parker House on Smith Street. The city of Perth Amboy was dramatically different from where my family lived. It was a real city, and it inspired awe and wonderment with its stores, theaters, office buildings, hospital, and hotels. Even the tone of voice that was used by my parents in discussing Perth Amboy indicated that they considered the amenities of this city with a sort of reverence. The real level of respect accorded to Perth Amboy is best demonstrated by the fact that my three older sisters were all born at Perth Amboy General, and it wasn't until I arrived in 1943 that my mother had sufficient confidence that New Brunswick (the county seat and the place where she was raised) had any adequate medical facility comparable to those provided by Perth Amboy.

Growing up, I remember being taken to the still-bustling dockyards, the polyglot open markets, the crowded shops, and of course my first movie. The city had movie theaters, and was in the movies. Walter Mitty came to life on the silver screen, residing in a small unassuming house on a tree-lined street in Perth Amboy. There was nothing unusual to me about the fact that Danny Kaye was commuting from the train station there. To me there was a very logical constellation of metropolitan centers involved in this movie—Hollywood, New York City, and Perth Amboy—three places all in the same league.

Later, as a teenager, I learned that the great metropolis of New York City was separated from Perth Amboy not by a harbor, but by a cultural, financial, and psychological gulf.

Still later, I came again to be charmed by Perth Amboy, this gritty, hardworking city with its tenacity, its openness to change, its diversity, and most of all its warm and loyal voters, who assured me reelection even in the bleakest of political years.

Now I have come to appreciate the might-have-been quality that is associated with Perth Amboy's long and mostly distinguished history. Existing now in the shadow cast across the harbor by New York City, and even by the penumbra of its larger urban sisters of Elizabeth, Newark, and Jersey City, this original port city once was considered to be the rival of New York. So too was the port city of Burlington, on the Delaware River, suggested as the potential rival to Philadelphia.

What happened in these two port cities, once the respective capitals of East and West Jersey, is illustrative of both external and internal political manipulations that have thwarted and frustrated the emergence of any urban center in New Jersey as a world-class city. The die was cast for the destiny of both of these cities as early as the seventeenth century when decision making rested in the hands of the courtiers, bureaucrats, and land speculators in England, and choices were made that gave a definite edge to Philadelphia and New York City.

The quantity and quality of the literature devoted to the early history of New Jersey requires that I defer all but the most cursory attempt to summarize the salient facts, and concentrate only on the matters that are directly relevant to our present inquiry. Charles II returned to the throne of England in 1660, and immediate attention was turned toward further colonization of the New World. Of particular interest was the consolidation of English interests, which meant closing the gap between Connecticut and Maryland. That land was then held by the Dutch and Swedes.

On March 12, 1664, Charles granted all lands between the Connecticut and Delaware Rivers to his brother, James, the Duke of York, knowing full well that the territory in question would have to be taken by conquest. The duke moved immediately to accomplish just that by ordering Colonel Robert Nicolls to take four ships and 450 men and seize control of New Amsterdam. Nicolls did so, but while he was still at sea, the duke gave the land between the Hudson and Delaware Rivers to his loyal supporters, Sir George Carteret and John, Lord Berkeley. The importance of the transfer from James to Berkeley and Carteret is that it consisted of two elements:

1. The right of ownership of the land, and the privilege of exploiting that ownership.
2. The right and power to govern the territory, provided that nothing be done that would be adverse to the interests of the British Crown.

Lord Berkeley, in desperate need of hard cash, sold his half interest in 1673 to a group of Quakers, fronted by a man named John Fenwick. The following year brought William Penn to America to mediate a dispute among his co-religionists. In 1676 an agreement was reached between the Quaker holders of Berkeley's interest and Sir George Carteret. This agreement divided the territory into West Jersey, containing 4,600 square miles, and East Jersey, to be owned by Carteret, consisting of 3,000 square miles. By 1681 Burlington had been laid out and was rapidly being built up as the central market for the almost 1,500 Quakers who had come to West Jersey.

In 1680, Carteret died and his interest in East Jersey was sold at auction to William Penn and eleven others, and for a brief time Quakers were the dominant landholders in both East and West Jersey. These twelve buyers soon sold portions of their stake to twelve others, and the new group of twenty-four began quickly to sell fractions of their shares to others. By 1684 the Board of Proprietors of East Jersey had organized itself and established Perth Amboy as their center of business in East Jersey. Anxious for growth, the board lured settlers to the new development, and the population of Perth Amboy received a large boost in 1688 when the Earl of Perth arranged for 200 Scots, all of whom were in disfavor with the Established Church, to emigrate to East Jersey. These Proprietors not only continued to sell fractions of their shares, but voted themselves regular dividends in the form of acreage. By 1702 each of the twenty-four shares had realized land dividends of 17,500 acres. There was therefore almost 500,000 acres of land in the open market in addition to a brisk market in fractional shares of the proprietors' original twenty-four shares.

Meanwhile the Council of Proprietors of West Jersey had organized and set up headquarters in Burlington. Edward Byllynge, one of the Quakers who had bought up Lord Berkeley's interest, had rights of ownership plus the right of governance in West Jersey until his death in 1687, at which time his lands and power transferred to Dr. Daniel Coxe, a man obsessed with land speculation. Coxe packaged his West Jersey holdings and sold the package consisting of his shares, his outright real estate holdings and his right to govern to a corporation known as the West Jersey Society. All forty-eight members of the society were businessmen and land speculators, primarily interested in profits from the resale of their holdings.

It is one thing to own land; it is an entirely different proposition to govern the people to whom you are actively selling or leasing the land, and who are actually inhabiting it while you are back in England waiting for your next dividend. It would be an exaggeration to say that anarchy ensued under the Proprietors, but the term "serious political instability" is totally appropriate.

The situation required a decisive resolution, and that came when the Proprietors of both East and West Jersey surrendered their rights to govern. These were turned back to the Crown in 1702.

This brief description of the events occurring in New Jersey between 1664 and 1702 fails to do adequate justice to a subject that is fascinating and important. For those interested in this critical period in the state's history, I commend to your attention a number of wonderful books that concentrate on the intrigue and maneuvering that was the hallmark of this time. A half dozen of these are included in the bibliography.

What is essential to understand is the following:

1. In 1702, the Quakers—the quintessential dissenters, refusing to swear allegiance to, or bear arms for, the Crown—were present in West Jersey and centered in the city of Burlington.
2. At the same time Perth Amboy was the center of Scottish influence, and populated by a majority whose loyalty to the Church and Crown of England was in doubt.
3. The Proprietors, while containing some Quakers and Scottish shareholders, were predominantly wealthy Anglicans, who were in the ventures for investment and speculation purposes.
4. The Proprietors were willing to surrender their rights of governance to the Crown in order that political stability would be imposed, and so that they could concentrate on what interested them most—land speculation.

From its original capture by Colonel Nicolls in 1664, New York City was considered to have exceptional strategic importance because of its location, but just as important was the symbolism involved. The British had taken New Amsterdam by force—it was a prize of war. The Dutch reclaimed it during the brief War of 1673, but the English regained control in the spring of 1674. From then on the city was a trophy to be displayed to their European neighbors—a symbol of England's dominance—London lavished care, attention, and concern on the new city. This small settlement, clustered at the tip of Manhattan Island, was cherished and nurtured as a showpiece of English strength and power in the New World.

That New Jersey was considered to have a lower standing within the British Empire of the seventeenth century, one need only cite the attitude of Nicholls's successor as governor of New York, Sir Edward Andros. We need not dwell on the details of the power struggle between Andros and Philip Carteret, the young nephew of Sir George, who had been duly authorized by his uncle to serve as the lawful governor of New Jersey. Suffice it to say that Andros prevailed, not even hesitating to send troops from New York to arrest and remove Carteret to New York to stand trial for the charges of riot and treason. Carteret was acquitted in 1680, but Andros ruled East Jersey, effectively usurping the powers of Carteret and the proprietors.

Perth Amboy was to be a free port. This meant ships could enter and discharge cargo without having to pay any customs duty. In this regard it was to be entirely independent of New York, but after England's glorious revolution of 1688 drove James II from the throne, New York once again exercised hegemony over the entire harbor, forcing ships destined for Perth Amboy to land there without first paying custom duties in New York. The fact that Perth Amboy was perceived to be a Scottish settlement, with all of the associated connections to the deposed king, undoubtedly emboldened New York in asserting its control of the harbor and denying free port status to Perth Amboy.

Even after New York's domination was curtailed, and the independent governing power of the East Jersey Proprietors was reestablished, their tenuous governance did not enjoy a long tenure. From the very inception of its status as a Crown colony in 1703, New Jersey found itself treated as the satellite of New York.

It was during these first critical years of rule by a royal governor that the fates of Perth Amboy and Burlington were sealed once and for all.

The period during which all of New Jersey was governed as a province of New York provided such an advantage to New York City that little could be done for Perth Amboy, or by its residents, to compensate for the head start afforded New York. The same may be said concerning Burlington, which was allowed to fend for itself while ever-greater resources were committed to and privileges granted for Philadelphia, a city founded almost a decade after Burlington had been thought of as the center of Quaker life in America.

I suggest that there is much more to this story of the fates of these two cities than meets the eye, although even on the surface New York had the distinct advantage of carrying the name of a hero, while Perth Amboy was burdened by a designation associated with questionable loyalty to the restored monarchy. As with so much else in the history of New Jersey there is a subtext that warrants closer inspection. In this case, as with others involving the fate of the state, the critical factor was which faction was willing to pay the higher bribe.

Queen Anne, in 1703, appointed her cousin, Edward Hyde, Lord Cornbury, as the first royal governor for the now united provinces of East and West Jersey. He was greedy, profligate, and an alleged transvestite. To compound these deficiencies, he was rumored to be more cunning than intelligent. Moreover, he was determined to govern New Jersey and its fifteen thousand citizens from New York City. He aspired never to set one high-heeled foot in New Jersey, but rather to judge the applications of the various delegations that traveled to his residence in New York City to petition his support. During the few months of the year that he did enter New Jersey, his presence was merely inconvenient for him, but truly unpleasant for those who dwelt here. Not often did he come to the colony of New Jersey unless well attended by his armed guards.

At this time there existed within the colony two major factions, which did not break down along the geographic lines that might have been expected as the natural legacy of the division of the former East and West provinces. Factional alliances had formed that bridged the old divisions. The first alliance was composed of Scotch Proprietors of East Jersey and the Quaker Proprietors of West Jersey. The second alliance vying for power consisted of English Proprietors with Anglican affiliations. Despite his early sympathies for the Scotch-Quaker group, Cornbury quickly turned on them when he realized that the High-Church/low-scruples group were ready to give him a substantial piece of the action. Cornbury was able to indulge his expensive tastes with the bribes he received from what was labeled the "Cornbury Ring." The Scotch-Quaker alliance was frustrated and impotent.

The story of Cornbury's corruption is as instructive, at least for our present purposes, as it is sordid. The power of the Scotch interests was concentrated in Perth Amboy, the city that appreciatively adopted its name to honor the Earl of Perth, who you will remember, had been instrumental in assisting 200 Scots, who were in serious trouble with the Church of England, to immigrate to this settlement at the mouth of the Raritan River. The city of Burlington was the center of

Quaker life on the east bank of the Delaware River. Therefore both cities, despite their natural advantages, were viewed as being unorthodox—different ethnically and religiously—and therefore considered slightly suspect by the Anglican landed gentry.

The bias against the Scots of Perth Amboy is reflected by Lord Cornbury's prosecution of Francis Makemie, a Presbyterian minister, for the offense of preaching without a license. But to prove he was even-handed in his persecution of independent clergy, in another instance Cornbury deigned to come to Perth Amboy specifically to arrest an Anglican clergyman, the Reverend Thorowgood Moore, who had the temerity to criticize Cornbury's penchant for cross-dressing. Moore escaped from the fort in New York while Cornbury was traveling to Albany, and made his way to the protection of Boston.

That Perth Amboy had suffered from the ill will of Cornbury is categorically proven by the very language used in the preamble of its charter, obtained from his successor, Governor Robert Hunter, on August 24, 1718. Following the expected effusive praise of King George and words of appreciation to their beloved Governor Hunter, the document recites: "That the said town hath for many years languished under designed and unjust impositions to prevent its growth, to the loss and detriment of the province." This clause leaves little doubt that the residents of Perth Amboy clearly understood and resented their treatment by Cornbury.

If Cornbury had been a man of probity, integrity, and vision the story might have been different. As it was, Perth Amboy and Burlington must be considered victims of the power struggle that Cornbury avariciously resolved on the side of the English land speculators. Albeit that both Perth Amboy and Burlington continued to be chartered by the British Crown as legal ports, they were limited to local and regional trade, with very little international activity.

Should the entire blame be placed on Lord Cornbury, and attributed to what was his not so thinly disguised prejudice against the Scots of Perth Amboy and the Quakers of Burlington? The real answer, or what might better be expressed as the other part of the answer, is that the forces with whom Cornbury ultimately aligned himself hold the key.

New Jersey was a multicultural, ethnically heterogeneous, religiously diverse, and religiously tolerant community at the start of the eighteenth century. It was not, however, a state where wealth was equally distributed. One of the most extensive scholarly examinations of this period appears in *Prologue to Independence: New Jersey in the Coming of the American Revolution*. The author, Larry R. Gerlach, points out that one-third of the population was landless, and that only one percent of the population owned tracts in excess of five hundred acres. Clustered at the apex of the society were the proprietors of both East and West Jersey, who owned enormous tracts. He also says, "The colony lacked a port of sufficient size and quality to handle a large volume of ocean shipping, and New Jersey merchants lacked the capital and commercial connections to establish a viable direct trade with Europe." Much of this is accurate, but something more should be added. First the natural harbor at Perth Amboy had unlimited potential, and was capable of being developed to handle any reasonable volume of international trade in this period. What was lacking was the investment necessary to build first-rate facilities. My position is that it was the absentee landowners who saw cash flow as going in one direction. Their focus, concentration, and interest, was on land speculation and not on building up any manufacturing or commerce in the mercantile sense. Their profit came from rents and resales. It is the dichotomy of the landed versus the merchant. Land was the only stock in trade of the proprietors, and as a result no attention was given to developing the harbor at Perth Amboy or the port at Burlington. The fate of these facilities was not in local hands. Gerlach is unquestionably correct in asserting that the local merchants lacked the capital. What he does not say is that the absentee proprietors had more than sufficient capital to develop these ports, but chose not to make the investment, being interested in selling land for short-term profits rather than investing in facilities for long-term sustained growth.

The Revolution did not improve the position of either Burlington or Perth Amboy, and, in fact, may have worsened their competitive condition. During the years between Lord Cornbury's governance and the onset of the Revolution, the population of Perth Amboy had taken on a distinctive English-Anglican air. Leonard Lundin in his book, *Cockpit of the Revolution: The War for Independence in New Jersey*, expresses the view that Perth Amboy, as the provincial capital, had become the center of conservatism—loyal to the church and loyal to the Crown—in a word, "Tory." This report of the politics of Perth Amboy during the Revolution is strongly seconded by New Jersey's eminent historian Richard T. McCormick in his *Experiment in Democracy*.

What both men call the "Perth Amboy Group" consisted of the wealthiest and most powerful families in the province. Mercantile agreements and interfamily marriages had produced a clique that constituted the penumbra of economic and political power that held sway over vast interests in New York as well as New Jersey. The Johnstons, Skinners, Kearnys, and Parkers of Perth Amboy were closely allied with the Delanceys, the Rutherfords, and other power families in New York. So powerful was the "Perth Amboy Group" that when their friend and fellow city resident William Franklin called together the council for 1775, three of its twelve members were directly involved with the "Perth Amboy Group," and four additional members were closely associated with it.

On the last pages of his book, Lundin sums up the fate of this group that had dominated the affairs of New Jersey for over fifty years. He writes, "The power of the Perth Amboy Group had been forever shattered, and its members dispersed. The pleasant little town where their wealth, prestige, and self-assurance had been so long displayed was now a desolate and deserted village, its primacy usurped by rising Trenton."

Perth Amboy found itself once again on the wrong side. Its Scotch connections had made it suspect in the eyes of Lord Cornbury in 1703. Over the ensuing decades it had overcompensated by becoming the bastion of Toryism. Once again Perth Amboy was viewed as being suspect, as it fought to recover from the effects of the Revolution.

During the years that the Confederation governed, the arbitrary and often discriminatory tariffs and other economic advantages enjoyed by New York and Pennsylvania exacerbated the problem. New Jersey supported the new Federal Constitution so strongly as a result of the unfair advantage that New York City and Philadelphia had as trading centers that were suffocating New Jersey commerce. A national currency was viewed as a major reform as were uniform custom and tariff duties.

In 1785, both Perth Amboy and Burlington were made free ports by charters voted by the new state government, but the charters also provided that the principal officers of the communities would be selected by the legislature. This particular restriction reflects the lingering view that the loyalty of these cities was still suspect. In effect they were denied the privilege of self-governance, and even more importantly their ability to raise revenues was severely hampered. In effect Quaker Burlington and Tory Perth Amboy were placed on probation.

The new state made them free ports for a period of twenty-five years. This was done at the height of the rivalry between New York and New Jersey, and was designed to lure trade away from New York and Philadelphia, which had imposed high tariffs and duties on the British goods that had flooded the market at such low prices as to destroy American-made products. At the same time New Jersey farm products shipped from Perth Amboy to New York were being charged duty as if they were luxuries from Europe. All of this maneuvering served to hasten the demise of the Confederation and the adoption of the U.S. Constitution, but that is an entirely other story. While the free-port status of Perth Amboy and Burlington may have been a catalyst for the creation of the country, it did very little for the development of these two cities.

After the new constitution was ratified, the revenues that they were able to generate as ports, instead of being used for local improvements and expansion of their ports and markets, were siphoned away to be used for the general support of the state's new government. It appears that even the granting of free-port status was done begrudgingly. Animosity left over from the revolutionary struggle did not dissipate quickly, and had it not been for the desperate financial condition of the new state, it might be assumed that this particular privilege would never have been granted by a legislature dominated by Revolutionary War veterans.

The control of the state government by the rural interests, who wore their patriotism on their sleeves, coupled with regional rivalry between the former East and West Jersey, starved both ports of the improvements that they required to develop and expand into viable competitors with their larger neighbors. Sadder still is the fact that New Jersey failed to learn the lessons that now seem so obvious, and therefore stifled what chances later presented themselves for Jersey City and/ or Newark to emerge as an equal to Manhattan, or for Camden to be a significant rival to Philadelphia. The failure of Perth Amboy and Burlington to fulfill the expectations entertained by their founders may be blamed originally on external forces, specifically the corruption of the first royal governor, Lord Cornbury. Their failure to emerge after the Revolution must be attributed to the fact that they were then viewed as communities whose allegiance was in doubt, and whose conduct during the war warranted retribution and not reward. However, the later failure of

Jersey City, Newark, and Camden to reach their potential must be attributed exclusively to the counterproductive policies of our own state government.

In more recent times, the mayor of Perth Amboy during most of the 1970s and 1980s, George Otlowski, and the former and once-more mayor of Burlington, Herman Costello, served with me in the New Jersey General Assembly. Even the briefest conversation with these fine legislators revealed the deep and abiding affection they had for their cities. While not all they tried was successful in revitalizing these two ancient urban areas, both tried their best against great challenges. A visit to either place shows the love and faith they both have for their respective cities, as revealed in the emerging vitality and struggling renaissance of the two former capitals of East and West Jersey.

CHAPTER 13

Camden

THE MISSED OPPORTUNITIES

I see a city invincible.
Walt Whitman

The City of Camden was, as anyone would agree, a definite late starter as compared to the other major cities of New Jersey. Part of the reason must be attributed to the fact that all of Camden County was a late starter, coming into existence only in 1844. When it was set off from Gloucester, Camden County consisted of only seven townships, and in 1871 it returned a portion of its jurisdiction back to Gloucester, and likewise ceded a portion to Burlington County in 1902.

As with other municipalities, the story of Camden City might have been different but for the outcome of a close election. In 1824, the grand jury of Gloucester County, which then consisted of the area that still bears that name, as well as all of Atlantic County, and most of present-day Camden County, lamented that the public buildings, including the court and the jail located in the county seat of Woodbury, were in deplorable condition, and should be replaced. The village of Camden was not yet a significant community even by the standards of this large and predominantly rural county, no less by state standards. However, Camden did have a number of things going for it. First, it was the only community south of Trenton authorized by the legislature to host a bank. In 1812 the legislature had granted this privilege to only five towns in the entire state. Second, it had a weekly newspaper, a rarity that provided an editorial boost to the commercial interests of the community. Third, it was the terminus of a network of roads leading to the ferries that plied the Delaware, not only to Philadelphia, but also up to Trenton and Burlington, and down river to Salem. Fourth, and perhaps most important, it contained an energetic merchant and manufacturing middle class that possessed an entrepreneurial spirit, recognizing that their commercial interests were in concert with the growth of the area. In academic terms it was a trading center that wished to legitimize its stature by becoming the administrative center as well. The local boosters stepped forward and offered the village of Camden as the new county seat. A referendum was held in February of 1825.

Voter alignment on this referendum augured ill for the future of Gloucester County as it was then constituted. The voters of Egg Harbor Township, stretching from the Atlantic Ocean to the border of what is now Winslow Township, sided with Camden, because traveling to this village was much more convenient and direct than going to Woodbury. Camden also received the support of its immediate neighbors, Gloucester Township and Waterford Township. The trouble came from two areas: one was predictable, Woodbury itself, where there was great suspicion of ballot stuffing and other illegal voting, the other trouble spot was Haddonfield, literally in Camden's backyard.

Both Camden and Haddonfield were villages within the Township of Newton. Their existed a certain tension between the villages, with Haddonfield representing the staid, bucolic, conservative interests of the landed elite, while Camden was already synonymous with the new, polyglot, secular interests of the tradesmen class. Distrustful of the commercial interests, and suspicious of their motives, Haddonfield had failed to support wholeheartedly the ambitions of their fellow township residents. Even if Haddonfield had thrown their entire support to Camden, it is still unlikely that it would have been enough to carry the day in the face of the voting irregularities in and around Woodbury; but Haddonfield's failure to rally to Camden's cause left very hard feelings—hard feelings that resulted in an immediate suit for divorce, hard feelings so intense that the ill will persisted well into this century.

On the pretense of wanting to have its own police force, Camden petitioned the legislature for incorporation, and after initially being rejected, finally persuaded the assembly to pass an act in 1828 incorporating Camden as an independent municipality.

By the time of the Civil War, Camden had become a full-fledged city. The major impetus for the transition from settlement to city came in the 1830s, as the ferries at Cooper's Landing had new customers deposited by the southern terminus of the Camden-Amboy Railroad. The coming of the railroad brought independent status for Camden County, and with full county status came additional tensions between Camden and Haddonfield. These two towns—Camden, now an incorporated municipality, and Haddonfield, a town, still within the geographic borders of Newton Township—now vied to be the county seat. Other communities stepped forward as well, but the real fight remained between Haddonfield and Camden. After seven years, four elections, and two Supreme Court decisions, Camden finally prevailed, but only by virtue of a court order directing the freeholders to build the new county court house in Camden. The city finally attained the position of administrative center that it had failed to acquire twenty-seven years before. The city was posed to make a major advance in statewide status, but with the first railroad bridge across the Delaware at Trenton in 1840 the city was forced to be satisfied with settling onto a comfortable commercial plateau. It would maintain its steady growth right through the next four decades, until a unique group of business and political leaders combined to make the city a real contender for national prominence.

As the saying goes, "only in America." The truth of this familiar expression was to be demonstrated to its fullest in Camden. Here it was that three Irish-born leaders would play out political careers that are the stuff of legends, and would leave indelible marks upon the history of the area.

William Joyce Sewell and David Baird would build a Republican machine that would dominate that party in the state for two generations, and control state government on and off for the same period. As for Camden County itself, the political operation the Sewell-Baird machine created was, without question or challenge, the dominant and controlling influence for the entire period from 1880 through 1933, with scant exceptions.

One of those rare interregnums was during the meteoric rise of William J. Thompson, who, as with Baird, was born in County Derry, Ireland, but, unlike Baird, chose the Democratic Party as his vehicle to fame and fortune. Fame and fortune it was in the 1890s, as Thompson parlayed his entertainment interests in Gloucester City into political control of the entire state. Believing the old adage about fighting fire with fire, Thompson and his fellow tavernowners, together with brewery and distilling interests from throughout the state, wary of the growing prohibitionist political strength, sponsored their own candidates on the Democratic tickets. Emboldened by their victories on the coattails of New Jersey's favorite Democratic son, President Grover Cleveland, in 1983 Thompson had the legislature approve, over the vetoes of Democratic Governor George Werts, bills allowing the local licensing of racetracks (Thompson owned both the racetrack and the governing body in Gloucester city) and the decriminalization of book-making. Spoil-sport reformers were galvanized in reaction, and Thompson's power crumbled around him in the elections of 1893. He attempted to hold on by having the Democrats in the Senate refuse to seat some newly elected reformers, but the Supreme Court stepped in at the behest of Sewell, and fair play.

Sewell and Baird marched from this victory to collaboration with their Republican colleagues in north Jersey to the nomination and election of Garrett Hobart of Passaic County as vice-president of the United States. The Republican machine of Camden never looked back, and was able, under the leadership of Baird's son, to muster a clear plurality even for Herbert Hoover in 1932, in the face of the Depression that was ravaging the industrial and commercial base of Camden County.

That industrial and commercial base of Camden was in large measure the work of Sewell-Baird and their intimate circle of business and political allies, who, working primarily through the Camden Board of Trade, made a concerted effort to emerge from the shadow of Philadelphia, and develop an economic area to rival the cross-river municipal behemoth. Campbell Soup, New York Shipyards, Victor Talking Machine Company joined more established companies, such as the Esterbrook Pen Company, to lead the list of dozens of companies lured to Camden by the political and business leadership of these men. Ironically, Sewell, when he wasn't in Trenton as a state senator (1872–1881), or in Washington, D.C., as a U.S. senator, (1881–1887 and 1895–1901), guided the development of Camden from his office in Philadelphia, where, despite the modest title of superintendent of the West Jersey Railroad, he was virtually the number two man in the operation of the nation's leading enterprise, the Pennsylvania Railroad. It is my opinion that Sewell's connection with the railroad interests chilled any effort to change the political boundaries of Camden City during the period of its most significant growth.

The city had severely and critically undersized itself from the very start, and, had no annexations taken place, the city would be only a little over two square miles in size. It is today still the second smallest in area of the six most populated New Jersey cities. Even with the annexation of Stockton Town, in 1899, a subject that will be discussed at length, Camden does not total nine square miles. Sewell and the Pennsylvania Railroad Company liked it that way. Prior to the adoption of the Railroad Tax Act of 1884, the physical location of railroad assets had not been a major consideration. However, the provisions of the new act made local tax rates a consideration in all future planning. The railroads obviously preferred to have their major properties in low-service, low-tax, low-cost towns if that could be arranged. They did not want their Class-two property taxes going to support large school systems or paid fire and police departments if they could avoid it. New and extensive railroad yards were built in Stockton and Gloucester Townships in the last two decades of the nineteenth century. Manufacturers who relied on the railroads also began to choose locations outside higher taxed urban centers if such locations were available.

The ten square miles of Pennsauken Borough were created from Stockton Township in 1892, and what remained as Stockton Town was annexed to the City of Camden by legislative fiat in 1899. Stockton, which had originally been set off from Delaware Township in a street fight of 1859, had already given up a part of its territory in 1874 for the formation of the Borough of Merchantville, which is less than a mile square. All of Stockton Township had begun in the early 1850s as a real estate development.

The railroads lived by a policy of divide and conquer. This meant that the companies were anxious to diversify their markets, their customers, and, even more importantly, their labor pool. Just as they tried to protect themselves from labor unrest by dividing their labor force on ethnic, religious, and geographic lines in hope of preventing the formation of successful unions, the railroad executives were not interested in fostering a large, consolidated, and strong regional government that might rein in their unbridled power. Fragmented local governments could not be large or powerful enough to fight to see that the railroads were adequately assessed, and made to pay their fair share of local expenses for the upkeep of such frills as schools, hospitals, parks and such. The railroads were great adherents of reductionism in their corporate policies as well. The Railroad Tax Act had made four different classes of railroad property. Class I was the main line or as it was expressed in the legislation, "the main stem." This received the most favorable tax treatment, being made subject to only a nominal, one-half of one percent of value, tax payable to the state. Class II property was all other real estate owned by the railroad, but the use of which was ancillary to the operation of the "main stem." This was taxable by both the state and the community in which it was situated. It did not take the railroads long to start creating dozens of subsidiaries some of which held title to only a siding, but that siding was then classified as the new company's "main stem." The railroads may have been rapacious, but they certainly were not stupid.

The logical time for a major consolidation in Camden would have been the period contemporaneous with its phenomenal growth from 1880 to 1900. It did not happen because it would have been contrary to the financial interests of the railroads, who through Sewell controlled the public policies of Camden County and its constituent municipalities.

The new century saw ever-increasing growth in Camden. World War I and the industrial buildup that presaged America's entry into the conflict served as the catalyst for the ever-expanding manufacturing might of the region. So successful were Camden businesses that the very existence of the city's Chamber of Commerce seemed to be superfluous, and for a brief time it ceased operation. The City of Camden did not need any more business—it needed more space. At the war's end, Camden was a major New Jersey city with a population of approximately 120,000. It was one of only six cities to boast a population in six figures, and the only city of stature in all of South Jersey. More important, since the entire county's population, was only 190,000, the city represented 60 percent. When one added Gloucester City and Pennsauken, more than 80 percent of the county population was concentrated in a five-mile-wide swath running north to south along the riverfront.

There can be no doubt that the leaders of the City of Camden were in earnest when they launched the idea of unifying all of Camden County into one metropolitan entity. This would be the best solution to the need for more growing room. Furthermore, it would be more efficient and more businesslike, and, if Camden aspired to anything, it was to be businesslike—the business of Camden was business. Moreover, with the death of General William Sewell in 1901, the stage was set for a new era. Although the political machine that he had constructed, now operated under the aegis of the elder and younger Bairds, was still firmly in control, the Pennsylvania Railroad no longer dominated the public agenda to the inordinate degree it had during Sewell's lifetime.

The real power of Camden during the first decades of the this century was highly concentrated and reposed in a handful of institutions:

> The first and strongest institution was the Republican Party, presided over by the Bairds, who were the intimates of presidents, coronators of governors, and makers of mayors.

> The second most powerful institution was the Camden Board of Trade and its affiliates, composed for the most part of interlocking directorates, the Chamber of Commerce, and the Manufacturers' Club of Camden.

> The third most powerful institution was the Masons, and the vast majority of the members of the first and second institutions mentioned were also members of this organization.

> Finally there was the elected leadership of the various communities within

the county—a substantial majority of whom were also affiliated with one
or more, and many with all three of the power elites.

These four groups, working together, promoted the concept of the Greater
Camden Movement, and hired nationally recognized planners to develop a plan
and guide its implementation. The corporate directors insured that the Greater
Camden Movement would also have the benefit of the services of some of the
finest public relations firms in the East.

What went wrong? In a previous chapter we examined the various factors
that operated and applied statewide to stifle the emergence of any metropolitan
area in New Jersey. All of those factors are relevant to the Camden experience.
The following analysis demonstrates local application of some of these factors,
but also shows that there were very specific local considerations—parochial concerns that might well be the dispositive factors in undermining attempts to create
a Greater Camden.

The very first test to address is whether the plan was well conceived. In my
judgment the plan was as good as or better than other comparable plans, at least
as far as it went. Its failure resulted from two inadequacies, which in retrospect
seem blatantly obvious. First, a misconception as to the impact of infrastructure
improvements, and second, an almost religious faith that infrastructure could create community instead of the other way around. The dynamic that created the plan
was the same dynamic that created gargantuan public housing projects in the un-
shakable belief that the brick and mortar would somehow forge a community. The
creators of these projects were always shocked that they had built vertical asy-
lums for alienated families. Communities grow organically; there can be no specific mold or model. The *build* of a specific modern city is akin to the *timbering*
of the medieval settlement as it grew from village to borough, and ultimately to
city status. It is a phenomenon that must grow from the bottom up, and resists
any efforts to have it imposed from the top down. What we see in Camden, with
its overreliance on the beneficent effects of infrastructure improvements, is the
law of unanticipated consequences operating to the fullest. This is particularly
graphic when one reviews the impact of the very symbol of the Greater Camden
Movement, the Benjamin Franklin (originally called the Camden) Bridge.

Begun in 1922, after years of planning, the bridge was dedicated by President Calvin Coolidge on July 5, 1926. The bridge was an engineering achievement, very expensive in terms of money, and costly in lives lost in its construction.
Finally, it was popular beyond anyone's wildest expectations. Interestingly, a not
insubstantial portion of the stupendous sum required to construct the bridge went
for acquiring the land for the approaches. The plaza on the New Jersey side and
the rights of ways over the riparian rights on both sides of the river had to be acquired by negotiation or condemnation. Of the myriad options presented in the
planning stage, the final plan required that the project pay the Baird family for
the lumberyard and chandlery that had been the source of the family's wealth, but
whose activity had slackened as the demand for its major product, wooden spars,
had declined. The bridge was so popular that no sooner was it completed than the

Board of Freeholders were discussing the need for a second bridge—a plan that would come to fruition in 1956 with the opening of the Walt Whitman Bridge—and represents the final demise of Camden as a major city of the state.

All of the factors mentioned previously played a role in thwarting Camden's ambitions, but, in addition, the following reasons can be identified as contributing to the failure of the Greater Camden Movement:

1. *The planners concentrated on the infrastructure, and ignored the tax-rate disparities.*

One cannot help but be impressed with the work done by such notables as Charles W. Leavitt of New York, who had a national reputation. Designs and plans for everything from highways and interconnecting parks, to a coordinated school system were planned, studied, and discussed. Regrettably, the extensive planning never seemed to take into account the most important consideration and the greatest obstacle, the disparate tax rates of the various sections of the county. So for all of the time, attention, and enterprise devoted to planning Greater Camden, no constructive program was ever suggested for equalizing the tax burdens, or for the phasing-in of a unified rate. Nor was any effort exerted to enlist the support and cooperation of the state government in expediting and encouraging the consolidation efforts. The equalizing of tax rates was the most intractable of the problems confronted, and without successful determination of at least a process by which such equalization could occur, all other planning was fruitless.

2. *The battery of public relations experts employed by the Greater Camden Movement focused their considerable skills on promoting the idea to the wrong audience.*

Much of what they did was in the category of preaching to the choir, and the bulk of their other efforts was addressed to a national audience, extolling Camden's benefits. A great deal of what was going on was also shared with municipal and county officials throughout the country. The one major audience that the public relations seemed to overlook was the voting public of Camden County. The enthusiastic support of county residents seemed to be taken for granted, and therefore little effort was expended to persuade the bulk of the population, who were not members of the power elite, that a consolidated Camden would indeed make them participants in a more dynamic market and vibrant political entity.

3. *The symbolic role of the Camden Bridge and its approaches made it somewhat of a sacred cow immune from scrutiny or criticism.*

It was the old story of the emperor's new clothes, and by the time people awakened to the fact that the bridge might be counterproductive to the goals of the Greater Camden Movement it was already too late. Prior to 1926, at the height of enthusiasm for the Greater Camden Movement, the power axis of the county ran north to south along the waterfront. The opening of the bridge radically shifted the axis to one that ran east to west. The dramatic shift in population in the decades following the opening of the bridge clearly evidences this shift in orientation.

4. *The political upset that occurred in the 1922 city elections caused the dominant Republican Party to temporarily rethink its commitment to the Greater Camden Movement.*

The city had been led for an extended period, from 1905 to 1922, by an able Republican mayor, Charles H. Ellis, whose reward for his good efforts and loyal service to his party was in being appointed by President Warren G. Harding to be the postmaster of the city. The organization had been grooming his successor, Frank S. Van Hart. He was the stereotype of the candidate that had brought countless prior victories to the Sewell-Baird machine. A corporation man employed in a responsible position by the Esterbrook Pen Company, Van Hart was also a strong supporter of the Greater Camden Movement. While serving as the president of the Camden City Council, he did not hesitate to speak bluntly about the inexorable annexation by the city of the surrounding towns. In the election of 1922, Democratic Councilman Victor King was considered a very long shot. King's election rocked the Republican organization, and for a period caused the powers-that-be to rethink their wholehearted support of the Greater Camden program.

5. *Confronted by the shock of having a Democrat in city hall, the Republicans considered their options and quickly concluded that the annexation of suburban townships would provide the best alternative for the dilution of the urban political base of the Democrats.*

King, for his part, was either still in shock or just too busy to devote much attention to the Greater Camden Movement. It does not appear that annexation or consolidation was much of a priority for him during his five memorable years as a Democratic reformer in Camden's City Hall. While the Republicans waited to regain control of the city, they rose to the principal positions of leadership in the Greater Camden Movement. That King's election was an aberration can be seen from the fact that during the 1920s the Republican Party held almost unanimous control of the thirty-two-member Board of Chosen Freeholders. However, the primary rule of political dominance for any party is to keep peace in your own house, and that was proving to be a challenge for the Baird machine, as local quarrels erupted throughout suburban Camden. The only way to peacefully resolve these often bitter conflicts was to allow the local chieftains to have fiefdoms of their own. The decade, therefore, witnessed the strange schizoid behavior of the Republican Party, who on the one hand was aggressively promoting the Greater Camden Movement, while on the other hand was resolving classic road and school appropriation battles by almost doubling the number of municipalities within the county. The truly unique genesis of some of these towns, such as Tavistock, has been dealt with elsewhere in this study. Only the sad commentary on the creation of Berlin Borough and Lawnside warrant additional mention, as they were categorically race-driven decisions, and their configurations are the product of mind sets more readily associated with South African apartheid than with twentieth-century New Jersey. It also must be pointed out that the Ku Klux Klan was marching thousands strong through the streets of Camden in the twenties and burning crosses on the lawns of Catholic convents. The infamous anti-nun bill of 1895, designed to prevent Roman Catholic sisters from teaching classes while garbed in their traditional uniforms or habits, had been sponsored by a Camden County senator.

6. *The Republican machine probably felt that once it had reestablished itself*

in city hall, the existence of all the additional municipalities would constitute nothing more than a minor inconvenience in welding together a Greater Camden political entity, but in truth the goal and focus of the Greater Camden Movement was already shifting by the time immediately preceding the Great Depression.

Instead of a Greater Camden, united under the political domination of the city, the leaders turned their focus to the growing power of the suburbs and the importance of control of the region under whatever administrative format no matter how complex. The onset of the Great Depression should have forced municipalities to ban together in common support, but what ensued was neighbor turning against neighbor with towns seeking relief from the state government as a better alternative than casting their lot with the declining fortunes of Camden City. The mayors of adjoining towns, which had once paid lip service to the Greater Camden idea, now felt it safe to verbalize their constituents' fears of being forced to board what was perceived to be a sinking ship.

The war years caused an economic revival in Camden where its shipyards worked round the clock employing tens of thousands in war-related enterprises. The war also caused demographic shifts that served to intensify the historic divisions within the county based on ethnic, religious, and racial groups.

7. *The war only served as a temporary reprieve for the city, whose ultimate demise was symbolized by the second bridge across the Delaware.*

It must be mentioned that from 1936 to 1959 Camden's strongest asset was the leadership of Mayor George E. Brunner, a man of energy, compassion, and common sense. As discussion of a second bridge heated up during the postwar years, Brunner spoke out against the proposed bridge. He knew that the Benjamin Franklin Bridge, once hailed as the start of a new era, had, in retrospect, been the beginning of the end of a Greater Camden, centered along the waterfront. As mayor, and as the Democratic leader of South Jersey, he argued vigorously and prophetically against the construction of the Walt Whitman Bridge. He predicted accurately, as well, that the new bridge would blight the very heart of the city. Indeed, he has been proven right. However, his warnings were not heeded by the person who mattered most in the deliberations, New Jersey Governor Alfred Driscoll.

It is impossible to escape the irony of the construction of the Walt Whitman Bridge, under the leadership of a Haddonfield native, Governor Driscoll. The tension between the two villages that had reached the boiling point in 1825, with the betrayal of Camden's ambitions by the conservatives of Haddonfield, had resulted in the emergence of the city that would grow and prosper for a hundred years. The decline of the city had been the result of the unforeseen consequences of the first bridge. This time the betrayal came in the form of Driscoll's refusal to stop a project, the consequences of which could be clearly seen. The Harvard-educated governor from Haddonfield wrote the obituary for Camden's dreams, as he refused to listen to the pleas of Mayor Brunner. The drama of the rivalry between Camden and Philadelphia came to an end with the completion of the one-hundred-and-thirty-year cycle of rivalry between Camden and its diminutive and suspicious neighbor to the east.

Camden's fate may accurately be described as tragic. In 1997, its population shrunken to barely 75,000, Camden became an issue in the gubernatorial campaign. The candidate of the Democratic Party, Senator James McGreevey—the candidate who might expect (and did in fact receive) a strong majority in the City of Camden—was criticized for being too candid and forthright in his description of the city. He compared it to the target of aerial bombing raids, or an American Beirut. I thought it refreshing that a candidate would be accused of being too candid. Camden that year had one reported murder for every 380 residents—one must think the highest rate in the allegedly civilized world. Under the circumstances it is strongly felt that maybe the public discourse should, if anything, become more candid and open. Something must be done to save this city and its residents.

Chapter 14

Newark

The Mistakes

Wherever America's cities are going, Newark will get there first.
Former Mayor Kenneth Gibson

$\mathcal{T}$he City of Newark, perpetually a dollar short and a day late, has endured a terrible run of bad luck. Suffering from the same anti-urban bias that afflicted its sister cities, Newark saw its problems compounded by a number of other unique situations, both internal and external.

Looking at other states along the eastern seaboard, one finds that today's major metropolitan areas already were asserting their commanding positions long before the Revolutionary War. Boston, New York, Philadelphia, and Baltimore were the dominant trading and manufacturing centers of their respective areas in 1776, while Newark was merely a large village, with an estimated population of barely a thousand people at that time. By 1800 Newark boasted 4500 residents. But putting that figure into context, one should note that all of Essex County contained 22,000 people in that year and trailed Sussex County as the most populous county, despite still containing all of what is now Union County.

Elizabethtown to the south had an estimated population of an amount nearly equal to Newark's at this time, and a better port as well. It was in the time period of 1800 to 1811 that crucial opportunities between Newark and Elizabeth were missed. During this critical time the merger of the two centers, Newark and Elizabeth, might have been possible. Instead of pooling their resources, the two fledgling cities set upon a protracted and bitter rivalry that failed to resolve itself for generations. The underlying controversies included all the usual suspects—status, religion, economics, and politics. The opposing forces particularly dwelt on questions of loyalty to the new country, and many a rash charge was hurled concerning Tory sympathies. In fact, neither city distinguished itself as being solidly behind the Revolution. And those sympathetic to the Revolution may well have been a minority, but a minority that included legendary heroes, such as Abraham Clark, Elijah Boudinot, Joseph Bloomfield, and the Reverend James Caldwell.

The issues of status and economics were central to the competition. Elizabethtown pointed out, somewhat haughtily, that it was the first capital; the first English-speaking settlement in the state; and the home of a leather industry, a hundred years before John Combs established his tanning operation in Newark. The partisans of Newark, while bristling at such claims, asserted that their founder, Robert Treat, had been in America longer than anyone.

The issues today seem somewhat picayune, but the rivalry was brought to trial by a referendum conducted in 1807 to determine which of the rival sister cities would be the site of the new court house. The judges of the election thought something was askew when more ballots were cast than there were voters. There are actually a range of stories surrounding this momentous election. The referendum was conducted over three days of balloting with the citizens of Elizabeth getting their chance at ballot-stuffing on the first two days. The polls in Newark opened at shortly after midnight on the third day, and the electorate went at their solemn duty with a vengeance.

Under the constitution in effect at the time, the one adopted hastily in Burlington in the summer of 1776, women were eligible to vote. The reports of the process contain extensive allegations of women casting multiple ballots, and men dressed in women's clothing, casting ballots. Some men allegedly exhausted their wives' and daughters' wardrobes, returning to the polls in new outfits on a regular basis throughout the day.

The fight intensified with the additional charges of "cheat" and "fraud" now being added to each side's litany of invective. The neutrality and measured judgment of the judiciary was called upon and the court ruled in favor of Elizabethtown.

Newark, however, exercising its political muscle, arranged to have the new courthouse built there in 1811. Smarting from what they viewed as a terrible miscarriage of justice, the people of Elizabeth continued to maintain their court.

The saddest fallout of this infamous election was that the widespread fraud on both sides was used as the justification for the legislature denying the franchise to women and blacks, notwithstanding the provisions of the State Constitution. African Americans would be denied the privilege to vote in New Jersey, until the adoption of the Fifteenth Amendment to the Constitution; and women would be kept from the polls in political contests until 1920.

Once having established itself as the region's governmental center of gravity, Newark grew rapidly as the commercial center of the region as well. The late-starting leather industry mushroomed. Newark became the largest manufacturer of shoes and harnesses in the country and monopolized the market in the southern states. Before the railroads were even built, sailing vessels from Newark were sending thousands of pairs of shoes to the South.

The tension that persisted was only resolved in 1857 when Union County broke off from Essex County. The City of Newark now boasted a population of 67,000, double the number of all Union County, and representing two out of three residents in Essex County.

The bitter rivalry destroyed the chance for Newark and Elizabethtown to build on one another's strengths. Newark would have benefited from the port facilities of Elizabethtown. All of Union County was more accessible for Newark's expansion than were the western sections of Essex County, separated as they were by imposing mountains. Thus, a united entity would enjoy not merely a decent harbor, but also unimpeded expansion possibilities to the south and southwest. Elizabeth in turn would have benefited from Newark's location on the Passaic River, and its easy accessibility to the raw materials of the northwestern quadrant of the state. However, such an ideal marriage of interests was not meant to be.

Already handicapped by its late start, Newark proceeded to curtail its potential by purposely shrinking its borders. Its inadequate size is dramatically evident by the fact that the bulk of Newark Airport is in Elizabeth. Its opportunities for expansion were severely and myopically curtailed by its willingness to surrender hegemony over Bloomfield (then including Belleville, Montclair, and Glen Ridge) and all the Oranges, East, West, and South. With its land base of less than 24 square miles, Newark never could hope to be a major player in terms of metropolitan areas. In comparison: New York City is 365 square miles, with Manhattan Island being the smallest of the five boroughs with a land mass of 31 square miles—still 25 percent larger than all of Newark. Boston is 48 square miles; Baltimore, 78 square miles; Philadelphia, 130 square miles. Among international capitals, Paris is the smallest at 41 square miles. (Ironically Newark owned areas in the watersheds of northwest Jersey that amounted to treble or quadruple its own size.)

Newark made two additional miscalculations during the period of 1830 to 1860. The first error in judgment concerned the enormous faith it placed in the success of the Morris and Essex Canal. This misplaced confidence probably led to Newark's disdain for Elizabeth and the balance of Union County. The question of the alignment of the canal led to further strife between these two cities, already at each other's throats. Despite the presentation of some cogent arguments, Elizabeth, which desperately wanted to be included in the canal project, was passed over, and the terminus was designated at Newark. Actually the route was a compromise involving Paterson and Newark with Jersey City added as the final partner later. Elizabeth was not even considered as part of this compromise.

Why, after all, would Newark have considered the prospect of expansion to the south or the use of Elizabeth's port? Newark's attitude was that the new center of commercial life would be concentrated on the banks of the Passaic River and its additional access to the west via this canal. Why even worry about the loss of the Orange Mountain and the land beyond? Trade by roads through that mountain range would be obviated by the construction of the canal, whose barges could haul a hundred more times coal and iron than could be transported in a day by wagon. The canal would transport the mineral wealth of the west to the doorstep of Newark.

Work on the canal began in 1826, with over a thousand Irish diggers employed. The engineering was difficult—the ground was hard in many places, and Lake Hopatcong, the source of the water for the canal, sits almost a thousand feet above the sea level at the Newark tidewater. Water began to flow in the summer of 1829, and the first coal barge from all the way at Phillipsburg on the Delaware made the five-day journey in 1832. The impact that the canal initially had on the city should not be underestimated. The population of the city virtually doubled from ten to twenty thousand in the first six years of the canal's operation.

The Morris and Essex Canal struggled for decades and really did not expire until after World War I. However, it never could sustain its competitive position after the east-west train routes were opened across New Jersey. It was inflexible in that it was designed primarily for the transport of commodities, and not passengers. But most devastating to its future was the fact that a barge took five days to travel the same distance a freight train could cover in six or seven hours. Under any circumstances, the canal certainly fell short of expectations. What minor short-term advantage it gave to Newark was vastly outweighed by the terrible nuisance the canal became. The canal was ultimately bought by the Lehigh Valley Railroad Company, who claimed that they would use the canal to augment their extensive operations, but who really wanted to snuff out any vestiges of competition of its coal-hauling monopoly. What had been dreamt of as a trophy, elevating Newark to premier status among New Jersey's cities, ironically became a filthy ditch languishing in the heart of Newark. Ultimately, the bed of the canal was innovatively converted into the Newark subway system by one of Newark's most visionary and hardworking mayors, Thomas L. Raymond.

Perhaps the strangest turn of events is that Elizabeth—which coveted the canal and was left empty-handed—shared only in the canal's destruction. Much of the fill excavated from the bed of the canal to make it deep enough for the proposed subway was hauled to the site of the new airport, where it was used to fill in the meadows to provide for adequate runways. Most of those runways are in the City of Elizabeth.

Newark's second profound miscalculation involved its overly pessimistic view of the impact of the Civil War. Perhaps because of its close economic ties to the South, Newark was late in realizing that what had appeared to be the disastrous loss of its markets was really an opportunity to diversify its products and markets.

Thirteen years after the Civil War, Joseph Atkinson wrote *A History of Newark: A Narrative of Its Rise and Progress,* which was published to much acclaim, by William B. Guild of Newark. By page 313, the author suggests that the city do a little soul-searching. He comments, "The city (in 1878) is yet unable to attract the eye of the visitor with a single imposing public building. It has no art gallery, no public statues, no monuments or fountains. Out of about one hundred and twenty miles of streets there are paved only twenty-two miles, and even that extent is wretchedly paved in the main." Some were saying that Newark's day in the sun was over. The nay-sayers fell into two categories: those who said Newark was too close to New York ever to allow it to become a great city, and those who pointed out that the areas that were once Newark's major markets were now manufacturing for themselves and no longer needed Newark's goods.

Atkinson sees Newark's future as being inextricably linked to the fate of New York City. If, in his words, New York is to become the "monster warehouse—the grand bazaar of the continent," then it will need Newark as the "adjacent workshop, correspondingly extensive."

As to the second argument of declining markets, Atkinson already sees "the clouds breaking and the silvery linings beginning to peep out as harbingers of hope and cheer." He has now hit full stride and is ready to give his prescription for gratifying results: "frugality in the cost of local government, securing a low rate of taxation and cheap rents—liberal encouragement to manufacturing capitalists." If his advice is followed, he sees the not-so-distant day when "the vacant spaces between the towns of Essex and Union Counties are built up; when Newark and Elizabeth will be practically united, and when Newark the happy home of a third of a million people is the seat of industrial art famed the world over."

This is an extremely interesting perspective in that it reflects, for all its optimism, a very limited horizon. Newark is not to be the shining city on the hill, but must be satisfied to be the backroom workshop of New York. The city must content itself, not with being a center of learning or the state's cultural and governmental hub; its goal, instead, must be to acquire fame for its industrial arts.

This particular history was widely read and broadly quoted. It became a self-fulfilling prophecy for Newark. It sold the potential of the city short.

Newark drew back to itself a modicum of the property it had jettisoned with such liberality. Parts of Clinton Township (Irvington) were reannexed in 1869, 1897, and 1902; the area known as Woodside was brought back in 1871, and the Vailsburg section was incorporated into Newark in 1905. By that time it was too late to undertake a significant consolidation effort that would have given Newark some room to grow. As early as the end of the Civil War, Newark's neighbors were considering themselves far too good to allow themselves to be invaded by the denizens of Newark, even if they were just passing through on their way to an afternoon in the countryside of the Caldwells. The residents on the western hills of Essex County considered themselves elevated not merely by altitude, but much more importantly, by social status. Newark had boxed itself in geographically and socially.

Regrettably, Newark realized it was necessary to expand only after witnessing the successful efforts of New York City to consolidate its five boroughs in 1898. Newark set out on three separate occasions to annex regions it had divested in the past. Referendums were conducted in 1903 and 1908 to annex Irvington, and in 1904 an effort was made to retrieve what still remained of Bloomfield. These efforts failed and it is difficult to find anyone active in Essex County politics today who has even the vaguest notion that Newark had once set out to reclaim lost territory, in order to establish itself as an adequate rival to New York.

That Newark's efforts at annexation failed is a factual certainty, but the legislature's attitude toward annexation between 1899 and 1903 is not so certain; although two alternative and reasonable hypotheses are possible. Indeed the legislature changed its mind about annexation after the session of 1899. During that session, both houses had adopted a measure that was known as Chapter 157 of the Public Laws of that year. Its two brief paragraphs simply read:

1. The town of Stockton, in the County of Camden and the territory embraced therein shall be and hereby is annexed to the City of Camden, in the said County of *Camden: provided,* that nothing herein contained shall in any way effect or impair any contract or contracts heretofore made by and between the town of Stockton and any persons or persons, corporation or corporations.

2. This act shall take effect immediately.

The citizens of Stockton went to sleep on the evening of March 24, 1899, and awoke the next morning as citizens of Camden City. This proved most disturbing to Mr. Peter Greenwalt, who had gone to bed being the treasurer of Stockton and awoke unemployed. So disturbed was Mr. Greenwalt that he refused the demand of Richard R. Miller, the treasurer of the City of Camden, that the records of Stockton Town be turned over to him, forthwith. From this refusal stems the matter of *Miller v. Greenwalt*, 64 N.J.L. 197. This matter involved the request of Mr. Miller that a writ of mandamus issue, compelling Greenwalt to surrender the records. Greenwalt was probably doubly offended by the sepulchral tone adopted by the city of Camden's pleadings, which referred to him as the "late treasurer." He fought back, claiming the action of the legislature was unconstitutional. The case was argued on June 6, 1899, before Justices Dixon and Collins of the state's Supreme Court, and Justice Collins issued the opinion of the court, after the legislative elections, on November 13, 1899.

The opinion resolves the dispute in the course of the first two sentences: "The challenged statute is, we think, constitutional. The power of creating municipal corporations is inherent and exclusive in the legislative department of the government," wrote the court.

This is about as straightforward and empowering as any legislature could ever wish. The matter was not appealed to the state's highest court, the Court of Errors and Appeals, and therefore this language stands as the official pronouncement on the issue of legislative powers. Camden's legislative delegation of Senator Herbert W. Johnson and the assemblymen William Bradley, John McMurray, and Edgar Coles must have been extremely gratified.

In this same session, Essex had a delegation in the Assembly that was four times as great as Camden's, yet no bill was introduced to annex any territory to Newark by legislative fiat. Foster M. Voorhees was the governor—a Republican—a former assemblyman, senator, senate president—a man who knew well, and was sympathetic to legislative machinations. Moreover, the Republicans had a powerful grip on the legislature. The question must be asked: Why did Newark not act in concert with Camden and logroll an omnibus annexation package?

In 1900, three bills were signed into law that shed some light about annexation legislation. On page 152 of the Public Laws of 1900 is found a supplement to the annexation law. The adoption of this law clarified some of the problems that had occurred in Camden's swallowing of Stockton. The early date of its adoption in the session and the long delay in the Supreme Court's decision in the Greenwalt case, the previous year, lead one to believe that the final outcome of the litigation was a worrisome matter to the political forces of South Jersey. It also makes me very suspicious as to why no additional annexation by legislative fiat was attempted after 1900, but we will deal with those suspicions subsequently.

Comforted by the new legislation, the City of Trenton made two annexations later in the same legislative session. The first acquisition gave Trenton a portion of Ewing Township, and before final adjournment Trenton also annexed a portion of Hamilton Township. These would be the last pieces of the mosaic of Trenton, which had previously annexed Wilbur Township in 1898 and both Chambersburg and Millham in 1888; all three were accomplished by legislation as opposed to a referendum of any type. Most important to note is that after these bills, no further annexations of this type ever took place, despite the amendment to the annexation law.

Perhaps, the Essex delegation, headed by its distinguished senator, Thomas N. McCarter, felt confident that with the annexation statute strengthened, Newark could take its time. Perhaps Newark thought it best to wait until other expected court challenges had been resolved. That certainly would have been a sensible approach. Neither Ewing nor Hamilton challenged the annexations by Trenton.

The time for annexations by Newark appears to have been extremely ripe. The state's second-highest court had provided its imprimatur in firm and unequivocal terms. Moreover in the session of 1900 the annexation law was bolstered, ratified, and confirmed. Republicans held two-to-one majorities in both houses. If ever there were to be a time for Newark to reestablish its historic borders, that time was at the beginning of the twentieth century when Newark was at its economic and political peak.

Newark waited until 1903 to have legislation adopted for the annexation of Irvington Town. What a difference a few years made—from the time of the Camden and Trenton annexation laws. Chapter 99 of the Public Laws of 1903 calls for the annexation by Newark of Irvington—*provided that the voters of Irvington approve the proposition at their next election, and the voters of Newark approve the question at the election following that.* The transition from annexation by legislative fiat to annexation only by a legislative and local obstacle course was a radical change in public policy.

The legislative obstacle course was prescribed for the annexation of Bloomfield in Chapter 65 of the Public Laws of 1904. The law even set the date for a special election to be held in Bloomfield on a Thursday, April 7, 1904—and then, only if it were to pass in Bloomfield would the annexation be considered by Newark.

In 1908, the legislature adopted Chapter 257, which provided for one more attempt to annex Irvington. This time the voters of Irvington still had to approve the annexation, and if it were to pass, then only the governing body of Newark, and not its voters, must consent to the annexation by adoption of an ordinance.

The question of what happened in those critical years between 1900 and 1903 is intriguing with two possible theories that can be put forth to explain events. By 1900 in South Jersey the political star of General Sewell was in slight decline. Sewell had been the dominant Republican in statewide affairs for a period spanning two decades. However, the party over which he presided was a "Legislative" party. The Democrats were the party that controlled the governorship. The Republicans in North Jersey had deferred to Sewell for many years, and the first challenge to his leadership was easily rebuffed. That initial challenge had been mounted by a man named Franklin Murphy.

Best known as an extremely wealthy manufacturer of varnish, Murphy had built his business over the years after the Civil War. He was also very interested in public service and was elected to the City Council of Newark in 1883. He rose to become the president of the Council in 1886, by which time he was also serving in the Assembly and as a charter member of the Essex County Parks Commission. In addition, he was active as a director of various banks and other corporations and associations.

In 1892, his persistence paid off in his election to the chairmanship of the Republican State Committee. That, of course, was not the best year to be a Republican, as New Jersey's own Democrat Grover Cleveland led his party to victory at every level. However, the ensuing excesses of the Democrats triggered a backlash of tidal-wave proportions, and the Republicans were successful in electing John Griggs governor in 1895, and William McKinley president in 1896.

Both of these men were very impressed with the fine work done by Newark businessman Franklin Murphy. President McKinley offered him a number of positions, including the ambassadorship to the Imperial Court of Russia. Murphy declined, but accepted the president's appointment as Special Delegate to the Universal Exposition in Paris. The North Jersey Republicans were in the ascendancy not only within the state, but also in the nation. Garrett Hobart had been McKinley's running mate. Governor Griggs resigned that position to become the attorney-general of the United States, and was succeeded by Foster Voorhees of Union County, who as president of the Senate became acting governor. Murphy, for his part, became a member of the Republican National Committee in 1900, replacing Garret Hobart, who had met an untimely death. This was still a year prior to the death of Senator William Sewell, who apparently coveted the seat on the National Committee.

Acting Governor Voorhees, blocked by the Constitution from succeeding himself, did the smart thing, and resigned so that he could be elected to a full term, which would not expire until January 1902. In departing from the governor's office, Voorhees turned the duties of the state's chief executive over to Franklin Murphy.

If ever there were a time for Newark to fulfill any intentions for territory restoration, it was during Murphy's tenure. To the wealth of benefits that Newark enjoyed in having the largest and wealthiest city, was added one of their own in the governor's chair, and a legislative delegation that was experienced and able. In the common vernacular of present-day politics, Newark possessed enormous clout.

Why then do we find this insipid special bill providing for the annexation of Irvington only after the proposal has been approved by a vote by the residents of both communities? The first answer may lie in the decade-long Murphy-Sewell struggle over control of the Republican Party. In that battle, Murphy had championed greater participation in the decision-making process. Franklin Murphy was as stalwart a Republican as the state has ever seen. In Newark—then throughout Essex County—and finally statewide, he was Mr. Republican, but he rose on the strength of his advocacy of more democracy. He was a small "d" Democrat, whose most enduring contribution to the state's political system during his three years in the governor's office was to reform the primary elections. Murphy believed that the people, not local and county political bosses, should be an indispensable part of the process.

The outcry from the Democrats was enormous, and every succeeding Democratic nominee, up to and including Woodrow Wilson, promised repeal of the "direct primary" reforms of Governor Murphy. To his credit, Wilson after his election recognized the merits of Murphy's efforts and left the primary reforms in tact.

Murphy rarely gets the credit he deserves. Too often he is dismissed unfairly and inaccurately as just another wealthy businessman who parlayed his fortune into political position. Besides having created an Essex County park system of the highest standards—a lasting monument to his vision—he was an early environmentalist, calling for measures to stop the rampant pollution of the Passaic River. He was compassionate toward those suffering from disease and personally generous to his Civil War comrades-in-arms.

Critical to the issue at hand is that Murphy led by example. As a successful businessman, he used regular audits to enforce accountability in his own firm, and therefore, he insisted that audits be routinely performed on the various departments of state government. At his factory, employee safety was preeminent, and thus he imposed stricter rules for factory inspection throughout the state. The day after his inauguration he showed up for work at the state house, and was shocked to find that no one else joined him until around lunch time. This story reminds me of the person who asked the question, "How many people work in the governor's office?" and got the answer, "Oh, about half." He set the example in his own work habits and made the political process practice what he preached. He would not allow a city, even his own, to annex a neighbor by a legislative fiat. That might have been tolerated—even encouraged—by the likes of Sewell, but Murphy would not condone such heavy-handed manipulations. He campaigned promising the people a greater role in the political process, and he stayed true to his principles.

It was Murphy's adherence to his beliefs in the democratic process that forced the change from forced annexations to consolidation by referendum. Murphy's commitment to change manifested itself with the Republican organization. Murphy repudiated boss Lentz, the chairman of the Republican Essex County Committee, whose old-fashioned methods the governor regarded as repugnant to his more open and participatory ways. Murphy also encouraged a new breed of leaders in the Republican ranks of Essex—men such as Colby and Colgate, who would go on to champion some of the governor's electoral reforms, along with other "new ideas" that were a bit too progressive, even for Murphy.

Once again Newark acted too late. If Newark struck while the annexation iron was hot at the turn of the century, it may have imposed its brand on Irvington and Bloomfield and had enough political muscle to have reacquired the bulk of the county. By the time Republican Murphy with his democratic ideals became governor, it was already too late; the opportunity had passed.

The alternate theory as to why Newark blew its chances is less idealistic and more startling in its consequences. The legislature contained a number of extremely able and intelligent men. The Senate alone was graced by a future member of the United States Supreme Court, Mahlon Pitney. He was joined by Thomas N. McCarter, one of the most distinguished attorneys in the history of the state. They may have known all along that the annexation of Stockton by Camden, as well as the annexations for Trenton in 1900, were categorically unconstitutional. They also would have known that the decision in the *Miller* case was wrong. It was simply bad law, and if Greenwalt had had the resources to pursue an appeal to the Court of Errors and Appeals, he would probably have won.

The legislature, between 1875 when the constitution had been amended and 1900, had ignored the fact that it could no longer pass bills that affected the internal operations of a specific community—without resorting to the formula of classifications to make the laws "general," instead of "special." The decision of Justice Collins in the *Miller* case was as tortured as it was delayed.

Five things must be pointed out as evidence that the unconstitutionality of annexation by legislative fiat was common knowledge:

- First, the inordinate amount of time taken by the court in deciding on the issuance of a writ of mandamus. Given the nature of the issue involved, one would have anticipated a prompt, if not immediate, resolution of the question raised.
- Second, the court uses the conditional modifying phrase "we think" in its decision, rather than asserting that the act simply "is constitutional."
- Third, the court relies on references to the sovereignty of the legislature, and avoids referring to the specific prohibition of such laws contained in the clear language of the 1875 amendment to the constitution.
- Fourth, the matter was not appealed to the Court of Errors and Appeals, yet the next legislature felt compelled to attempt to buttress the existing annexation statute.
- Fifth, no attempt was made to annex a municipality, or a part thereof, against its will, by legislative fiat, after 1900.

The legislature was content to keep the lid on this particular Pandora's box. Having escaped without a dispositive ruling from the highest court on its annexation methods, the legislature did not wish to provide the vehicle for another test case. The risks were too great, and there was too much at stake. The high court was probably equally as happy to avoid the question of forced annexations. The clear wording of the constitution, as amended, left little room to maneuver—except for the same misplaced reliance on the nebulous concept of sovereignty to which Justice Collins had resorted in *Miller*. The consequences of overturning that wrong decision were frightening, as they would require the dismantling of Trenton and Camden. If this second theory were to be correct, then the consequences of the unconstitutional annexations of Chambersburg by Trenton and Stockton by Camden must remain troubling to this day.

Whatever the accurate interpretation of the facts may be, the outcome was plain and simple for Newark—the city now was faced with insurmountable hurdles in its attempts to obtain more territory by voluntary consolidations. The experience with the Morris and Essex Canal left a "once-burnt attitude" in its wake. Newark did not turn to the sea in a major way again until the eve of World War I. Newark started too late on the harbor project and the widening of the channel. One gets the sense that the efforts with regard to port development were the result of: 1. the disappointment in the failure of the Morris and Essex Canal; and 2. a nostalgic desire to return to the days when water-borne commerce had provided such an enormous boost to the economy. Compounding the interest in turning eastward to the harbor was the fact that Newark now knew that the harbor was the last open frontier; expansion to the south (Elizabeth), the west (Irvington), and the north (Bloomfield) were foreclosed.

Newark experienced a tremendous surge during the period of World War I and the decade that followed. It was by far the most populous and the wealthiest city in the state. It contained thousands of industries and businesses and had a tax base that represented over 10 percent of the entire real estate value of the state. The economic base was serviced by a new airport, hundreds of bus routes, a subway system, and six separate railroad lines that shipped the goods manufactured in Newark to every state in the nation.

In Newark's case those same rail lines provided an escape route for laborers in western Pennsylvania, West Virginia, and Kentucky, who had to face the Great Depression's powerful and painful lessons: oil was replacing what demand still existed for coal, and machines could mine cheaper and faster than the most determined man with pick and shovel.

There no longer existed opportunities for laborers no matter how swift the hand or strong the back. Whether whites were disgorged from the mines of Appalachia or blacks were thrown off the fields of the south, they came north depositing into the city, a diaspora of the economically, educationally, and socially disadvantaged.

Newark, which had absorbed such an enormous labor pool in the past, had become a magnet and found itself deluged with a new and unexpected migration of fellow Americans. These were not the pools of cheap labor that had been earlier welcomed for their exploitability, coming from Ireland, Italy, and the empires of the Hapsburgs, and the Romanovs. The lingering aftereffects of the Depression, the mechanization and early suburbanization of industry, and an ever-increasing role of government in social programs had changed all that. The war effort starting as early as 1939 provided only temporary relief for the first wave of the migration.

To Newark's credit, it remained an open city, refusing to block the influx of African Americans as other communities did. A sad aspect of the military buildup is seen in the employment patterns of North Jersey. While the dirty, dangerous munitions and armaments industries of Morris County provided employment, no collateral housing opportunities were provided. Convoys of buses shuttled black workers from their dangerous jobs loading munitions in Morris to the tenements where they slept in Newark. The economic activity of World War II and the Korean conflict provided enough income for the first wave, which had consisted of the mobile and employable, to have sufficient resources to underwrite a second wave of migration, which brought to the northeast corridor, primarily Newark, those who were previously stranded and often lacking any skills.

Newark failed to plan for the rapidly changing demographics and for the postwar realities of declining industries, suburbanization, population shifts, and new transportation modes. This led inevitably to the serious problems Newark encountered in the late 1960s. The problem was most clearly articulated by one of the most able and intelligent men that ever blessed Newark—Felix Fuld.

The partner of Louis Bamberger, Fuld helped build a merchandising empire centered in Newark. His leadership, energy, vision, and generosity are legendary. The following is taken from *New Jersey: A History*, published in the late 1920s.

> Mr. Fuld saw for the future a much greater Newark than that existing today. On occasion he pointed out the need for greater cooperation between Newark and its existing suburbs in working out the problems presented. "The contrast between Newark and some of the municipalities abroad is striking when one gets back," he remarked upon returning from his last European trip. "I was surprised. Newark is growing. There is no doubt of that, but that growth is spasmodic, here and there, with no apparent effort at planning." Far-seeing planning, he considered the outstanding need of the city.

To summarize the missed opportunities:

1. Newark and Elizabeth started with sufficient territory, as opposed to Trenton, Camden, Jersey City, and Paterson, which started small and tried to expand. However, both allowed themselves to shrink and shrink significantly.
2. Newark and Elizabeth from the outset considered themselves rivals, so that the natural religious and ethnic tensions exacerbated driving a wedge between areas that should have been pooling resources.
3. Newark caused an irreparable breach in its relations with Elizabeth by insisting that it become the county seat in disregard of Elizabeth's historic position.
4. At the same time as it was insisting on recognition as the administrative center of the county, Newark was allowing the prime areas of the Oranges and Bloomfield to become independent.
5. Newark placed too much reliance on the Morris and Essex Canal. It once again insisted that it be the terminus of the canal, further foreclosing its relationship with Elizabeth. The canal, after an initial boost to the economy of Newark, ultimately proved to be a significant handicap to the rational development of the central city, and finally discouraged growth in its vicinity because of the its derelict condition.
6. Newark continued to play out the self-fulfilling prophecy that it would be the backroom workshop for New York's role as the "bazaar of the world."
7. When it finally became obvious that it must expand, Newark—for a variety of reasons—failed to take part in the annexation-by-legislative fiat that allowed other cities to add territory in the 1880s and 1890s. Governor Murphy, a Newark native, was an electoral reformer who disapproved of annexation by fiat. Newark's efforts to annex Irvington and Bloomfield were made subject to referendums that failed. The alternative theory is that after 1900, it

became obvious that annexation by legislative fiat was unconstitutional. Either way, Newark's efforts at enlargement were thwarted.

8. The city started extremely late in attempting to create a cultural infrastructure. Although the effort of the city in constructing its library, museum, and parks was impressive it was also very late in happening.

9. The city assumed that its growth and development would never end, and therefore eschewed major long-term planning efforts until such efforts became moot.

*I*t is impossible to leave this subject without some comment on the recent history of Newark. I must confess that having attended law school there and taken the bar exam in the summer of 1967 at the height of the civil disturbances, I arrived in the legislature with some strong opinions and misconceptions about the city. While return to its once-dominant position is improbable, Newark has made a remarkable recovery. I've worked personally with two of Newark's finest mayors: Sharpe James and Ken Gibson. I found both men to be hard-working, sincere, and committed to the revival of their community. They both made enormous strides in the face of overwhelming obstacles. Occasionally those obstacles included suburban legislators such as myself during my first few terms in office. I want to take a final moment and pay tribute to the memory of the man who sensitized me to the real Newark and removed the blinders that hindered me in perceiving what needed to be done to assist the city. My friend and colleague Michael Adubato represented the city in Trenton for eighteen years. The city never had a prouder son or better advocate.

CHAPTER 15

Jersey City

THE EXPLOITED VICTIM

It is not really a place so much as it is a way of thinking.
Joseph Sullivan

*I*n 1998, the State of New Jersey, represented by the attorney general, entered the Supreme Court of the United States to continue an argument with the State of New York that began in 1664. This most recent round in the ongoing dispute about the ownership of Ellis Island centered on the nagging controversy over which jurisdiction has the right to impose and collect sales tax on the souvenirs sold there.

The island once consisted of a speck of land—about three and half acres—when the tide was low. There was no debate over the fact that New York owned those 3.5 acres, but over the past 160 years, the island had been supplemented by 20 acres of dredged fill. The original commission that had established the boundary had acknowledged ownership by New Jersey of all the lands under the water surrounding Ellis Island. New Jersey's argument, as presented to the highest court, was that the additional 20 acres of dry ground belongs to New Jersey. This land is particularly valuable, not only for the sales tax revenues paid by the visitors, but also for the nostalgic aura associated with this historic site. The justices in Washington agreed with New Jersey.

In 1664, no one, least of all King Charles II and his brother James, spent much time reflecting on this issue. The king had granted to James, Duke of York, all the lands between the Connecticut River and the Delaware River, i.e., all of present-day New York and New Jersey. The duke wasted little time conveying a substantial portion of this property, specifically the area between the Hudson River and the Delaware, to his friends, Berkeley and Carteret. However, when James conveyed the land between the Hudson and the Delaware, it is unclear whether he meant from the east bank of the Hudson, the west bank of the Hudson, or from the center of the river.

The transfer raised many questions:

- Was the nature of the title held by James altered in 1685, when he himself became king of England?
- Were his proprietary rights to New York, that he had held by grant from his royal brother, enlarged by his own elevation to sovereignty?
- Did the riparian rights he held as sovereign between 1685 and 1688 merge with his proprietary rights, giving him all the lands under the flowing water of the Hudson River and the tidewaters of the bay?
- What effect did this potential merger of interests have on the transfers James already made to Berkeley and Carteret?

Neither the colonial governors of New York nor its legislature could be bothered with the complex issues. They were convinced that the duke had been profligate in deeding a portion of his property to his friends Berkeley and Carteret. To compensate for his extravagance, the legislators minimized the deeding by interpreting that the grant to Berkeley and Carteret started at the west shore of the Hudson. The early powers-that-were in New York considered that the Hudson River continued beyond the harbor and that it actually flowed down the Kill Van Kull. Therefore, New York owned everything to the high-water mark in places such as Elizabeth Town, Woodbridge, and Perth Amboy.

The issue originally arose in the context of the free-port status of Perth Amboy. If the Kill Van Kull were simply an extension of the Hudson River, then customs duties were payable in New York for ships entering the port of Perth Amboy. Once it was determined that Perth Amboy, the capital of East Jersey, was actually on the Raritan Bay, the issue became moot. It reared its head again when Robert Fulton got his steamboat up the Hudson to Albany in 1807.

In recognition of his accomplishment, the New York legislature awarded to Fulton and his chief financial backer, Robert Livingston, a monopoly on water traffic in the New York Harbor. Fulton began building steamboats in the Paulus Hook section of Bergen Township, an area that would become downtown Jersey City. Livingston concentrated on enforcing the New York monopoly, and forcing ferry operators located in New Jersey to pay a licensing fee or run the risk of having their crafts seized by law-enforcement officers in New York.

The New Jersey legislature responded to the New York monopoly by granting its own monopoly in 1811 to Aaron Ogden, who for many years operated sailing vessels between Elizabeth Town and New York and thus was familiar with the harbor. In current parlance, push came to shove. The New York courts stoutly defended the Fulton-Livingston monopoly, while the New Jersey courts just as adamantly claimed that Ogden held valid rights granted by New Jersey. Ogden folded, and, rather than run the risk of having his vessels impounded when reaching New York, he agreed to pay Livingston a licensing fee. As part of the franchise, Ogden also agreed to defend the Livingston-Fulton monopoly against any upstart competitors attempting to operate from New Jersey.

Then Thomas Gibbons, a former partner of Ogden's, hired the young Cornelius Vanderbilt to captain his unlicensed steamboat from New Jersey to New

York. For seventeen years, the New York monopoly had exercised total political, economic, and commercial hegemony over the shared harbor before the issue came before the U.S. Supreme Court. In a decision that usually finds its way into the first fifty pages of any text on constitutional law, Chief Justice John Marshall in 1824 wrote that the authors of the Constitution had intended that only the Congress could regulate interstate commerce, and the New York monopoly was therefore unenforceable.

Nine years later both states appointed commissioners to determine their mutual boundary line. In 1834, each state ratified the recommendations, including the fact that Ellis Island (pre-landfilling) would continue under the jurisdiction of New York. The members of the commission had made great progress in resolving the dispute arising from the untidy draftsmanship of the Royal Grants of 1664, but left enough open issues to warrant New Jersey's most recent trip back to court.

The Court's decision in *Ogden v. Gibbon* led to the Inter-state Boundary Agreement of 1834. These actions, as salutary as they were, did nothing to compensate for decades of treating the west bank of the Hudson like a step-child—a mere outpost—a satellite of the city on Manhattan Island. Moreover the commissioners had only resolved that the west bank of the Hudson was located in New Jersey; they had not dealt with the serious problem of who owned the land along the riverbank. The issues of ownership, control, access, and development would plague Jersey City, and retard its rational growth, for the next fifty years.

For those next fifty years the railroad would serve as the principal enemy of Jersey City by thwarting any aspirations Jersey City might have entertained of becoming a first-class city—perhaps a shocking contention, but one that is difficult to contradict. The story of nineteenth-century Jersey City is the story of its victimization. The railroads, from their initial charters in the 1830s to the passage of the Railroad Tax Act of 1884, paid virtually no taxes to the city. They had bought up almost a quarter of the land in Jersey City and held it tax free during this period. Finally, the railroad companies attempted to steal the Jersey City waterfront, filled it in with garbage, and then paid only nominal values for this priceless property to the state and not to the city.

In a knock-down blow, the railroads turned their vast holdings within the city into a veritable jungle of steel, tangled with lines, sidings, crossings, switches, and switch-backs—all built at grade. This made the laying out of street patterns difficult, and the streets themselves treacherous to traffic. Atlases indicate that the principal vector of all the rail lines was toward the tidewater of the Hudson River. These lines bifurcated the community—they fractured and paralyzed the development of the city.

Long forgotten now is the extraordinary foresight exhibited by Alexander Hamilton in 1804, when he persuaded the state's legislature to authorize the formation of a stock company known as The Associates of the Jersey Company. This company held the ferry franchise across the Hudson, as well as controlled the prime upland and the principal riparian rights of a huge stretch of waterfront. These lands and the rights attached to them would be pivotal in the development of Jersey City.

Not surprisingly, the owners of the 100 shares of this company included a number of governors and relatives of governors. New Jersey Railroad and Transportation Company acquired these rights and then merged into the United Railroads of New Jersey, which then leased all of their tracks and tidewater riparian rights to the Pennsylvania Railroad. The significance of all this is that Jersey City could not reach its own waterfront. Decades of attempts to extend city streets in an easterly direction to the tidewater were thwarted by the railroads. The railroads continually won in court because the justices upheld the 1804 grant to Hamilton's company from the legislature.

As if this were not sufficiently horrendous, the period immediately after the Civil War saw the commencement of a legal battle that occasionally spilled out of the corporate board rooms and into the streets and along the tracks. It is usually referred to as the "battle of the basin." This term refers to the basin of the Morris and Essex Canal. The protracted and complex story has been recounted so well by many others that it serves no purpose to attempt to expand on the excellent work by such writers as William Sackett, Robert Fleming, and John Cunningham. A particularly detailed account of the fight is provided by Barbara Kalata, who wrote the history of the canal entitled *A Hundred Years a Hundred Miles*.

The continuing fight over the canal and over the rights to bridge the canal by rail or by street made up the hottest fight that transpired in Jersey City for the course of the next forty years. The battle reached its zenith in 1879 to 1880, when Jersey City insisted that candidates take a pledge supporting legislation to close the gap or at the very least bridge the gap to join the main part of the city to the southern section of Greenville, which had been annexed to the city in the early 1870s. The city had nowhere to grow. The Morris Canal's minor width yawned like the Grand Canyon, creating an impregnable barrier to the city's logical expansion.

The city was stymied by selfish motives of the Canal Company, now under the control of the Lehigh Valley Railroad. What jumps out from every account of the great battle of the basin is that the railroads gave no thought or consideration to the welfare of the city. The only consideration was the advantage that they might gain over their competitors. Although the city on one or more occasion was allied in its agenda with both the Central Railroad of New Jersey and/or the Baltimore and Ohio Railroad, these alliances were for the railroads' convenience only, with no thought given to the city's real needs.

Its expansion to the south effectively blocked by the intransigence of the railroads and the canal company, Jersey City had the alternative to turn its orientation to the north. Here again the railroads either blocked logical expansion or failed in their own efforts to build a viable operation along a north-south axis. The one great breakout to the north occurred when a rail line starting in Weehawken made its bid to become a dominant and unifying vehicle. If it had succeeded, an entirely different fate might have awaited Jersey City and the other Hudson County communities.

One of the best shots Jersey City ever had at the brass ring was thwarted in the 1880s by the Vanderbilt clique of railroad barons in New York. The Erie Railroad was allowed to leave Jersey City and head for Buffalo, but the attempts to run a logical and rational course up the west side of the Hudson to Kingston and Albany was unmercifully quashed by the men who controlled the monopoly on the highly profitable Harlem Line and the Central Railroad of New York. They gambled their fortunes on the success of the easterly side of the Hudson route and backed up their wager by buying enormous amounts of land along the route. The stakes were too high for William H. Vanderbilt, son of the commodore, to run the risk of finding himself in the unaccustomed position of losing. After all, his father had fought many a battle in New Jersey and won. Most notably the commodore had prevailed in the first battle of this railroad war for the control of the Erie Railroad. That fight had pitted Daniel Drew against Commodore Vanderbilt, and included setting up "war rooms" and command posts on various sides of the Hudson. Vanderbilt won that legendary fight, which took place in the 1860s.

Twenty years later, the attempts of the West Shore Railroad were as ambitious and daring as those of any who had ever challenged the Vanderbilts by trying to break their stranglehold on the Mid-Atlantic railroad lines. The west shore faced three overwhelming problems:

- the engineering challenge presented by the Palisades themselves;
- the raising of sufficient capital;
- the ability to muster the staying power necessary to sustain the new line against the inevitable price war that was the established rail lines' tactic of choice, and a hallmark of the Vanderbilts.

The *New York Times* published an editorial on May 27, 1883, suggesting that the West Shore was in for a real battle. First, it would be tough for them to draw business away from the Central, which had been working for forty years. Second, the Central had established an enormous corporation with all sorts of connections through its vast interests. Finally, "the Central could starve that road into bankruptcy if only it chose to pay the cost of doing it."

Vanderbilt needed no coaching from the *Times*. He had already declared his own private and corporate war on the upstarts in New Jersey. He was outspoken in his contempt for the new West Shore Line, and gave the Herodesque order to "crush this competitor in the cradle." When it was rumored that the fledgling West Shore was ready to sell out to Vanderbilt's competitors, the railroad baron was equally candid in sharing with the public his opinions and strategy.

> The Central can pay as much as anybody, I guess, but if some one else wants the West Shore, he must understand that the war is not yet settled, and will not be until we have the West Shore. We would just as leave fight these men, and perhaps, rather, if they have some money. This fighting a bankrupt railroad is tedious work, I tell you, but no one shall buy the West Shore to make money out of us, and they shall not have any of our roads until we have that one.

I tell you, I look on the West Shore Road just as I would on a man whose hand I had found in my money drawer—a common miserable thief.

The New York Supreme Court ordered the sale of the bankrupt railroad for not less than $22 million, and on November 24, 1885, the West Shore, less than three years in operation, was sold to Vanderbilt's associates, J. Pierpont Morgan, Chauncey M. Depew, and Ashbel Green, for the minimum price required. This action completed Vanderbilt's acquisitions of potential competitors and ended any chance of a connection between Hudson County and Albany other than by ferry.

In spite of the havoc wreaked upon the city by the railroads, the canal company, and the state government, Jersey City has managed to succeed. Unquestionably, many of the problems it experienced—the graft and corruption, the payroll padding, and the nepotism—Jersey City brought on itself. However, several other New Jersey cities prospered, notwithstanding the foibles and larcenies of their mayors. Jersey City's fate as a second-rate contender cannot be attributed to the venality of its succession of colorful and questionable leaders.

However, a major consolidation effort of the nineteenth century turned into a disaster and left everyone with misgivings about the alleged virtues of growth. This first major consolidation effort came after the Civil War, and was sponsored by the all the wrong people—for all the wrong reasons. The reasons for the proposed consolidations were complex, but were essentially driven by those who wished to dilute the growing strength of the Democrats in Jersey City by annexing adjoining areas that voted Republican. Ancillary motivations included the expectation that the bridging of the Morris Canal would take place in the immediate future and open up great opportunities in the area of Greenville and Communipaw. The Jersey City consolidation story—predictably—involves road expenses, corruption, and unintended consequences.

The towns of Bergen, Hudson City, and Greenville Township were all incorporated into the City of Jersey City between 1869 and 1873—about the same time as the attempted riparian giveaways and the Republican-sponsored state takeover of the city government. The town fathers of both Bergen and Hudson City prepared for the merger by loading up on public debt, including the alleged improvement of a number of roads, all in anticipation of the debt being spread among all of the residents of the newly reconfigured Jersey City. Excessive spending and obvious theft of funds are the mildest terms to characterize what happened. The consolidated municipality was off to a very poor start. When the city treasurer absconded with the city's funds, the schoolteachers didn't get paid for a significant period. Bankruptcy was avoided, but only as the result of the railroad's properties being added to the tax rolls for the first time. The local officials, led by a man named William Bumstead, looted and plundered their community. The consequence of their spree was the public backlash that resulted in substantial constitutional reforms in 1875—reforms that to this day affect the manner in which the state operates.

In his *New Jersey: America's Main Road,* discussing the financial pressures of the 1870s, the insightful historian John T. Cunningham noted that "Jersey City fended off bankruptcy simply because it grew faster than its home-town leaders and its statewide enemies could ravage it." At the same time, Tammany Hall and its ruler, boss William Tweed, along with his lieutenant George Washington Plunkett, were exploiting opportunities on the right bank of the Hudson. However, the graft extracted by Tammany did not prevent New York from growing to be the center of the world. The rapacious nature of its statewide enemies, I believe, was more significant in the thwarted development of Jersey City, than was the petty greed of its indigenous leadership. The characters analogous to Tweed et al. were in Trenton, not in Jersey City.

The story of this first consolidation effort is retold for two reasons to reinforce two points:

1. The fallout of that consolidation in Jersey City generated serious reservations and misgivings about the value of territorial expansion. These reservations remained strong in Hudson County for decades, and served as a negative object lesson for other cities considering annexation or consolidation.
2. Hudson County's reputation for corruption not only spans the centuries, but also embraces both political parties. This leads us to reassess the man whose name became synonymous with Hudson County in the twentieth century.

The name of Frank Hague, mayor of Jersey City from 1917 to 1947, invariably arises in discussions of political corruption. I would like to offer a different view of his tenure—not an apologia, but a more measured view of his achievements and where and why he failed. Hague is perhaps one of the most maligned political figures of this century. A concerted effort has been made to rewrite history and distort the record of achievements of perhaps the most controversial municipal leader in the nation's history. As we approach the fiftieth year after his death, it is time for a more balanced assessment. Was he corrupt? Undoubtedly. Was he tyrannical? Yes. Was he humorless and pedestrian? By all accounts, very much so.

Was he efficient and pragmatic? Did he govern the safest and cleanest city in the state? Did he carry out some of the greatest relief efforts and social programs that any city undertook during the Great Depression? Was he a social visionary in the area of health care? Did he recognize the limitations of the city he governed and attempt to make it better and greater? The answer to all of these questions has to be in the affirmative.

Hague's reputation proves the truth of a sentence in Marc Antony's funeral oration: "The evil that men do lives after them; the good is oft interred with their bones." Hague's legacy was the target of a concerted attack launched with vigor and tenacity by the successful political machine of his successor, Mayor John V. Kenny. The ardor brought by Kenny to the task of tarnishing Hague's reputation was equaled by the unstinting efforts of the left wing of the Democratic Party, who, feeling their oats in the mid- and late 1940s, continued to label Hague a fascist. It was a strange marriage. Kenny was no fan of the liberals and the feelings were mutual; the only thing they did agree on was their hatred of Hague. Finally, the Republicans delighted in holding Hague up as an example of the worst of Democratic bossism. It is extremely difficult to find fair-minded appraisals of Hague. Most information is provided by sources who had specific agendas in besmirching him.

Ironically, one of the fairest comments comes from one of Hague's staunchest adversaries in the 1940s—Governor Walter Edge. In his memoirs entitled *A Jerseyman's Journal*, this two-time Republican chief executive acknowledged that Hague ran a tight ship and administered the affairs of Jersey City in an efficient and orderly manner. That opinion, of course, failed to stop Edge from going to war with Hague. Edge directed Attorney General Walter van Riper to raid every betting parlor and numbers operation in Jersey City in retaliation for Hague's having beaten Edge in court over the distribution of $15 million in accumulated interest that the railroads owed on back municipal taxes.

In fact, Hague did protect the bootleggers during Prohibition, and throughout his tenure was the paladin of the bookmakers and numbers runners. In retrospect, Hague's conduct was unquestionably venal; on the other hand, the Volstead Act was a matter of national insanity. As for the protection of the betting parlors and other operations involving games of chance, living in an urban environment during Prohibition, the Depression, and the war was itself a risk. Should Hague be vilified and demonized for refusing to enforce laws that enjoyed little public support? Perhaps he is a valid target of criticism for accepting payments for the protection provided, but how different philosophically is that from what the State of New Jersey presently does in extracting revenue from lotteries and casino gaming? One could argue that a higher percentage of Hague's illegal tribute system on gambling found its way back to the poor and needy than do the taxes imposed by the state on similar activities, now glorified under our current mores.

As to the constant charges of payroll padding, let's look at the figures provided by Professor Richard J. Connors, in his extensive study of the career of Frank Hague entitled *A Cycle of Power*. Reportedly, the city under Hague never exceeded a ratio of one employee per 750. At the height of the Depression in 1937, there were only 3,603 municipal employees, excluding educational personnel, at a time when the population of the city far exceeded 300,000. By comparison, the municipal payrolls in many New Jersey suburbs today reflect ratios of one employee for every 600 residents, and the ratio is much worse in many smaller towns.

Even Arthur Vanderbilt II, in his biography of his uncle, Chief Justice Vanderbilt, acknowledged that Hague was "forthright and efficient in his work." The younger Vanderbilt then goes on at length to rehash all of the allegations of corruption, comparing the increase of expenditures in Hudson County during Hague's reign to the modest increases in Essex County during the same time, under the watchful eye of his uncle's Republican machine. The book *Changing Law* was published in 1976, almost nine years after Governor Hughes's blue ribbon commission on the causes of the Newark riots suggested that it was not merely the corruption of Newark's administration, but also the parsimony of Essex County in its failure to address social ills, which were partly responsible for that social upheaval. The younger Vanderbilt, however, failed to mention that no similar civil disturbances occurred in Jersey City.

Hague's Jersey City had jobs, such as, "cuspidor cleaners" and "foreman of vacuum cleaners," but it had fewer empty bellies and cold-water flats than did Newark. It is annoying to read sanctimonious criticism of Hague from an heir of Vanderbilt's money. The late chief justice was able, talented, hardworking, and intelligent, but he benefited from his political connections as surely as did Hague, and without the drawback of Hague's limited education. They both worked hard, but what Vanderbilt did on behalf of the wealthy was considered honorable, while what Hague did on behalf of the poor was considered corrupt.

Perhaps the legend of Hague has grown out of all proportion over the years—perhaps distorted from the outset. When one revisits the most scathing exposé of the era, Dayton David McKean's *The Boss: The Hague Machine in Action*, the attacks seem woefully underdocumented and pallid in our post-Watergate world. McKean's bigotry and prissiness are glaringly evident in his condemnation of Hague's alleged profanity. McKean would have Hague tarred and feathered for denying his opponents their civil liberties, but hypocritically has no qualms about his own use of McCarthyesque tactics against Hague.

The centerpiece of every attack on Hague are transcripts of the infamous Case Commission Hearings; hearings, which today would be publicly condemned as the worst type of political witch-hunt. The background of those hearings was a resolution adopted by the Republican-dominated Senate. The court exonerated Hague of his alleged contempt of the Senate, and today such an unconstitutional investigation would be unthinkable. The motivation for that particular witch-hunt by the committee, headed by Senator Clarence Case of Somerset County, is usually attributed to Republican pique at Hague after he invaded the Republican primary to assist in securing the gubernatorial nomination for the benign Morgan Larson. The investigation was to teach all Democrats, especially Hague, to stay away from the inner workings of the Republican Party.

An alternative evaluation presents a different view of the events leading up to this noteworthy clash between the political parties. Outside of his inner circle, Hague's closest friend and political role model was Alfred Smith of New York—mayor, governor, presidential nominee of the Democrats in 1928. No one doubted that Hague admired Smith enormously, and that he wanted to emulate Smith's political model in the operation of the City and State of New York. Hague's goal was to give Jersey City a political position within the New Jersey political landscape analogous to that occupied and enjoyed by New York City in the affairs of New York State. No one would argue that Hague's sentiments were perceived as an enormous threat by the New Jersey Republican establishment. The Republicans felt they had to movee quickly to spike Hague's ambitions. The vehicle chosen to deflate Hague's efforts to consolidate Hudson County into an entity similar to the consolidated boroughs of New York City was the Case Investigation Committee.

Reviewing the transcripts today is akin to reading the libretto of a second-class *opera buffa*, but the Case Committee was successful in diverting Hague's attention, if not fully successful in keeping him from attempting to influence Republican primary elections. The combination of the Case Hearings and the onset of the Great Depression were enough to have Hague abandon his design for a consolidated Hudson City that would be the colossus of New Jersey politics, bestriding the state in the same manner as the five consolidated boroughs of New York City did New York State at that time.

Among the things that occupied Hague's attention was the construction of the Margaret Hague Medical Center. This hospital and the programs it conducted were models of urban health care. Visionary is not too powerful a word to describe the dream that Hague turned into a reality, if only for a brief period. This project opened the door for much broader discussions of health care as a fundamental right of all citizens, as opposed to a privilege reserved for the wealthy. Was it successful? This can only be answered in the context of expectations. The project and its programs became a financial burden impossible for the city to sustain, and in that regard it was unable to fulfill its goals over the long term. On the other hand, it helped to create expectations among millions of Americans, who were familiar with its work. Medicare and Medicaid had their roots in the foundations of this medical center. The ongoing debate on universal health-care coverage is a continuation of discussions initiated by Hague.

However, the credit he deserves for this significant contribution to the advancement of public health care must be balanced by the criticism that is warranted by his failure to promote any type of cultural infrastructure in the city he dominated for so long. Hague's fellow commissioner on the Jersey City Council was the Democratic nominee for governor in the election of 1925. A. Harry Moore would go on to victory that year, and twice more before finally retiring. During his first term Moore pushed for the Jersey City Normal School, which opened in 1927.

The school was not quite a college, but a two-year program for training teachers, and thus satisfying the insatiable demand for qualified teachers in the state's expanding public-school system. It was the first state institution of higher learning to be opened in a county that contained 20 percent of the state's residents. Jersey City had been home to Saint Peter's College, but that had closed during World War I; Jesuit politics being allegedly more byzantine than even New Jersey's, an internal dispute prevented its reopening until 1930. (Stevens Institute of Technology was operating in Hoboken, but was a small and highly specialized institution.) Because under the old Constitution of 1844 Moore could not succeed himself, it was Governor Morgan Larson, the prominent but innocuous Republican senator and an engineer from Perth Amboy, who had the honor of presiding over the elevation of Jersey City Normal School to a State Teacher's College in 1929.

All of this is related to a simple point about how Jersey City sees itself today, how it saw itself in 1929, and how the state saw it historically. Beginning in the late 1970s, Jersey City and the other waterfront communities of Hudson County started to consider themselves as the *gold coast,* with real estate speculation reaching the most fevered pitch it had seen since the 1870s. In order to nurture and foster the new spirit in the county, the Chamber of Commerce, in cooperation with the county government, commissioned *Hudson County: The Left Bank,* a fine history of the county prepared by the chief librarian of Jersey City, Joan Doherty, with excellent photos selected by Joseph C. Brooks. It was published in 1986.

I must confess that during my days as assemblyman for Perth Amboy, I occasionally described Perth Amboy as the "Sausalito of the East Coast." Many of my constituents weren't sure of the reference, and others simply wrote it off to provincial chauvinism or sheer hyperbole. Some knew it was a tongue in cheek reference to the fact that if Hudson County were the Rive Gauche of New York City, then Perth Amboy was the Atlantic Coast's Sausalito.

In 1929, one could stroll in a matter of minutes across a number of bridges to the Left Bank, to tour the Pantheon or visit Les Invalides—or ride to the top of the Eiffel Tower—perhaps to walk through the Luxembourg Gardens—followed by lunch in the Latin Quarter—perhaps strike up a conversation with students from the Sorbonne, or share a bottle of wine with Hemingway at Café Deux Magots. Albeit the Seine is narrower than the Hudson, the distance separating Manhattan from Hudson County cannot be measured in feet. The chasm separating the Rive Gauche and Hudson County is an immeasurable cultural, psychological and institutional chasm. Without colleges, universities, significant museums, recreational facilities, monuments, landmark structures, or other cultural amenities, Jersey City could hardly contend with New York City.

By way of comparison, Columbia University was chartered in 1756 by King George II; New York University opened in 1831 under the patronage of Albert Gallatin, who had served as U.S. treasurer under Presidents Jefferson and Madison. City University opened in 1892, offering free tuition to city residents. New York's cultural infrastructure goes far beyond educational institutions. Take for example the park system. Central Park was initiated by an editorial suggestion in 1850. The cost was staggering, and the logistics were intimidating as three million cubic yards of soil had to be moved in before the park could officially open in 1876. The comparison with what was occurring in Jersey City is depressing. The Jersey City waterfront was being filled with New York City's garbage, while New York was importing fill dirt to construct Central Park. As New York was preserving hundreds of acres for recreation, Jersey City made no effort to conserve open space. William E. Sackett, the author of *Modern Battles of Trenton: History of New Jersey's Politics and Legislation from the Year 1868 to the Year 1894,* wrote that he would have been hard-pressed to find one public park in the county more than ten acres in size. The ultimate irony is that Jersey City now has the state's largest urban park—Liberty State—which is the property that the state had almost gifted to the Jersey Central Railroad. Today New Jersey has title to the beautiful park only because of the financial collapse of the once-wealthy railroad.

While it may be unfair to point out that the left bank of the Hudson failed to have institutions comparable to the Sorbonne and the Polytechnic that its European counterpart possessed, it is reasonable to point to the fact that the second-largest city in the state was being out-paced by a small town in the interior of

Gloucester County. In 1920, all of Gloucester County contained fewer than 50,000 people, and the town of Glassboro had a population significantly below 10,000. Yet Glassboro opened the doors of its state teachers college two years prior to that of Jersey City.

Finally, Jersey City is still attempting to recover from the placement of the two major highway systems that are the major arteries within the city. Both the Pulaski Skyway and the New Jersey Turnpike Extension have done more harm than good. Each of these roadways is a corridor with few doors, whose goal is to deliver the motor vehicle to the Holland Tunnel entrance as quickly as possible. Arriving at the tunnel with dispatch, one often must wait in bumper to bumper traffic for thirty minutes or more at its entrance. Meanwhile, idling engines produce thousands of tons of pollutants that are released into Jersey City's environment annually. Reaching a bottleneck faster serves no purpose, and in the case of the Holland Tunnel, is actually counterproductive to the interests of Jersey City.

The construction of the Pulaski Skyway during the Great Depression was hailed as "one of the wonders of the modern world." The labor employed thousands of people who would have otherwise been thrown on relief. The project also served as a flash point for some of the ugliest moments in Hague's career, as he refused to require the use of union labor. Tensions escalated to the point that there were serious injuries, even a death related to the labor strife on the project.

The Turnpike Extension was constructed during the years that John V. Kenny, "the little guy," was the mayor of Jersey City. When I worked for Governor Richard J. Hughes, I remember meetings where Mayor Kenny would protest any proposed state improvements to Route 440 or Tonnelle Avenue as unneeded. Kenny always emphasized that any such widenings or upgradings would only take business away from the Turnpike. I was puzzled as to why Mayor Kenny would be so solicitous of the Turnpike's revenue stream. My initial thought was that he wanted to make sure it was making enough money to keep his army of payroll patriots employed. Only when I was much older and wiser did I find out that his concern for the Turnpike's fiscal soundness emanated from his having millions of dollars in unregistered Turnpike bearer bonds.

Both the Pulaski Skyway and the Turnpike "pass-overs" essentially bypassed the interior of Jersey City, never really servicing the needs of the area. Elevated above the tenements and factories, both roadways are disconnected from the reality of Jersey City and are simple conduits for traffic in and out of New York City. The roadways sliced the city in the same manner as the railroads had carved the area into a fragmented city planner's worst nightmare a hundred years before.

To reiterate, Jersey City's failure remains primarily the responsibility of a myopic state government, abusing and victimizing this city over the course of two centuries. No city in this state has been more exploited or abused, from a public-policy perspective, than has Jersey City. Each of the growth-retarding factors applies to Jersey City. Considering that Jersey City's resources were given away to the railroads, its tax base made exempt to benefit the railroads, its riparian lands sold by the state without the smallest token coming to the city, its banking institutions handcuffed from expanding to Bergen or Passaic, and its fair representation in the Senate being denied, Jersey City's survival is a miracle.

However, while the state must accept the lion's share of the blame, other factors, in summary, compounded the problem:

1. The city was hamstrung by New York City's claim to control of the Hudson River all the way to the west bank's tide line. This claim was enforced by the law and by literal force-of-arms, until resolution of the dispute by the U.S. Supreme Court in the 1824 case of *Gibbons v. Ogden.* Now the fallout from that case is argued proudly by the attorney general of New Jersey, but back when it counted, the state put up no fight, and the New Jersey interests footed their own expenses.

2. The Jersey Associates, who owned the waterfront under the legislative grant of 1804, were only interested in money and control. They made their decisions based on their private advantage rather than from any civic point of view. It was just land to be exploited rather than developed.

3. The railroads sliced and carved up the city with dozens of lines running to the tidewater. The railways not only made any rational development of street patterns impossible, but also removed most of the city's most valuable property from the tax rolls for half a century.

4. The fist major consolidation was done for the wrong reasons and by the wrong people. The Republicans wanted to dilute the concentration of Democratic voters in the core of the city. This was to be accomplished by adding peripheral areas that were more Republican. Prior to annexation, the leaders of these towns adjoining Jersey City looted, borrowed, and spent their communities to the brink of disaster in expectation that Jersey City would ultimately foot the bill.

5. The Vanderbilt clique in New York blocked the Erie Railroad from going to anywhere from Jersey City except Buffalo and forced the West Shore Railroad, which would have connected Jersey City to Albany, into bankruptcy.

6. The owners of the Morris and Essex Canal blocked any attempts to build a connecting road along the waterfront. In order to get to the south of Jersey City from Exchange Place it was necessary to travel all the way uptown to detour around the basin.

7. The one man who could have united the entire region, Mayor Frank Hague, was diverted from his goal by the extensive investigation known as the Case Commission. The Republicans were desperately afraid of Hague's unifying all of Hudson. The Democratic power of New York City dominated New York State, electing Al Smith and Franklin Roosevelt. The Republicans in New Jersey, fearing a New York replay, set out to harass Hague. Once Hague backed off his consolidation efforts, the Republicans backed off the investigations.

8. Jersey City never developed a cultural infrastructure necessary to sustain a world-class city.

9. The Pulaski Skyway and the New Jersey Turnpike pass over Jersey City and not through it. They are conduits, and not real corridors.

*M*y closing comment must be that while Hudson County may not be the Left Bank, one should give credit where credit is due. Jersey City and the balance of the county have proven themselves to be incredibly resilient. One cannot spend a day in Jersey City, nor for that matter in any part of Hudson County, without being impressed by the vitality and vibrancy that seems to push up from the pavement. Despite the diversity that is also apparent, this area is still the prime candidate for potential consolidation into a unified metropolitan district.

PART IV

Correcting Yesterday's Mistakes: Is It Possible?

CHAPTER 16

Once the Municipal Multiplication Madness Stopped

Better to reign in Hell than serve in Heaven.
John Milton

$\mathcal{T}$he Federal Census of 1930 showed enormous growth in New Jersey during the 1920s. The state's population had increased at an annual rate of almost 2 percent—a rate ten times greater than the growth rate in 1990s.

In 1930, New Jersey's 4 million people, were divided among 559 municipalities. It has taken the balance of the century for the state's population to double. Now our 8 million people live in 566 communities—a net increase of only 7 towns. Since 1930 only 10 new municipalities were created and 3 eliminated. Of the 10 created, the majority had populations of under 1,000, and half were War Orphans, as discussed in Chapter 10.

Loch Arbour Village, Monmouth County, created in 1957, population 350, holds the distinction of having been the last municipality created in New Jersey. Island Beach, Ocean County, was created in 1933, only to be abolished in 1965. In 1951, a consolidation occurred merging Landis Township and Vineland City into Vineland Township, Cumberland County. In 1997, the Township of Pahaquarry, Warren County, population 10, whose lands had been aggressively acquired by the federal government, ceased to exist.

In 1930, the average size of a municipality was approximately 15 square miles. The average population of a municipality at that time was 7,000. The largest was Landis Township with almost 68 square miles. Dozens of communities had less than a square mile. A few towns such as Longport in Atlantic County, East Newark, and Guttenberg in Hudson County, were under a half mile square—so small that they could be traversed on foot in a matter of minutes. The range in population was more dramatic in 1930, with Newark squeezing over 400,000 into its borders, while Pine Valley and Teterboro had fewer than 20 residents.

Thus far, this book has examined the origins of New Jersey's unique geopolitical map and focused on the specific dynamics of separation and division that resulted in the severe balkanization of the state. The end of municipal proliferation coincided with the onset of the Great Depression. However, the nation's fiscal disaster was not the reason for the end to the fragmentation. Rather, the citizens of the state accepted zoning as the instrument by which to preserve the status quo. The amendment to the constitution adopted in 1927 had removed all doubts that zoning was a legitimate exercise of the plenary police powers of the state. That power could be properly delegated by the state to municipalities. The last remaining dynamic that had historically driven the proliferation of municipalities became moot. The four other major operative dynamics of fragmentation—road maintenance, liquor sales, control of local schools, and accommodation of train commuters—lost their relevance. The boundary lines, then in place, began to fossilize. It is particularly surprising that even the wrenching, cataclysmic dynamics of the Depression were insufficient to shrink the number of jurisdictions.

One is tempted to dismiss the frenzy of town creation occurring between 1880 and 1930 as the product of a different era, the result of unique circumstances, the consequence of a different mind-set. Municipalities were not spreading—they were metastasizing, and when remission was achieved in the second half of this century, the state found itself with an extraordinary number of municipal entities. Even at the onset of the Great Depression, New Jersey was already considered an urbanized state. Today we are, by far, the most urbanized and most densely populated of the fifty states.

The municipal framework in place as of 1930 has absorbed an additional 4 million people. This alone is proof that the state by 1930 had too many jurisdictions. Since then, the population distribution has moved toward more equalization. Newark has suffered the most significant decline in population to under 300,000. Teterboro and Pine Valley still contain fewer than 20 people, but the average municipality now has over 14,000 residents.

These figures are not as significant as the data that indicates density per square mile. In this category New Jersey leads the nation, being the only state to surpass the figure of 1,000 per square mile. West New York, Union City, and Guttenberg, in Hudson County have populations that reflect approximately 40,000 people per square mile—populations nearly as dense as that of Bombay and almost twice as dense as the population of New York City. Pahaquarry was, until its demise in 1997, the least dense with a population of less than one person per square mile. The honor now goes to Teterboro and Pine Valley with a population density of 20 per square mile.

Rhode Island, New Jersey's nearest competitor in the density category with over 900 persons per square mile, manages its million residents within 39 municipalities. The average size is 30 square miles, double the average in New Jersey, and the average municipal population is nearly twice as large as New Jersey's. Indeed, no other state in the nation may be compared to New Jersey in its multiplicity of municipal jurisdictions.

This book also explored the reasons preventing any urban center from developing into a major city of national prominence. The year 1930 marks the effective end of the efforts of Camden and Jersey City to develop into larger governmental units. Newark's efforts had long before been put on hold.

Activity in other states demonstrates that New Jersey is aberrational in its failure to consolidate and regionalize. The U.S. Bureau of the Census has compiled data since 1972 on boundary changes and annexations in all fifty states. The resistance to change in municipal boundaries in New Jersey has been abnormally strong. The little boundary adjustment taking place in New Jersey was so insignificant that it was considered zero for statistical purposes. Only the New England states reflect a similar jurisdictional stasis. However, those states lack the great number of jurisdictions that New Jersey has. Rhode Island, as we've seen, manages to provide local services through its scant 39 municipalities. Connecticut, smaller in population and slightly smaller in size than New Jersey, manages with only 169 municipalities and has no county level of government. The average population per town is over 20,000, and each town bears a portion of the responsibilities carried in New Jersey by the counties. New York, Pennsylvania, Delaware, and Maryland, which share with New Jersey their early ratification of the U.S. Constitution, have light to moderate activity by way of boundary alterations.

Of the original states, North Carolina stands out for its active restructuring of municipal territories. In the five years between 1990 and 1995, North Carolina led the nation in the number of people living in unincorporated areas that were annexed to existing communities. A total of 287 square miles, containing 157,000 people, were added to existing North Carolina towns in that five-year period. The original states of South Carolina and Georgia were also busy during that period, bringing people in unincorporated areas into existing communities by way of annexation.

In those states such as Massachusetts, Vermont, and New Hampshire where boundary alterations have been few, the process of consolidation and regionalization of services has been most aggressive, setting an example for the nation. But in New Jersey it has been as if the jurisdictional boundaries existing in 1930 were cast in stone. The regionalization and sharing of services has proceeded slowly in New Jersey as compared to the activity of the rest of the Northeast.

By revisiting the historical data about New Jersey's unique balkanization, we may obtain a keener appreciation of how public policy, as reflected in various statutory enactments, has operated to encourage the multiplication and balkanization, while thwarting major consolidations of the state's municipalities. Understanding the forces that brought on conditions which prevailed in 1930 will give a foundation for exploring the larger public policy questions raised by this review of the historical material.

Since 1930 the dominant state policy has been to preserve New Jersey's municipal framework at all costs. This conclusion is supported by the gubernatorial initiatives and legislative enactments over this period. While it would be impossible to deal with each administration and every legislative session, the following review is sufficient to make the argument. Many of the governors who have served since 1930 have acknowledged that the surplus of jurisdictions constituted a problem warranting attention. Fundamental change, however, has been suggested rarely and never pursued aggressively. Rather, as we will see, program after program has been adopted to patch and repair a system that was often on the verge of collapse.

The dimensions of the economic collapse suffered by America in the 1930s elude us today. The world as people knew it seemed to fall apart, and the foundations of society appeared to crumble. An appropriate time to rethink the municipal system that had been created would have been during this convulsive decade. In retrospect, the official response is surprising. Every effort was directed to preserving the complex and bizarre arrangement designed and structured in the previous century. In many cases, the political forces that had drawn the boundary lines were rendered irrelevant. Also, the existence of ancient lines compounded intractable problems confronting the state's leaders. However dire, the new economic reality was insufficient to force consolidation of communities. Rather, the new economic reality appears simply to have spurred greater efforts to keep the municipal house of cards from tumbling. Officialdom clung to the old forms and institutions, hollow and useless as they were, in order to maintain some frame of known and accepted reference in a world that was spinning out of control.

The new economic realities of the Depression definitely impacted New Jersey's municipal system. At the economic nadir of the Great Depression in 1935, New Jersey municipalities were collecting less than half of the current tax levy. By way of comparison the collection rate has averaged 95 percent throughout the 1980s and 1990s. Statutes designed to place limits on the level of municipal and county borrowing were ignored or circumvented. The existing law provided that a town could borrow no more than 7 percent of the average assessed valuations for the preceding three years. The actual level of bonded indebtedness of municipalities exceeded 40 percent in some seashore communities. The tragic financial plight engendered legendary feats of fiscal ingenuity. For example, cities would include in anticipated revenue all of the current tax levy and the full amounts of delinquent taxes and accumulated interest as well. The budget officers of many towns included optimistic projections of the amounts of fees, fines, and miscellaneous revenues. Likewise, it was standard operating procedure to overlook emergency borrowings that had recently been undertaken for payroll and relief purposes.

Having exhausted every fiscal gimmick, new and old, by 1935, 87 municipalities and two counties simply defaulted on their obligations. Thirty-one additional communities and 7 counties were meeting their payrolls by issuing scrip in lieu of cash. The situation in 10 towns was so dire that they turned their internal operations over to the state's Municipal Finance Commission. In 1936, tax collections were increasing, and the canceling of capital improvement projects in many towns proved to be a temporary, if mixed, blessing. The number of towns in default was reduced to 79, and only 28 were paying in scrip, but the number of communities that had surrendered to their insolvency had reached 12.

Governor Harold Hoffman, although a Republican, was, in large measure, a creation of the Frank Hague political machine. Hague had tacitly agreed not to meddle in Republican primary elections, but his agreement did not extend to directing his troops to take a year off and let an occasional friendly Republican triumph. Hoffman was acceptable to the mayor of Jersey City primarily because they shared the same enemies. Just as the new governor was the beneficiary of Democratic defections in the general election, he was equally dependent on the votes of Democratic legislators to enact his agenda. The original agenda was extremely ambitious and very progressive for that time. Within the first few months of his inauguration he had accomplished the passage of New Jersey's first sales tax, effective July 1, 1935, at the rate of only 2 percent. This sales tax generated almost $7 million in state revenue prior to its repeal on October 25, 1935. It was struck from the books immediately preceding the legislative elections scheduled for the first week in November.

Hoffman spent a terrible few months after the signing of the sales tax. The enemies of Hoffman and Hague coalesced. Under the aegis of the Clean Government Group, the Republican conservative faction, headed by Arthur T. Vanderbilt in Essex County, filed slates of anti-Hoffman candidates who carried the Republican primary elections throughout the state. Hoffman realized that it would be impossible to have a working coalition in the next legislative session even with the help of Hague. Ever flamboyant, Hoffman signed the sales tax repeal using red ink, claiming he foresaw unbalanced budgets and *maybe hungry people.*

By 1935, at the very latest, the chickens were coming home to roost. The Trenton establishment, which had for over a century tolerated and sometimes encouraged policies that created the enormous numbers of separate communities, was now faced with reaping what they had sown.

The legislature that convened in 1936 was unwilling to consider new revenues, and the crisis mounted. The inheritance tax collected on the Dorrance Estate gave New Jersey a much needed respite. The state realized a windfall of over $15 million upon proving that the deceased Mr. John T. Dorrance, the moving force behind the Campbell Soup Company, was domiciled in New Jersey at the time of his death. The state was also beginning to see the tax advantages that came with the repeal of Prohibition. Revenues on liquor moved steadily toward the $8 million figure. While being far from out of the woods, the idea of new taxes was unthinkable. The Vanderbilt clique spoke piously about being progressive, and even hinted that they were more in tune with the New Deal than was Hoffman. In spite of all the sanctimonious posturing, the agenda of the Clean Government faction was reduction of taxes and cutting of government services, even emergency relief programs. With Hoffman relegated to political irrelevance, the Republican aristocracy in the Senate turned toward forcing municipalities to reform their bookkeeping, promising that better bookkeeping would return them to credit-worthiness.

As was previously mentioned, Vanderbilt, for purposes of political expediency, occasionally hinted that his Clean Government Group should be linked in the voters' minds with the progressive reforms of the New Deal. If President Franklin D. Roosevelt reached out to the academicians at Harvard for advice and counsel, then Vanderbilt could do the same thing by soliciting the assistance of a similar brain-trust from Princeton University. Vanderbilt, supported financially by large amounts of money pledged by conservative corporate special interests, persuaded the president of Princeton University, Harold W. Dodds, to assemble a group of faculty to study New Jersey's fiscal problems and make recommendations to the legislature. The faculty group taking the name Princeton Local Government Surveys started work after the elections of 1935. By 1936, the Princeton Local Government Surveys group was able to push through the legislature a law requiring that all municipalities prepare and adopt budgets on a cash basis. This reform restrained local officials from anticipating the collection of current and delinquent levies in excess of the actual amounts collected from these sources in the previous year. The act further limited the amounts that could be borrowed on an emergency basis and mandated that a reserve for uncollected taxes be factored into projected revenues. Finally, the act made all local budgets subject to review and approval by the office of the state auditor.

The transition period permitted by the act envisioned the statewide use of cash-basis budgets by 1944. This goal was accelerated, and by the outbreak of World War II, New Jersey's municipalities were on a standardized cash-basis system, whose structure was designed by the state with the guidance of the Princeton Survey team.

To Vanderbilt's dismay—and to the professors' credit—academic independence was alive and well in Princeton. The recommendations of the Princeton Surveys were not nearly as Draconian as those desired by their political and financial patrons. Despite the fact that Princeton Surveys substantially moderated the Clean Government Group's agenda, there was still a great deal of resistance and resentment at the local level. However, the real success of the imposed reforms must be measured by the fact that now, sixty years later, the fundamental framework of the Budget Act of 1936 remains operative and governs the municipal budget process for every town in the state.

Hoffman was both preceded and succeeded by A. Harry Moore, who in 1938 won his third term in the governor's office by a margin of almost fifty thousand votes. It was not the mandate Moore had received in his second campaign. In the election of 1931, he had defeated Camden's David Baird by an unprecedented plurality, approaching a quarter of a million votes. The veteran governor demonstrated that he had forgotten neither his background in municipal government nor the lesson taught by his Hudson County predecessor, Leon Abbett.

Governor Abbett had saved Jersey City from imminent disaster and rescued other cities, such as Elizabeth, from bankruptcy with the passage of the Railroad Tax Act of 1884. That law allowed the cities to share with the state the revenues generated by the railroads. The provision of the law, allowing for local taxation of the railroads' Class II properties, provided a much-needed new source of municipal revenue. The majority of the towns through which the railroad passed had some Class II property, and therefore numerous localities, large and small, were able to obtain some share in the total revenues. Moore adapted a variation on the theme struck by Abbett. The public utilities, carrying gas, electric, and telephone service throughout the state, were similar to the railroads in that they traversed many municipalities, but they were in better financial shape than the railroads in the 1930s.

The state imposed a franchise tax on most of the utilities as early as 1900. The Voorhees Act imposed an excise tax calculated at 2 percent of the gross receipts of each utility. During his second term, Moore increased taxes on the gross receipts of utilities, but left in place a system for their distribution that was open to abuse by desperate municipalities. The revenues were distributed to municipalities on the basis of local valuations of the public utility property within each jurisdiction. In 1935, when Newark doubled its valuations on the Public Service Company from $29 million to $60 million, it resulted in no greater tax being paid by Public Service, but it did result in Newark claiming twice as much as it had received the previous year. Moore's reforms of 1938 assured that the division of the pool of gross-receipts revenue could not be manipulated by operations internal to any one city. It created a formula that spread the revenues so that each town in the state received some portion of the total money collected by the state. This was a very significant change and a real boon to many of the smaller municipalities.

The formula, under constant siege since its inception, was radically altered in 1997, but that is an entirely different story. Moore's 1938 change in the gross-receipts tax distribution, while intended to thwart Newark's avarice, proved to be a life-saver for many municipalities. In the 1970s and 1980s the gross-receipts revenues accounted for 20 percent or more of all municipal revenues. In the 1930s the percentage was substantially higher for many hard-pressed communities, particularly the cities.

If an implosion of municipalities were to have occurred at any time, reversing the explosive multiplication witnessed prior to 1930, the Great Depression would have been that time. The statistics graphically depict the acute financial crisis that faced the state and its constituent municipalities.

Yet the response of Governors Hoffman and Moore, legislative leaders, as well as that of the influential Princeton Surveys, was to salvage the existing framework, save the communities from defaulting, and thus preserve the jurisdictional status quo. Many towns had crossed the line into insolvency and their independent existence as self-sustaining political subdivisions had become irretrievably fictional. Indeed, the depression era marked a dramatic increase in state aid; the initial term applied to such diversion of state revenues to the municipalities was called subventions, i.e, literally the sending under of money. By 1939 state aid and subventions had increased to over 50 percent of the total state budget, as compared to zero percent at the turn of the century. Whether they were called subventions, relief, grants, state aid, revenue sharing, or any other name, the state government was called upon to provide ever-increasing amounts of money to an ever-increasing number of municipalities simply to keep them operating.

Little if any serious consideration was given to the possibility of merger or consolidation of municipalities. Governor Moore's annual address of 1933 included an admonition that the legislature strongly encourage the consolidation of smaller jurisdictions. However, nothing came of his proposal. The actions of the Trenton establishment may have saved the cities, but in doing so they preserved a system acknowledged to be inefficient and protected the municipal status quo despite the clear understanding that thereafter it would require substantial subsidies. The technical problems of municipal accounting had been solved by the end of the Depression. Likewise a significantly higher and more equitable system for the distribution of certain tax revenues, primarily the Gross Receipts and Franchise Tax, had been established. Nothing, however, addressed the underlying insufficiency of local revenue. The new reality was that most municipalities would need state subsidies for the foreseeable future, and perhaps forever.

Year after year, decade after decade, political administration after political administration, the predominant public policy has been preservation of the jurisdictional status quo. Despite chaos, crisis, confusion and expense, the official response has been to patch the system and keep it working rather than address the problem of the overabundance of subsidy-dependent municipalities. An analysis of the major policies of each administration since 1930 demonstrates efforts, sometimes of heroic dimensions, to keep the gravely wounded system from collapse. In order to preserve the system, the state government has worked *with it, around it, over it,* and primarily *under it.* Here are some examples of each modality.

> *With it*: by the creation in 1966 of the Department of Community Affairs and the contemporaneous legislative establishment of the County and Local Government Study Commission.

> *Around it*: by the promotion and fostering of over 200 independent authorities whose financing is directed to municipal functions, but whose debt is allegedly self-liquidating and therefore carried off the books.

> *Over it*: by creation of such regional agencies as the Meadowlands Development Authority.

> *Under it*: by literally hundreds of programs whose sole aim is to subsidize the existence of the municipalities.

Call it what you wish—state aid, revenue sharing, subventions, grants, grants in aid—it all amounts to much the same thing, the use of state tax dollars to keep the towns afloat.

To understand why this system has endured despite economic collapse and why billions are still spent on its maintenance, it is necessary to assess the lessons of history. The deference paid to jurisdictional boundaries and the tribute by way of taxes paid to subsidize the system can only be appreciated within the context of New Jersey's unique past.

The first factor, one with the longest legacy, extends back to 1702. The original accord that was negotiated to merge East and West Jersey and to bring the united entity under the governance of the British Crown gave enduring legitimacy to the concept that geography contained inherent political power. That artful, diplomatic, and delicate political compromise has long been forgotten, but the progeny of that arranged marriage have continued to thrive and prosper. The idea of real estate having political power was encoded into our political genes and continues to live on in the collective unconscious of our governmental structures. A 300+year legacy is extremely difficult to abandon.

The power of this idea is reflected in three corollaries to the initial agreement of 1702:

1. Its influence was reflected in every New Jersey Constitution. The versions of 1776, 1844, and 1947 each provided guaranteed upper-house representation in the legislature for each county, notwithstanding a county's population or lack thereof. However, the New Jersey Supreme Court, given little latitude by rulings of the federal high court in the 1960s, had to declare that the practice violated the U.S. Constitution. The new section of the state's constitution providing for equal representation in both houses of the legislature was added only in 1966.
2. The New Jersey Plan, which provided the compromise that eased the way for the adoption the U.S. Constitution in 1787, reflected our state's firm belief that geography equals political power. Local leaders, anxious to preserve their disproportionate power, relied upon this stellar and almost irrefutable precedent. How indeed could anyone challenge a system so perfect that it had been incorporated into the U.S. Constitution?
3. The governing bodies of each county were known as the Chosen Board of Freeholders—*chosen* by each of the constituent jurisdictions within each county. Prior to 1902, the freeholder boards were constituted by members representing each township and borough within the county; cities were often accorded an additional seat on the freeholder board for every ward or precinct within the jurisdiction. County boards often had large numbers of representatives from small townships and boroughs, who often outnumbered, and therefore outvoted, the more populous areas of the county. The idea of geography having political power infected a large part of the entire system.

An additional fact regarding incorporation of property, makes New Jersey unique among the states. It traces its origin to the original creation of the proprietorships in 1668. Because of the nature of the ownership rights inherent in the concept of proprietorship, New Jersey never had any unclaimed lands. From a technical point of view, every square inch of land in the state was spoken for from the very outset. Every parcel was under the ownership and governance of the proprietors at the very beginning of early settlement. After 1702, all land was under the governance of the Crown, and under the ownership of the proprietors or their grantees. Unique among the colonies, New Jersey entered the Union in 1787 as the only state wherein all territory had been allocated either to a township or in the rare case to one of the few recognized cities.

The abiding endurance of the New Jersey municipal pattern and the influence it exerted upon the state's political system continued undiminished through the mid-twentieth century. Then, if anything, it was further strengthened. A Constitutional Convention by its very nature should hold plenary powers, but the question of boundaries was sacrosanct as the most recent convention met in 1947. The sanctity of county and municipal boundaries was regarded as of such importance that the legislative enactments convening the Constitutional Convention of 1947 and the miniconvention of 1966 prohibited those gatherings from undertaking any attempt to alter the established boundaries.

The Constitutional Convention of 1947 ratified and confirmed the power of the legislature to delegate zoning powers to the municipalities. The suggestion that the power be conferred on the counties was quickly and summarily rejected. No single decision made at that convention had greater ramifications or widespread consequences.

Historical legacy alone, however, could not have maintained the unique circumstances of New Jersey's municipal framework. There are those, including myself, who believe that municipal government has broader dimensions and higher aspirations than simply providing services. This broader, more expansive view of municipal government has a great deal of merit.

1. Local government is more accountable to its constituency. The highest endorsement one can receive in public life is to be trusted and supported by one's neighbors. Holding local office in New Jersey usually means knowing a goodly number of your voters by their first names. Just as the candidate knows the voters, the voters in turn know the kind of job the local official is doing.
2. Local government, lacking the multiple layers of bureaucracy, is most responsive to individual problems.
3. Local government provides a testing ground for aspiring leaders of both political parties and weans out those who are not ready for prime time while showcasing those who are suitable for elevation to higher office. This proposition is also defined as the *farm system* because it resembles the apprentice program preparing, evaluating, and testing young baseball players for possible promotion to the big leagues. An aspect of this system also helps preserve the present system. Members of the state legislature are permitted to serve also as local officials, either elected or appointed. This practice results in a number of legislators' having a strong commitment to maintain the current jurisdictional arrangement.
4. Local government allows ethnic, racial, and religious minorities to acquire some semblance of political power. If their numbers were constantly diluted in large jurisdictions, effective political power would remain beyond the reach of minorities. Related to this point, local government provides governmental experience to minorities who would otherwise have no opportunity to prepare themselves for participation in county or state politics.
5. Local government provides a sense of place.
6. Local government is the quintessential American institution. The town meeting represents our political values as does no other assemblage.

All of these arguments are valid. The question today is not the validity of the defense, but the weight to be accorded these factors when placed in the scale to be measured against the arguments of cost and efficiency of the services distributed at the local level. In the following chapter we will review other factors that must be placed on the scale to counterbalance these positive arguments. We will also observe how one of New Jersey's most treasured myths presently prevents the scale from giving true measure.

CHAPTER 17

Reasons for Change

New Jersey's state flower should be the concrete cloverleaf.
Lewis Mumford

*T*he downside of New Jersey's multiple municipal system boils down to inappropriate land use and redundant, expensive administration. Every town in New Jersey seems to have a sign saying that the town is *open for business*. The omnipresent signs that say "This township welcomes your business" never say that "you" are welcome; i.e., only a tax-paying ratable is welcome. The paradigm of the perfect ratable generates a lot of tax revenue, generates no traffic or pollution, and most importantly generates no school-aged children. At last count there are about 560 municipalities chasing after this fantasy facility.

The municipal ratable chase is not new, but it has intensified over the last few decades. The chapter on school-district boroughs contained the story of how competing factions in 1894 raced to the court house to file petition maps for the creation of one borough in Bergen County. The competing factions both tried to include the area's largest factory within the borders of their proposed new community. The situation a century ago was different from the standard modern chase in that the ratable was already in existence. Certain cities attempted, sometimes successfully and sometimes not, to increase their ratables by annexing adjoining areas. The City of Trenton pulled off a coup before the turn of the century by annexing Chambersburg with its Roebling steelworks. Shortly thereafter, the City of South Amboy was unsuccessful in its legislative efforts to reannex some of the territory it had jettisoned to Sayreville, upon which substantial ratables had been subsequently constructed.

The negative implications of any type of ratable chase within the state are, and have been for some time, well understood. The state's experience in the late 1930s and early 1940s with the ratable chase after business taxes on intangibles, such as stocks, bonds, mortgages, and good will, set a frightening example. In spite of that lesson, political leaders still allowed other types of ratable chases to continue unabated.

No one wanted to learn the ratable chase lesson, which bears witness to the contention that the pro-rural, anti-urban bias of the New Jersey legislature has been a force as pernicious as it was powerful. Looking at the administration of Governor Charles Edison, who served from 1941 to 1944, one can see how Edison's efforts at tax reform made a significant contribution by calling into sharper focus the counterproductive effect of the disparate tax rates that existed. In his advocacy for a statewide uniformity in tax treatment, Edison identified what would become the destructive "ratable chase" in future decades.

He argued unsuccessfully that a statewide uniform tax on intangibles would prevent what had happened during the depression. Desperately needing revenue, cities such as Newark and Jersey City would place assessments on the intangible "good will" of a corporation headquartered in their jurisdiction. This procedure was referred to as "tax lightning." The predictable response of the victimized corporation was to relocate their corporate headquarters to such places as Flemington, which harbored so many corporate refugees from the larger cities that it was able to drop its tax rate from $3.91 per $100 in 1937 to merely $0.28 in 1943.

While Edison was not able to solve the problem he so graphically identified, his Republican successor, Walter E. Edge, wasted little time in having a corporate-net-worth tax adopted. This tax replaced all other taxes on intangible property and immediately terminated the intramunicipal competition. By eliminating disparate rates, set by untrained assessors acting at the direction of their political leader, the counterproductive and often internecine competition between political subdivisions ceased. What an incredible achievement.

However, the results were not significant enough to encourage Edge or anyone else to suggest that the program be expanded to include a statewide uniform tax to replace the disparate property taxes—the principal disincentive to municipal consolidation.

By the time Edge left office, over 56 percent of all state revenues were consumed by state aid and other subventions. One can only wonder what would have occurred had he aggressively worked for total reform in the property tax and accomplished a statewide uniformity. The cities would have been spared the great ratable chase of the 1960s, 1970s, and 1980s, which saw Trenton attempting to compete with Plainsboro, and Newark with Roseland, while their effective tax rates were eight to ten times as great.

The ratable chase since 1950 has involved the disastrous competition to attract new construction of industries, research facilities, office complexes, and shopping malls to a municipality, while minimizing the amount of housing provided to shelter the employees working at these new sites. This situation gave birth to the phenomenon known as the reverse commute, with workers living in the cities and driving to work in suburban communities. The suburbs, who were victorious in the ratable chase, provided few housing opportunities within the reach of the budgets of those who worked on the new research campuses or did clerical work in the new office parks. The staff behind the counters at such places as the Mall at Short Hills were not receiving compensation adequate for them to maintain a residence in the same neighborhood.

Patterns of growth, which for time immemorial had followed a rational course parallel to the extension of transportation networks, were suddenly turned upside down. Projects were built without supporting or sustaining infrastructure resources, physical or human. New Jersey cannot lay claim to being the first state where the inversion took place; that dubious honor goes to New York, with Levittown on Long Island being the first pure automobile-dependent suburb. Levittown was more than just that—it was the first development whose simple existence would serve as a magnet pulling infrastructure to its borders to serve its purposes.

In 1982 the Canadian author W. P. Kinsella was startled by the success of his first novel, *Shoeless Joe.* He was more surprised when a few years later screenwriter Phil Alden Robinson persuaded Kevin Costner to read his script for a movie ultimately entitled *Field of Dreams,* nominated for an Academy Award in 1989. Its mystical leitmotif is the phrase: *if you build it they will come.* The closing aerial shot that is seen as they role the credits shows the headlights of bumper-to-bumper traffic extending for miles. One is left with the warm and fuzzy feeling that Kevin Costner has had his dream vindicated. Wonderful fantasy.

During the past few decades in New Jersey, hundreds of developers were invited to build their own fields of dreams in the form of shopping malls, apartment complexes, industrial parks, and research campuses. The phrase, *if you build it they will come,* was verified by the initial bumper-to-bumper traffic. However, as opposed to the fade-out shot where the movie ended so happily, New Jersey's taxpayers have been forced to ante-up billions of dollars to construct the new infrastructures required by these private *fields of dreams.*

The zoning powers conferred upon municipalities have been used in an unwise, unseemly, ill-advised, counterproductive, and unconstitutional manner. It is possible to document this allegation by citing the number of square miles of forest and farmland lost to the bulldozers—the linear miles of asphalt that accommodate our millions of daily trips to and from home, jobs, schools, shopping, etc. No greater indictment of the widespread abuses could be offered than the language of the Supreme Court in its series of decisions that are usually referred to collectively as *Mount Laurel.*

Another and the most dramatically negative aspect of the ratable chase concerns the neighborhood center. New Jersey's cities, large and small, were once active retail centers, providing a vast array of goods and supplies. In addition to the commercial cores, nearly every neighborhood had local markets for food and groceries, pharmacies, newsstands and soda fountains, clothing stores and shoe stores, service stations and auto service stations. Highways were used for getting from one center to another, or out to the suburbs and eventually to the farms or seashore. The highway shopping center changed habits and lifestyles. The mom and pop operations had little ability to compete. Small retail businesses all but disappeared from the commercial landscape by the mid-1980s, leaving block upon block where plywood shields pockmarked the face of once-thriving neighborhoods.

In what might be viewed as poetic justice, those same shopping centers that destroyed the commercial viability of so many downtowns enjoyed dominance for only a few decades. They in turn began to feel the unrelenting pressure of the discount chains with their superstores. Just as the mom and pop neighborhood store feared the advent of the shopping centers, the strip malls and smaller shopping centers now plead to be protected from the construction of a new Wal-Mart or Sam's Club. Meanwhile, some formerly boarded-up downtowns have regained vibrance by emphasis on their quaintness or by the influx of immigrants who have staked out an area as their own.

Perhaps most interesting is the apparent reassessment of transportation policy. In 1997 the *Wall Street Journal* carried a front-page article that dealt with the idea of abandoning any further consideration of urban by-passes and forcing traffic to travel through major cities rather than around them.

The most effective way to absorb all this depressing data is to put down this book and see for yourself. It is impossible to travel fifty miles in New Jersey without being overwhelmed by the sense of opportunities lost, open space jeopardized or wasted, unsightly and depressing commercial sprawl, inappropriate adjoining uses, once-vital cities now gutted and destroyed. As in every race, there were winners and losers. Unquestionably the cities lost the ratable chase, but what about the winners? What exactly have they won?

Note on this drive the second major negative consequence of our multiplicity of municipal jurisdictions—expensive redundancy or redundant expense. As the signs welcoming you to the suburban borough of *x* and the suburban township of *y* flash by, consider the price the citizens of New Jersey pay for their victory in the ratable chase. Consider, too, how you probably will be going through a community where the chief law-enforcement officer's salary is comparable to that of the director of the FBI; or where the school superintendent makes more than the president of a fine college; where the business manager or administrator is compensated more generously than corporate executives of billion-dollar corporations; where local officials' salaries are the envy of cabinet officers.

And the final bludgeon blow is that the property taxes supporting these 566 communities are double the national per-capita average. The Institute on Taxation and Economic Policy in Washington, D.C., determined in a national study in 1997 that New Jersey's average couple was paying $3,562 in property taxes. The very next highest state levy was in Connecticut, where the annual bill averaged a thousand dollars less at $2,573. After this the figures dropped precipitously.

The state average property tax is 25 percent higher than the next highest state and double the nation's average. The salt in the wound is that this occurs in a state with a 6 percent general sales tax and an income tax that is above the national average.

The system is complex, counterproductive, wasteful of land resources and more—and virtually fossilized. A construct of previous centuries, the structure was designed for the needs and problems of those eras—dynamic during its formation, but now frozen, institutionalized, virtually paralyzed.

Nicholas Negroponte, the author of *Being Digital,* has a vision of a time traveler who returns from the past century and visits various sites. Modalities of transportation and communication have taken quantum leaps. Office suites and medical facilities are miracles to the visitor from 1899. Negroponte uses this to preface a discussion about the one setting that might appear as a reassuring stabilizer for the otherwise bewildered guest. He suggests that the classroom with its front-of-the-room blackboard and rows of ordered desks is the institution that has most resisted change over the century. Negroponte's time traveler would certainly feel confused and disoriented on the modern highways of New Jersey, but would be comforted by the presence of municipal boundaries which are relatively unchanged since he was last in the state.

As with all systems, our municipal divisions are subject to change. However, the state's system of municipal jurisdictions has resisted change more successfully, for a longer duration, and more adamantly than anyone might have expected of a system that was once so fluid and protean. Indeed, it has resisted change even more than Negroponte's classroom.

The single greatest inhibitor of change is the myth of home rule. Two of the most prominent New Jersey myths are the existence of the Jersey Devil and the existence of home rule. The difference between the two is that there have been more sightings of the Devil than there has been of home rule. The credible evidence marshaled for the existence of the hellish creature from the Pine Barrens far outweighs any that might exist to demonstrate the viability of home rule as anything other than an empty and vitiated concept in our state's political structure.

Home rule has no constitutional recognition as it does in other states. Home rule has no Supreme Court precedent to lend it legitimacy as it does elsewhere. To the contrary, the decisions of the highest court uniformly assert the absence of home rule. All that exists is a certain amount of deference given to traditional methods of municipal governance. And when anyone threatens the status quo, the magic words "Home Rule" are invoked. The legislature has also adopted a great, but declining, amount of permissive legislation.

The idea of home rule has never gotten past the talking stage in New Jersey during the present century for one essential reason: money. Inherent in the concept of home rule is that a municipal jurisdiction is willing and able to pay for the areas of government over which it wishes to assert jurisdiction. For example, the idea is embodied in the following language taken from the Model State Constitution as prepared by the National Municipal League. Their recommended document would include an affirmative directive requiring the state's legislature to adopt a general law to provide:

> For the adoption or amendment of charters by any county or city for its own government, by a majority of the qualified voters of the city or county voting thereon, for methods and procedures for the selection of charter commissions, and for the framing, publishing, disseminating and adopting such charters or charter amendments and for meeting the expenses connected therewith

Home rule is reserved for those willing to pay for its privileges. As they would have said back home, *don't ask for requests unless you are paying for the band.* There are a relative handful of communities left in New Jersey that possess the financial wherewithal to pay their own way without the assistance of state aid in some form, whether it be by allocations of the Gross Receipts and Franchise Taxes or some other program. Add in school costs and the handful dwindles to almost none.

The reason the myth of home rule has been so persistent is the fact that it has been the centerpiece of political debates and campaigns for 120 years. It metamorphosed from a campaign slogan in the 1870s to a magical mantra in the second half of the twentieth century.

The movement of the cry of home rule into the political spotlight would more aptly be described as a movement into the torchlight of the political parades that wended their way through the streets of Jersey City from 1871 to 1875. As we know, the post–Civil War excesses resulted in a significant citizens' revolt. Ultimately the constitution was amended in 1875 to forever preclude intrusion by the legislature in the internal operations of Jersey City or in any other municipality. No longer could the legislature enact local or special laws—the constitution now provided for all laws to be of general application. This provision continues in our present constitution. It is one of the most widely ignored and abused of its provisions.

Ignoring the narrow margin of the general-law amendment of 1875, Jersey City and its champion, future governor Leon Abbett, reveled in a victory that they described inaccurately as having granted them home rule. The period of 1873 to 1897 was the only span in New Jersey's history when one might say accurately that a semblance of home rule was in effect. The examination of municipal births reveals wretched excess culminating in the borough boom of 1894. Citizens of various areas failed to use their powers to create new municipalities wisely or well. However, in defense of these actions it must be pointed out that each of these new communities was self-sustaining at the time and not dependent on state aid to support their local services.

The political shoe was on the other foot at the conclusion of Abbett's second term as governor in 1892. The Republicans, sensing disaffection for Abbett's autocratic handling of legislation that consolidated power in the hands of the various mayors throughout the state, adopted a platform promising real home rule, whatever that meant. For the following five years the Republicans made the promise of home rule a centerpiece of their promises to the statewide electorate. The political pendulum swung rapidly and dramatically in favor of the Republicans in 1893. The wave of new municipalities washing across the state and particularly in Bergen County from 1894 to 1895 must be attributed in part to the encouragement provided by the promise of municipal independence contained in the Republican Party platform. Even more proliferation might have occurred, but the Republican legislature stepped in on an emergency basis to halt all further locally initiated incorporations. In the second year of the administration of Republican governor John Griggs, sweeping overhauls of the laws governing both boroughs and townships were enacted. Once again the sponsors of these acts claimed that home rule was being granted, but a review of the laws indicates the exact opposite was occurring. The Borough and Township Acts of 1897 substantially lessened home rule rather than increased it.

The high-water mark of hypocrisy was attained in 1917. The gargantuan task of consolidating the thousands of existing statutes dealing with municipalities was undertaken and a new comprehensive statute was enacted having the misleading title of the *Home Rule Act.* As with so many statutes that claimed that they were *Acts to provide for the establishment of a thorough and efficient system of education,* this act failed to do what it claimed to do. However, its adoption constituted an enormous propaganda coup. For decades people thought that home rule existed because the legislature had adopted a law entitled the Home Rule Act. The abiding success of this ploy continues to the present.

In New Jersey, the concept of home rule is constructively a delusion. The law is clear-cut, categorical, and beyond debate. While our new constitution requires that laws governing municipalities are to be given liberal construction, it is obvious that all sovereign power remains with the state. Municipalities are mere creatures of the state, and nothing more. New Jersey fails to give even token acknowledgment of the municipalities' alleged powers. The constitution contains few other references to local government, but these deal with municipalities' being allowed to do certain things, provided the legislature has given its blessing.

The power granted by the constitution—and endorsed by the citizens of our state—reposes plenary power in the legislature. No residual or inherent power rests in our municipalities. All actions of every and any type taken by a municipal governing body are exercised in a derivative manner, and are restricted to those matters specifically delegated to them by the legislature.

The home-rule issue in New Jersey receives an extremely thorough and informative treatment in an essay by Ernest C. Reock, Jr., and Raymond D. Bodnar in 1979 for the County and Municipal Government Study Commission. That article, updated and condensed for the same commission in 1985, acknowledged that the *Mount Laurel* decisions further curtailed communities in their delegated zoning powers. The 1985 study also disclosed that the figures then available indicated that property taxes accounted for only 34 percent of the revenues upon which municipalities relied, and that the Gross Receipts Tax accounted for over 21 percent of all municipal revenue in 1982. These statistics are very telling. The articles are rewarding for anyone who wishes to know more about the subject. Ernest Reock, a man who has provided invaluable assistance to the state and particularly to the legislature over the course of his distinguished career as the director of the Bureau of Government Research at Rutgers University, presents very telling and important statistics. Anyone who has served in the legislature, including the author, has benefited from his dedicated service.

New Jersey falls into a small minority of states that have no home-rule provisions whatsoever. The majority of states provide constitutional recognition to the concept of home rule and constitutional protection to many municipal prerogatives. New Jersey has the weakest form of institutionalized protection for home rule, yet it is a state in which the multiplicity of municipalities dominates public policy.

A serious mistake is made, therefore, by those who contend that there is something sacrosanct about local government and who invoke the alleged mystical mantra: "home rule." This incantation, formerly somewhat effective, loses its force with each succeeding year. As costs mount, advocates for the status quo should emphasize the advantages of local governments rather than attempt to argue that the system is invulnerable to change because of "home rule."

Apologists for the plethora of municipal jurisdictions are on relatively strong ground when they argue that the system was intended to provide for administrative efficiency; the huge 100+square-mile townships existing at the outset of the Revolutionary War constituted units that were unwieldy and impossible to govern. The firm historical ground of that position rapidly transforms to quicksand when the argument is advanced that the system, so long tolerated, has become institutionalized and therefore unalterable. A great disservice to the political process is the contention that alternative systems of providing service should be ignored because change would create social tensions and political dislocations.

CHAPTER 18

Some Suggested Solutions

The times, they are a changin'.
Bob Dylan

*I*magine a web woven by a spider on LSD and you might see a frightening similarity to the map showing the jurisdictional outlines of our 566 municipalities in New Jersey. Present the current facts and statistics of the situation to a systems analyst and you can expect howls of laughter. Given a free hand to reconstruct and reconfigure the present map, no one would attempt to justify a replication of the existing system. We do not have the luxury of a clean slate upon which to reconfigure, but we do have the power to address the prospects of change.

Legislation allows voters to initiate studies and approve recommendations for consolidation. That legislation has been in place, with minor amendments, for almost one hundred years. So seldom has it been used that one must wonder how it has escaped being repealed for lack of interest. The statutory scheme is cumbersome, complex, and provides for a protracted and complicated process, while offering no meaningful incentives to consolidate. Small wonder it has been resorted to so rarely. The attempt to consolidate the Princetons (borough and township) in 1996 also brought to light a number of technical shortcomings. The legislature, despite being placed on notice of the technical problems, has not acted on corrective amendments.

The present laws governing municipal consolidation provide no real incentives, other than the offer of some technical assistance from the Department of Community Affairs. Experience has shown that the state's assistance, well intentioned as it may be, has no meaningful value.

In 1972 the County and Municipal Government Study Commission published a report entitled, *Consolidation: Prospects and Problems.* This study pointed out the difficulties with the existing legislation, such as the requirement that concurrent petitions signed by 20 percent of the registered voters of each municipality be submitted just to initiate the process. Anyone who has ever participated in a petition drive recognizes this as an intimidating threshold obstacle; also, since municipal clerks, who must certify that the required number of valid signatures have been obtained, may have a vested interest in the status quo and feel their jobs in jeopardy, they might exercise meticulous scrutiny in reviewing the submitted petitions.

The 1972 report contained meritorious recommendations, such as:

- the Department of Community Affairs should award grants to qualifying communities to underwrite some of the feasibility studies that would be necessary to expedite any consolidation;
- the threshold number of signatures should be cut in half to 10 percent of the registered voters;
- and most importantly, the state should enact a program of incentives for communities that undertook consolidation.

The keystone of the incentives recommendation was a state payment that would *save harmless* the community with the lower tax rate, i.e., the town with the lower tax rate would not have to fear that their tax rate would suddenly escalate as the result of the consolidation. The recommendation provided that this incentive be phased out over a period of five years following consolidation, thereby affording ample opportunity for the merged communities to adjust fully to the new realities. This fine and intelligent suggestion found few sponsors in the legislature and was never acted upon by either house.

The valid proposals of this 1972 report still provide a useful starting point for intelligent discussion about the challenges of consolidation. This report made reference to a report the commission had issued the previous year: *Joint Services— A Local Response to Area Wide Problems*. Many of the recommendations made by the commission in that 1971 report, concerning interlocal joint services, were ultimately adopted. While it took some time for municipalities to get accustomed to the idea of cooperative action, joint agreements are now pursued aggressively and enthusiastically by cost-conscious towns.

Since the century-old consolidation statutes have been so inadequate, it may be time to revisit the subject, not merely with some technical corrections, but with substantive changes. Perhaps the state government should take a proactive role in the restructuring of municipal governments, rather than relying on permissive legislation. Such a proactive stance would reflect the state's sovereignty and the absence of any home-rule prohibitions, i.e., reform from the top down rather than from the bottom up. Undoubtedly such state-directed changes would be more expeditious. On the other hand, such action would be unique and untraditional. The question to address is whether or not present circumstances warrant a new and different approach.

State-directed changes potentially could come in two fashions, first, by adoption of meaningful incentives, or, second, by compulsory legislation. The *save harmless* incentive is only one possibility. The State could create a whole spectrum of incentives, including a specific program of state aid that would reward both consolidating communities by initially subsidizing a lower effective tax rate than either town had prior to their merger. A wide spectrum of other possible incentives is available.

However, the state has the power to effectuate the greatest possible incentive of all: a uniform statewide property tax rate. The advantages of such a statewide property tax structure are as promising and luminous as its prospects for adoption are abject and bleak. The most recent of New Jersey's myriad tax policy study commissions, initiated during the second term of Governor Thomas H. Kean, was the State and Local Expenditure and Revenue Policy Commission, known by its unfortunate acronym SLERP. Having served on this commission, I thought SLERP's work, including its suggestion that the state adopt a more uniform system of property taxation, should have served as the basis for meaningful discussions about reforming what is presently a scandalously unfair and disuniform system. My enthusiasm was shared—most regrettably—only by my fellow commissioners. Thus, the thoughtful Report and Recommendations were pronounced *dead on arrival* at the State House.

Fair and uniform tax treatment is the other great New Jersey myth that has been around since the 1860s. In 1875, the state took a significant step by amending the constitution to include the following:

> Property shall be assessed for taxes under general laws, and by uniform
> rules, according to its true value.

The meaning and significance of this clause were among the two or three issues that dominated the debate at the Convention of 1947. The constitution produced by that gathering changed the wording to read:

> Property shall be assessed for taxation under general laws, and by uniform rules. All real property assessed and taxed locally or by the State for allotment and payment to taxing districts shall be assessed according to the same standard of value; and such real property shall be taxed at the general tax rate of the taxing district in which the property is situated, for the use of such taxing district.

It must also be noted that Article Eight of the constitution dealing with taxation and finance has been subject to sixteen amendments since its adoption, far more than any other section of the constitution. Many of those amendments carved out exceptions to the basic standard. The language when analyzed provides for no uniformity or equity on a statewide basis or even a countywide basis. The state's organic document guarantees only that you won't be treated any worse than your fellow townspeople are treated. The promise of a constitutional protection that ensures taxation by general laws and uniform rules extends only to the borders of your municipality; thus, it is a constitutional myth. Life would be breathed into this constitution if a statewide property tax were put into effect.

However, the state could begin to force consolidations, even without incentives for municipalities. Knowing that municipalities are not protected by any constitutional guarantee of home rule, the legislature is free to act as they wish. However, the few instances of consolidation by legislative fiat that we observed at the turn of the last century in Trenton and Camden were met with resistance and political backlash. That might not be the case today, if the heavy-handedness of past efforts were eliminated.

The fairness associated with general laws, uniformly applied, pursuant to objective criteria, is the absolute condition precedent to the political acceptance of any state-imposed changes. The general laws required to begin the process of mandated merger must have categorical and objective standards as the criteria for whether or not a community is subject to such a required merger. Such objective criteria may, however, fall into two separate categories: physical, i.e., geographic size and/or census population data; or fiscal, i.e., ratables, ratables per capita, effective tax rate, any one of a number of objective standards.

Using the purely physical standards of territory and population, a suggested approach might be the use of a minimum of two square miles as an appropriate initial standard. Size of population might be just as good an example. A combined formula taking both size and population into account might well be the most acceptable criterion. Nothing in the state's constitution would preclude the adoption of a general law formulating public policy that prevented any community from continuing independent existence unless its population exceeded 2,000 in an area of no less than two square miles.

I suggest that the state allow a two-year grace period for municipalities in this category to find an appropriate partner. If a merger candidate were not found in the third year, the state would step in and fill the role of matchmaker; by the fifth year the merger would be accomplished, by state fiat if necessary. Of course the towns in this category would be prohibited from either borrowing heavily to make themselves unattractive, or granting tenure to any of their employees during this period. Poison pills are excellent strategies to prevent takeovers in the private corporate world, but would have to be outlawed in municipal consolidation.

In the following five-year period, the state could raise the standard to a minimum of 10,000 population and ten square miles of territory, thus paring its municipal subdivisions in half within the next ten years. The immediate goal for the next generation would be to have a state with approximately 200 administrative subdivisions with minimum populations of approximately 40,000.

The use of fiscal standards as a criterion for mandated consolidation is just as practical and perhaps even more logical. The state and its people have a hundred year history of state-sanctioned regulation of banks, insurance companies, and other industries that provide services to the public. These private enterprises must meet established standards or run the risk of forfeiting their right to do business in the state. If any of these businesses falls into a questionable condition, the state heightens its supervision. If the condition becomes serious or critical, the state moves in to force a consolidation, merger, acquisition, or liquidation. Each of these private enterprises knows that it must function within the acknowledged guidelines—maintaining capital and reserves to cover liabilities, as well as meeting other benchmarks that provide adequate assurance as to its financial condition.

An analogous set of standards applied to the financial condition of municipalities would trigger review proceedings in hundreds of communities. The truth is that almost two hundred towns in the state are totally reliant on state subsidies to function even at a minimal service level.

If the state were to turn a blind eye to any of the financial institutions, insurance companies, or regulated utilities that it supervises in the same cavalier fashion as it has acted toward municipalities, the results would be indictments for malfeasance. Year after year the inadequacies of municipal operations are papered over and patched up with some form of subsidy while there are chants about "home-rule." Adopting strict standards for municipalities similar to the regulations used for supervising regulated industries would shrink the number of jurisdictions radically and rapidly from 566 to 200.

The use of physical or fiscal criteria should not be mutually exclusive. Combinations, variations, hybrids, and use of other appropriate objective criteria are all acceptable. However, there are other ways to approach the consolidation issue.

Counties could be given the option of consolidating traditional municipal services in a metropolitan area, as has been done successfully in other places in America and Europe. I broached this possibility in the late 1980s relative to the prospects for the creation of Atlantic County as a metropolitan region. I believed that New Jersey's successful experiment with casino gaming should not be jeopardized by the inability of Atlantic City, with a relatively small population of 40,000, to deal properly with the manifold problems that had arisen consequent to having an influx of 25 million annual visitors.

I made my argument by quoting from Flaubert, but without attribution—*a statue cannot be larger than the pedestal that holds it.* I might have been better received if I had recommended that *Eboli virus* be adopted as a new flavor of salt water taffy. The howls of protest were deafening and dismal in their lack of logic and substance. The chorus of local officeholders chanting *home rule—home rule— home rule* was depressing. In spite of the negative reaction, I received many invitations to speak at civic, social, fraternal, and service clubs whose members were interested in hearing about the proposal. Those invitations proved to me that there are a large number of citizens interested in alternatives and anxious to have a forum that would offer possible options to the expensive status quo.

During the research undertaken in conjunction with the controversial proposal, I was struck by the progressive attitudes demonstrated in various areas throughout the country. With the impressive economic benefits realized elsewhere, it is startling that New Jersey continues to cling so adamantly to its present system.

My experience with the suggested metropolitanization of Atlantic County was not my first quixotic tilt with the windmill of home rule. During my days as Speaker of the New Jersey State Assembly in the early 1980s, I had proposed a special planning commission embracing all of the towns in southern Middlesex County and in Mercer County that made up the *Route 1 Corridor* between New Brunswick and Trenton. Although that legislation never became law, I have the continuing satisfaction that its introduction and the widespread discussion it engendered made a positive contribution by raising the consciousness of many planning and transportation officials at the state, county, and local levels. The debate became the genesis for a substantial amount of remedial policy that fore-stalled the nightmare that might have occurred in the region had an alarm bell not been rung.

During the countless discussions with people, both in and out of public of-fice, concerning these two legislative initiatives, I was constantly impressed by how strongly people felt about geographic identity—the sense of place—the ca-chet that came from a certain address. I felt that the idea of address was invested with too much significance, especially since the name of the town in which one lived was rapidly losing importance. I found it difficult to persuade many of my listeners of this fact in the 1980s. The truth is that we are no longer evaluated on the basis of the name of the town in which we reside or even by the section of that town which we call home. Wall Street, Madison Avenue, and the decision-makers at both ends of Pennsylvania Avenue have abandoned the relevance of place names. Preferences, whether they be made for consumer purchases or political can-didates, are assumed to be reflected by your zip code. As consumer and/or voters we have been reduced to a set of integers.

Municipal governments as service industries should look to the postal ser-vice for guidance as to how to cope with today's challenges. The United States Post Office once filled the description of the largest single service of the federal government, and at one time it was the single most significant enterprise, public or private, in the entire country. Those days are long past, and the postal service has evolved into a new and different entity—an entity that competes for custom-ers with other similar services.

For all of the criticism directed at the post office, and for all the humor that has made it a target, it has been able to stay ahead of the curve and has been the source of many innovations. In this latter category, Postmaster General, Charles E. Walker instituted a new system in 178 cities throughout the country on May 5, 1943. That new system, designed to speed the flow of mail, recognized that merely identifying a destination by the name of a city or town was insufficient and cum-bersome. Starting on that day in the middle of World War II, the U.S. Post Office initiated a system based upon the numerical identification of geographic areas. Starting as postal zones, the system soon evolved into a nationwide zip code system.

The smart money of mass marketers, lenders, and risk underwriters recog-nizes the validity of the demarcations. The name and location of your hometown has already become irrelevant in the business world. Your zip code defines you for a vast array of economic purposes, while your local jurisdiction simply pro-vides you with police protection or your library card.

Equally important is that the service provided by the postal service and all of its competitors is rendered on a system that has long abandoned municipal boundary lines. If what was once the country's stodgiest bureaucracy could es-cape the trap of history, I have faith that we can recognize that the delivery of services such as police protection, snow removal, trash pick-up, functioning sew-ers, and tax collection might be accomplished on a more logical, progressive, ra-tional, and streamlined basis than our existing 566 municipal jurisdictions.

Also, we should not spend too much time worrying about loss of geographic identity. Chambersburg lives on despite its absorption into Trenton a century ago. I once lived in Sayreville, but my boyhood friends came from all over town: Parlin, Morgan, Melrose, President Park, Laurel Park, and MacArthur Manor. The size of the lettering of a place name on a map is often irrelevant. It is the vitality, character, and spirit of a community that give it identity, and not the other way around.

Citizens of Connecticut reside in one of eight counties, but those counties serve only as geographic indicators and have no governmental function. Throughout the nation people live in villages and hamlets and unincorporated territories without much concern for their identity. They are more concerned, I believe, with the quality of the nearest school, whether their road will get plowed after the next snowfall or how a threatening fire will get extinguished. For those in New Jersey who identify their lives only by the status of their address, my best advice would be: You have an address, now get a life.

The success of municipal joint service agreements was mentioned earlier. Consolidation of services is already a major trend in New Jersey municipalities. A parallel trend that appears to be inexorable is the redefining of the traditional roles of municipal government.

Perhaps the most interesting development of the past decade has been the trend toward privatization of local services. Nontraditional areas of services, formerly called proprietary functions, grew exponentially during the period of municipal expansion. These proprietary services were distinguished from core governmental functions such as public safety, road maintenance, judicial administration, care of the indigenous poor, and the assessment and collection of taxes.

Hundreds of communities, following the example of the state's largest cities, found themselves in businesses, proprietary functions, that historically had been the province of private enterprise. Towns and cities rushed to be in the water business, the sewage disposal business, the trash collection business, even the stadium and transit business. Shore communities did more than charge for admission to their beaches; occasionally they ventured into the real estate business, building stores along their boardwalks and leasing to the highest bidders by way of concessions. Back in the cities the governing bodies found themselves engaged in a wide variety of enterprises. Supervising weights and measures had been a function of ancient tradition in European commercial centers, but now New Jersey had cities that were actually operating as well as supervising public markets. Some cities owned and maintained their own municipal bathhouses, where their citizens could enjoy a luxury seldom afforded in the tenement in which they lived. The forerunner of the municipal parking deck was the municipal stable.

Some proprietary ventures passed with the Depression. Others, such as the public baths, declined as building codes mandated indoor plumbing, and the last city-run stables became nothing more than photos in an anniversary booklet. More and more, the proprietary functions of supplying water, sewage disposal, and garbage collection are slowly but surely reverting to the private sector.

It is not necessary to document the extensive number of privatizations. What is important is that municipal government is in the process of rethinking itself.

Local governments are rapidly retreating from the number of proprietary functions that once seemed so attractive. It is one thing for a city to terminate its active operation of a bathhouse; it is more significant when the operation of water systems is surrendered to private operators, a redefining of core services is taking place.

Local officials ought to ponder why private security guards have been the fastest growing job opportunity of the 1990s. Every large manufacturing or distribution facility employs full-time security personnel, and apartment and condominium complexes usually list the presence of a private security force as a major amenity. Even such basics as police protection are being subtly changed as private security becomes the norm in shopping centers, defined by the New Jersey Supreme Court in a recent decision as the new "downtowns" of America.

School administrators, likewise, must find the growing interest in school vouchers and charter schools to be troublesome. New Jersey spends the highest amount of money on a per-pupil basis of any state, yet when an alternative appears in the form of a charter school, lotteries must be conducted as there are ten applicants for every seat.

Municipal governments are presently feeling the early tremors of the same type of earthquake that rocked so many other service industries with the advent of deregulation. The constant theme of every election since the mid-sixties has been the most effective way to generate funds for local use. Although every race has had its own unique nuances, I think it fair to say that both political parties have promised more state aid to hard-pressed property taxpayers. The debate has centered around just how to accomplish such a task. One party has focused on increasing broad-based taxes in a progressive manner, while the other party has concentrated on paring down state expenditures and placing more accountability on local officials.

This debate appears to be a no-win zero-sum game. Increase state taxes and you can lower local property taxes through increased state aid, or lower state taxes and cause an increase in local taxes as a result of decreased state aid.

The most telling—and consequently the one most successfully repressed—statistic is the one that defines the overall aggregate cost of government at the state, county, and local levels. Add the average property tax to income and sales taxes, factor in all the nuisance taxes and fees for services, and the result is that New Jersey, with its complex and convoluted system, leads the nation.

Consolidation of municipalities appears to be an attractive possibility for transcending the unproductive debate in which we have been enmeshed for the past thirty years. The restructuring of the system with its promised reduction of overall costs of government should be a solution that is hard to resist.

Conclusion

The world of civil society has certainly been made by men, and its principles are therefore to be found within modifications of our own human mind. Whoever reflects on this cannot but marvel that the philosophers should bend all their energies to the study of the world of nature, which since God made it, God alone knows; and that they should have neglected the study of the world of nations or civil world, which, since men had made it, men could come to know.
Giambattista Vico

I have chosen this quote from Vico because it reflects the theme of this study. We are masters of the created institutions of our culture. No immutable natural law precludes us from change in the present system constructed by our predecessors. Nothing stays our hand from reconfiguring our jurisdictions in a manner reflecting the advances in our attitudes toward local government and the ability of our modern technologies to service our present needs.

Earlier the observation was offered that we no longer are identified by our community but by our zip code. Tomorrow our address on the World Wide Web will have more practical application than does either the name of our town or even our nine-digit zip code that narrows down to our specific neighborhood. Our E-mail address is mobile, and our physical location can already be tracked by the military's system of satellite identification, a system so sophisticated that it can define any point in the world by a system of coordinates.

These changes have all been made possible by the dynamics of computer technology—dynamics that are diametrically opposite from those that created the fragmented jurisdictions of municipal governments. New Jersey's present geopolitical map is one drawn by the dynamic of reductionism. While reductionism was once the dominant world view, it is a world view that is passé nowadays in the computer age.

The colonization of America occurred at a time almost contemporaneous to the construction of this reductionist paradigm for understanding the operation of the physical world's reality. One legend has it that the Township of Newton—which eventually gave birth to Camden, Haddonfield, and Collingswood—was not simply the contraction of the words *new town,* as one might imagine. Rather, it was named in honor of the scientist, mathematician—and reductionist—Sir Isaac Newton.

The new nation developed, and the already diminutive State of New Jersey divided time and time again almost on a parallel course with what was the dominant theme of scientific explorations. The English-speaking world advanced its investigations into all of the natural sciences—physics, biology, mechanics, and astronomy—by cutting, separating, and dividing.

The instruments developed to aid the reductionist world view were the microscope and the telescope—instruments that allowed us to see and study smaller and smaller parts of the whole. It is uncanny that while he was working on the invention of the microscope, Anton van Leeuwenhoek was employed as the maintenance supervisor of the town hall in the Dutch city of Guelph.

The economy during these centuries followed the reductionist suit, with tasks being ever more segregated and refined until the culmination of the reductionist paradigm was represented on the assembly line, with each worker performing a repetitive task within the set time period that expired as the small part of the whole passed in front of his or her work station. It is no surprise that a society which worshipped reductionism in its material and economic life applied the same concept to the operation of its political culture.

The state's early townships, consisting of areas that could not be walked across in less than a day, were obviously difficult to govern, but at the time, government was rudimentary and extremely limited in its obligations and aspirations. The unfettered operation of the reductionist dynamic led to the quartering, cutting, paring, peeling, slicing, slivering, dividing, and redividing of the body politic. In retrospect this hyperdivision has proven to be counterproductive. Mere dissection has no inherent benefit, and gains value only when the reduced subject matter is carefully examined, evaluated, and analyzed.

I hope that the reader has gained something from this effort to place some of the present pieces under a microscope, while using the telescope of history to reach back and study the fragmentation process. The dominance of the reductionist world view has ended, but the political and governmental institutions created during its reign may be with us for a long and very expensive time.

The computer operates in precisely the opposite direction of all previous tools of scientific investigation. Computer technology and the products of its use are potentially holistic. Instead of dividing and redividing in order to make the universe more understandable and manageable, the computer aggregates information, assembles and arranges data, compares alternatives simultaneously, and provides solutions by construction instead of deconstruction. The new paradigm is the maximum utilization of all components, not the paring down or specialization of function. Yesterday the expert was the one who knew more and more about less and less. Tomorrow's problem-solver will be the one who knows more and more about more and more.

Above all, I hope that this study will stimulate you to participate in the predicted debate on new government structures that must ensue over the following decade. For myself, I disavow any special expertise or insight. However, I do entertain the abiding conviction that we are not simple prisoners of history. There is a better, more intelligent, and less expensive way to provide local services, and we have it in our collective power to bring about changes for the better.

BIBLIOGRAPHY

Barber, John, and Ward Henry Howe. *Historical Collections of the State of New Jersey.* New Haven: John Barber, 1857.

Bebout, John E. "Introduction." In *Proceedings of the New Jersey State Constitutional Convention of 1844.* Trenton: State House Commission, 1942.

Bebout, John E., and Ronald J. Grele. *Where Cities Meet: The Urbanization of New Jersey.* The New Jersey Historical Series, vol. 22. Princeton, N.J.: D. Van Nostrand Company, 1964.

Beck, Henry Charlton. *Forgotten Towns of Southern New Jersey.* 1936. Reprint. New Brunswick, N.J.: Rutgers University Press, 1961.

———. *Jersey Genesis: The Story of the Mullica River.* New Brunswick, N.J. Rutgers University Press, 1963.

———. *The Roads of Home: Lanes and Legends of New Jersey.* New Brunswick, N.J.: Rutgers University Press, 1956.

———. *Tales and Towns of Northern New Jersey.* New Brunswick, N.J.: Rutgers University Press, 1964.

Bello, Carla Vivian, and Arthur T. Vanderbilt, II. *Jersey Justice: Three Hundred Years of The New Jersey Judiciary.* Newark, N.J.: The Institute for Continuing Legal Education, 1978.

Black, Charles C. *Law of Taxation with Special Reference to Its Application in the State of New Jersey.* Newark: Soney & Sage Co., 1935.

Bowie, Norman E., ed. *Ethical Issues in Government.* Philosophical Monographs. Philadelphia: Temple University Press, 1981.

Boyd, Julian P., ed. *Fundamental Laws and Constitutions of New Jersey.* The New Jersey Historical Series, vol. 17. Princeton, N.J.: D. Van Nostrand Company, The New Jersey Tercentenary Commission, 1964.

Carlisle, Robert D. B. *Water Ways: A History of the Elizabethtown Water Company.* Elizabeth, N.J.: Elizabethtown Water Company, 1982.

Cawley, James and Margaret. *Along the Old York Road.* New Brunswick, N.J.: Rutgers University Press, 1965.

———. *Exploring the Little Rivers of New Jersey.* Princeton, N.J.: Princeton University Press, 1942.

Connors, Richard J. *A Cycle of Power.* Metuchen, N.J.: Scarecrow Press, 1971.

Crowther, Samuel. *Consider Middlesex County*, Garden City, N.Y.: The Country Life Press, 1926.

Cunningham, John T. *New Jersey, America's Main Road*. Revised ed. Garden City, N.Y.: Doubleday, 1976.

Cushing, Thomas, and Charles Sheppard. *History of the Counties of Gloucester, Salem, and Cumberland*. Philadelphia: Everts & Peck, 1883.

Doherty, Joan F. *Hudson County: The Left Bank*. Northridge, Calif.: Windsor Publications, 1986.

Dorwart, Jeffrey M. *Cape May County, New Jersey: The Making of an American Resort Community*. New Brunswick, N.J.: Rutgers University Press, 1992.

Edge, Water E. *A Jerseyman's Journal: The Autobiography of a Businessman, Governor, Diplomat*. Princeton, N.J.: Princeton University Press, 1948.

Eisenberg, Eileen. *Jewish Agricultural Colonies in New Jersey 1882–1920*. Syracuse: Syracuse University Press, 1995.

Ellis, Franklin. *History of Monmouth County, New Jersey*. Philadelphia: R. T. Peck, 1885.

Erdman, Charles R. *The New Jersey Constitution of 1776*. Princeton, N.J.: Princeton University Press, 1929.

Federal Writers' Project. *New Jersey: A Guide to Its Present and Past*. American Guide Series. New York: Viking, 1939.

———. *New Jersey: A Profile in Pictures*. New York: Barrows, 1939.

———. *Proceedings of the New Jersey State Constitutional Convention of 1844*. New Jersey State House Commission, WPA, 1942.

———. *Stories of New Jersey: Significant Places, People and Activities*. New York: Barrows, 1938.

Fleming, Thomas. *New Jersey: A History*. American Association for State and Local History. New York: W. W. Norton, 1984.

Fitzgerald, Thomas F. *Manual of the Legislature of New Jersey, Two Hundred and Eighth Legislature (First Session)*. Newark, N.J.: Skinder-Strauss, 1998. Annual, 1875– .

Gerlach, Larry R. *Prologue to Independence: New Jersey in the Coming of the American Revolution*. New Brunswick, N.J.: Rutgers University Press, 1976.

Gordon, Thomas F. *Gazetteer of the State of New Jersey*. Trenton: D. Fenton, 1834.

Hornor, Edith R., ed. *The New Jersey Municipal Data Book, 1994–95 Edition*. Palo Alto, Calif.: Information Publications, 1994.

Johnson, James P. *New Jersey: History of Ingenuity and Industry*. Northridge, Calif.: Windsor Publications, 1987.

Kalata, Barbara. *A Hundred Years a Hundred Miles: New Jersey's Morris Canal*. Morristown, N.J.: Morris County Historical Society, 1983.

Karcher, Joseph T. *Main Street Lawyer*. Boston: The Meador Publishing Company, 1959.

———. *A Municipal History of the Township of Sayreville, 1876–1920*. Boston: Meador Publishing Company, 1958.

Kemmerer, Donald L. *Path to Freedom: The Struggle for Self-Government in Colonial New Jersey 1703–1776*. Princeton, N.J.: Princeton University Press, 1940.

Kerney, James. *The Political Education of Woodrow Wilson*. New York: Century, 1926.

Kobbe, Gustav. *The New Jersey Coast and Pines, an Illustrated Guide Book*. 1889. Reprint. Baltimore: Gateway Press, 1977.

Kraybill, Richard. *The Story of Shrewsbury 1664–1964*. Red Bank, N.J.: The Commercial Press, 1964.

Leaming, Aaron, and Jacob Spicer. *The Grants, Concessions and Original Constitutions of the Province of New Jersey*. 2d ed. Somerville, N.J.: Honeyman, 1881.

Lewis, Alice Blackwell. *Hopewell Valley Heritage*. Hopewell, N.J.: The Hopewell Museum, 1973.

Lockard, Duane. *The New Jersey Governor: A Study in Political Power.* The New Jersey Historical Series, vol. 14. Princeton, N.J.: D. Van Nostrand Company, The New Jersey Tercentenary Commission, 1964.

Lundin, Leonard. *Cockpit of the Revolution: The War for Independence in New Jersey.* Princeton, N.J.: Princeton University Press, 1940.

McCormick, Richard P. *Experiment in Independence: New Jersey in the Critical Period (1781–1789).* New Brunswick, N.J.: Rutgers University Press, 1950.

McKean, Dayton David. *The Boss: The Hague Machine in Action.* Boston: Houghton Mifflin, 1940.

McMahon, William. *South Jersey Towns: History and Legend.* New Brunswick, N.J.: Rutgers University Press, 1973.

McPhee, John. *The Pine Barrens.* New York: Farrar, Straus & Giroux, 1967.

Meinig, D. W. *The Shaping of America: A Geographical Perspective on 500 Years of History.* Vol. 1, *Atlantic America, 1492–1800.* New Haven: Yale University Press, 1986.

————. *The Shaping of America: A Geographical Perspective on 500 Years of History.* Vol. 2, *Continental America, 1800–1867.* New Haven: Yale University Press, 1986.

Menzies, Elizabeth G. D. *Passage Between Rivers: A Portfolio of Photographs with a History of the Delaware and Raritan Canal.* New Brunswick, N.J.: Rutgers University Press, 1976.

Mumford, Lewis. *The Culture of Cities.* New York: Harcourt Brace, 1938.

Murray, Davis. *History of Education in New Jersey.* Washington, D.C.: Government Printing Office, 1899.

Negroponte, Nicholas. *Being Digital.* New York: Random House, 1996.

New Jersey, County Municipal and Government Study Commission. *Corrections Policy for the '90s.* Trenton, N.J.: County and Municipal Government Study Commission, a Legislative Agency, May 1989.

————. *County Mandates: The State Judicial System and Human Services.* Trenton, N.J.: County and Municipal Government Study Commission, a Legislative Agency, October 1984.

————. *The Delivery of Human Services Within New Jersey.* Trenton, N.J.: County and Municipal Government Study Commission, a Legislative Agency, June 1990.

————. *Functional Fragmentation and the Traditional Forms of Municipal Government in New Jersey.* Trenton, N.J.: County and Municipal Government Study Commission, a Legislative Agency, November 1985.

————. *Intergovernmental Funding Within New Jersey.* Trenton, N.J.: County and Municipal Government Study Commission, a Legislative Agency, May 1992.

————. *Judicial Unification.* Trenton, N.J.: County and Municipal Government Study Commission, a Legislative Agency, July 1987.

————. *Local Redevelopment in New Jersey: Structuring a New Partnership.* Trenton, N.J.: County and Municipal Government Study Commission, a Legislative Agency, January 1987.

————. *Modern Forms of Municipal Government.* Trenton, N.J.: County and Municipal Government Study Commission, a Legislative Agency, May 1992.

————. *Optional Municipal Charter Law (Faulkner Act) as Amended, January, 1987.* Trenton, N.J.: County and Municipal Government Study Commission, a Legislative Agency, October 1987.

————. *Optional Municipal Charter Law (Faulkner Act) as Amended, June 1983.* Trenton, N.J.: County and Municipal Government Study Commission, a Legislative Agency, July 1983.

————. *Services for the Elderly: Current and Future Needs*. Trenton, N.J.: County and Municipal Government Study Commission, a Legislative Agency, October 1988.

————. *Solid Waste Management in New Jersey: Today and Tomorrow*. Trenton, N.J.: County and Municipal Government Study Commission, a Legislative Agency, November 1987.

————. *The Structure of County Government: Current Status and Needs*. Trenton, N.J.: County and Municipal Government Study Commission, a Legislative Agency, July 1986.

New Jersey, History Committee. *Outline History of New Jersey*. New Brunswick, N.J.: Rutgers University Press, 1950.

Noble, Ransome E., Jr. *New Jersey Progressivism before Wilson*. Princeton, N.J.: Princeton University Press, 1946.

Pierce, Arthur D. *Iron in the Pines: The Story of New Jersey's Ghost Towns and Bog Iron*. New Brunswick, N.J.: Rutgers University Press, 1957.

Pierce, Arthur D. *Smugglers' Woods: Jaunts and Journeys in Colonial and Revolutionary New Jersey*. New Brunswick, N.J.: Rutgers University Press, 1960.

Princeton Local Government Survey. *Legislative Proposals (1938) Preliminary Statement (December 7, 1937)*. Princeton, N.J.: Princeton Local Government Survey, 1937.

————. *Local Government in New Jersey: A Political Patchwork*. Local Government Bulletins Nos. 1–5. Princeton, N.J.: Princeton Local Government Survey, 1936.

Prowell, George. *History of Camden County*. Philadelphia: L. J. Richards, 1886.

Raftis, Edmund B. *Summit, New Jersey: From Poverty Hill to the Hill City*. Seattle: Great Swamp Press, 1996.

Reock, Ernest C. *The Changing Structure of New Jersey Municipal Government*. Trenton, N.J.: State of New Jersey, County and Municipal Government Study Commission, a Legislative Agency, April 1985.

Roberts, Russell, and Rich Youmans. *Down the Jersey Shore*. New Brunswick, N.J.: Rutgers University Press, 1993.

Sackett, William Edgar. *Modern Battles of Trenton: History of New Jersey's Politics and Legislation from the Year 1868 to the Year 1894,*. New York: Neale Publishing Co., 1914.

Sepinwall, Harriet Lipman. "The History of the 1875 'Thorough and Efficient' Amendment to the New Jersey Constitution in the Context of Nineteenth Century Social Thought on Education: The Civil War to the Centennial." Ph.D. Diss., Rutgers University, 1986.

Shaw, William H. *History of Essex and Hudson Counties*. Philadelphia: Everts & Peck, 1884.

Short, John R., ed. *The Illustrated Encyclopedia of World Geography: Human Settlement*. New York: Oxford University Press, 1992.

Smith, Samuel. *The History of the Colony of Nova Caesaria or New Jersey*. Trenton: W. S. Sharp, 1890.

Smith, Thomas F. X. *The Powerticians*. Secaucus, N.J.: Lyle Stuart, 1982.

Spearman, Frank. H. *The Strategy of the Great Railroads*. New York: Scribner's, 1904.

Stockton, Frank R. *Stories of New Jersey*. New Brunswick, N.J.: Rutgers University Press, 1961.

Stokes, Edward C. *Memorial Upon William J. Sewell, United States Senator from New Jersey, March 24, 1902*. Trenton, N.J.: John L. Murphy, 1902.

Vanderbilt, Arthur II. *Changing Law*. New Brunswick, N.J.: Rutgers University Press, 1976.

Village of Ridgewood State Tercentenary Committee, Oscar T. Conner, Chairman, Ridgewood History Committee, Esther Baker Fishler, Chairman. *The History of a Village: Ridgewood, New Jersey*. 1964.

Walker, E. R., et al. *History of Trenton 1679–1929*. Princeton, N.J.: Princeton University Press, 1929.

Weis, Eleanor. *Saga of a Crossroads: Florham Park*. Historical Society of Florham Park, 1988.

Whitehead, William A. *Early History of Perth Amboy and Adjoining Country*. New York, 1856.

Whitehead, William A. *East Jersey under the Proprietary Governments*. Newark: M. R. Dennis, 1875.

Woodward, E. M., and J. F. Hageman. *History of Burlington and Mercer Counties*. Philadelphia: Everts & Peck, 1883.

Wooster, Benjamin C. Chapter on "Public Education." In Frances A. Westervelt, ed., *History of Bergen County*. New York: Lewis Historical Publishing Company, 1923.

INDEX

CPSIA information can be obtained at www.ICGtesting.com
Printed in the USA
BVOW031540240212

283740BV00003B/7/A